S0-ASE-311

Pioneers Of France In The New World

France and England in North America

Part First

Francis Parkman, Jr.

Alpha Editions

Copyright © 2018

ISBN : 9789352971350

Design and Setting By
Alpha Editions
email - alphaedis@gmail.com

All rights reserved. No part of this publication may be
reproduced, distributed, or transmitted in any form or by
means, including photocopying, recording, or other
electronic or mechanical methods, without the prior
written permission of the publisher.

The views and characters expressed in the book are of the
author and his/her imagination and do not represent the
views of the Publisher.

Contents

INTRODUCTION

The springs of American civilization, unlike those of the elder world, lie revealed in the clear light of History. In appearance they are feeble; in reality, copious and full of force. Acting at the sources of life, instruments otherwise weak become mighty for good and evil, and men, lost elsewhere in the crowd, stand forth as agents of Destiny. In their toils, their sufferings, their conflicts, momentous questions were at stake, and issues vital to the future world,—the prevalence of races, the triumph of principles, health or disease, a blessing or a curse. On the obscure strife where men died by tens or by scores hung questions of as deep import for posterity as on those mighty contests of national adolescence where carnage is reckoned by thousands.

The subject to which the proposed series will be devoted is that of "France in the New World,"—the attempt of Feudalism, Monarchy, and Rome to master a continent where, at this hour, half a million of bayonets are vindicating the ascendency of a regulated freedom;—Feudalism still strong in life, though enveloped and overborne by new-born Centralization; Monarchy in the flush of triumphant power; Rome, nerved by disaster, springing with renewed vitality from ashes and corruption, and ranging the earth to reconquer abroad what she had lost at home. These banded powers, pushing into the wilderness their indomitable soldiers and devoted priests, unveiled the secrets of the barbarous continent, pierced the forests, traced and mapped out the streams, planted their emblems, built their forts, and claimed all as their own. New France was all head. Under king, noble, and Jesuit, the lank, lean body would not thrive. Even commerce wore the sword, decked itself with badges of nobility, aspired to forest seigniories and hordes of savage retainers.

Along the borders of the sea an adverse power was strengthening and widening, with slow but steadfast growth, full of blood and muscle,—a body without a head. Each had its strength, each its weakness, each its own modes of vigorous life: but the one was fruitful, the other barren; the one instinct with hope, the other darkening with shadows of despair.

By name, local position, and character, one of these communities of freemen stands forth as the most conspicuous representative of this antagonism,—Liberty and Absolutism, New England and New France. The one was the offspring of a triumphant government; the other, of an oppressed and fugitive people: the one, an unflinching champion of the Roman Catholic reaction; the other, a vanguard of the Reform. Each followed its natural laws of growth, and each came to its natural result. Vitalized by the principles of its foundation, the Puritan commonwealth grew apace. New England was preeminently the land of material progress. Here the prize was within every man's reach: patient industry need never doubt its reward; nay, in defiance of the four Gospels, assiduity in pursuit of gain was promoted to the rank of a duty, and thrift and godliness were linked in equivocal wedlock. Politically she was free; socially she suffered from that subtle and searching oppression which the dominant opinion of a free community may exercise over the members who compose it. As a whole, she grew upon the gaze of the world, a signal example of expansive energy; but she has not been fruitful in those salient and striking forms of character which often give a dramatic life to the annals of nations far less prosperous.

We turn to New France, and all is reversed. Here was a bold attempt to crush under the exactions of a grasping hierarchy, to stifle under the curbs and trappings of a feudal monarchy, a people compassed by influences of the wildest freedom,—whose schools were the forest and the sea, whose trade was an armed barter with savages, and whose daily life a lesson of lawless independence. But this fierce spirit had its vent. The story of New France is from the first a story of war: of war—for so her founders believed—with the adversary of mankind himself; war with savage tribes and potent forest commonwealths; war with the encroaching powers of Heresy and of England. Her brave, unthinking people were stamped with the soldier's virtues and the soldier's faults; and in their leaders were displayed, on a grand and novel stage, the energies, aspirations, and passions which belong to hopes vast and vague, ill-restricted powers, and stations of command.

The growth of New England was a result of the aggregate efforts of a busy multitude, each in his narrow circle toiling for himself, to gather competence or wealth. The expansion of New France was the achievement of a gigantic ambition striving to grasp a continent. It was a vain attempt. Long and valiantly her chiefs upheld their cause, leading to battle a vassal population, warlike as themselves. Borne down by numbers from without, wasted by corruption from within, New France fell at last; and out of her fall grew revolutions whose influence to this hour is felt through every nation of the civilized world.

The French dominion is a memory of the past; and when we evoke its departed shades, they rise upon us from their graves in strange, romantic guise. Again their ghostly camp-fires seem to burn, and the fitful light is cast around on lord and vassal and black-robed priest, mingled with wild forms of savage warriors, knit in close fellowship on the same stern errand. A boundless vision grows upon us; an untamed continent; vast wastes of forest verdure; mountains silent in primeval sleep; river, lake, and glimmering pool; wilderness oceans mingling with the sky. Such was the domain which France conquered for Civilization. Plumed helmets gleamed in the shade of its forests, priestly vestments in its dens and fastnesses of ancient barbarism. Men steeped in antique learning, pale with the close breath of the cloister, here spent the noon and evening of their lives, ruled savage hordes with a mild, parental sway, and stood serene before the direst shapes of death. Men of courtly nurture, heirs to the polish of a far-reaching ancestry, here, with their dauntless hardihood, put to shame the boldest sons of toil.

This memorable but half-forgotten chapter in the book of human life can be rightly read only by lights numerous and widely scattered. The earlier period of New France was prolific in a class of publications which are often of much historic value, but of which many are exceedingly rare. The writer, however, has at length gained access to them all. Of the unpublished records of the colonies, the archives of France are of course the grand deposit; but many documents of important bearing on the subject are to be found scattered in public and private libraries, chiefly in France and Canada. The task of collection has proved abundantly irksome and laborious. It has, however, been greatly lightened by the action of the governments of New York, Massachusetts, and Canada, in collecting from Europe copies of documents having more or less relation to their own history. It has been greatly lightened, too, by a most kind co-operation, for which the writer owes obligations too many for recognition at present, but of which he trusts to make fitting acknowledgment hereafter. Yet he cannot forbear to mention the name of Mr. John Gilmary Shea of New York, to whose labors this department of American history has been so deeply indebted, and that of the Hon. Henry Black of Quebec. Nor can he refrain from expressing his obligation to the skilful and friendly criticism of Mr. Charles Folsom.

In this, and still more must it be the case in succeeding volumes, the amount of reading applied to their composition is far greater than the citations represent, much of it being of a collateral and illustrative nature. This was essential to a plan whose aim it was, while scrupulously and rigorously adhering to the truth of facts, to animate them with the life of the past, and, so far as might be, clothe the skeleton with flesh. If, at times, it may seem that range has been allowed to fancy, it is so in appearance only; since the minutest details of narrative or description rest on authentic documents or on personal observation.

Faithfulness to the truth of history involves far more than a research, however patient and scrupulous, into special facts. Such facts may be detailed with the most minute exactness, and yet the narrative, taken as a whole, may be unmeaning or untrue. The narrator must seek to imbue himself with the life and spirit of the time. He must study events in their bearings near and remote; in the character, habits, and manners of those who took part in them, he must himself be, as it were, a sharer or a spectator of the action he describes.

With respect to that special research which, if inadequate, is still in the most emphatic sense indispensable, it has been the writer's aim to exhaust the existing material of every subject treated. While it would be folly to claim success in such an attempt, he has reason to hope that, so far at least as relates to the present volume, nothing of much importance has escaped him. With respect to the general preparation just alluded to, he has long been too fond of his theme to neglect any means within his reach of making his conception of it distinct and true.

To those who have aided him with information and documents, the extreme slowness in the progress of the work will naturally have caused surprise. This slowness was unavoidable. During the past eighteen years, the state of his health has exacted throughout an extreme caution in regard to mental application, reducing it at best within narrow and precarious limits, and often precluding it. Indeed, for two periods, each of several years, any attempt at bookish occupation would have been merely suicidal. A condition of sight arising from kindred sources has also retarded the work, since it has never permitted reading or writing continuously for much more than five minutes, and often has not permitted them at all. A previous work, "The Conspiracy of Pontiac," was written in similar circumstances.

The writer means, if possible, to carry the present design to its completion. Such a completion, however, will by no means be essential as regards the individual volumes of the series, since each will form a separate and independent work. The present work, it will be seen, contains two distinct and completed narratives. Some progress has been made in others.

Boston. January 1, 1865.

Part One
HUGOENOTS IN FLORIDA

PREFATORY NOTE
TO THE HUGUENOTS IN FLORIDA

The story of New France opens with a tragedy. The political and religious enmities which were soon to bathe Europe in blood broke out with an intense and concentrated fury in the distant wilds of Florida. It was under equivocal auspices that Coligny and his partisans essayed to build up a Calvinist France in America, and the attempt was met by all the forces of national rivalry, personal interest, and religious hate.

This striking passage of our early history is remarkable for the fullness and precision of the authorities that illustrate it. The incidents of the Huguenot occupation of Florida are recorded by eight eye-witnesses. Their evidence is marked by an unusual accord in respect to essential facts, as well as by a minuteness of statement which vividly pictures the events described. The following are the principal authorities consulted for the main body of the narrative.

Ribauld, 'The Whole and True Discovery of Terra Florida,' This is Captain Jean Ribaut's account of his voyage to Florida in 1562. It was "prynted at London," "newly set forthe in Englishe," in 1563, and reprinted by Hakluyt in 1582 in his black-letter tract entitled 'Divers Voyages.' It is not known to exist in the original French.

'L'Histoire Notable de la Floride, mise en lumiere par M. Basanier' (Paris, 1586). The most valuable portion of this work consists of the letters of Rene de Laudonniere, the French commandant in Florida in 1564-65. They are interesting, and, with necessary allowance for the position and prejudices of the writer, trustworthy.

Challeux, Discours de l'Histoire de la Floride (Dieppe, 1566). Challeux was a carpenter, who went to Florida in 1565. He was above sixty years of age, a zealous Huguenot, and a philosopher in his way. His story is affecting from its simplicity. Various editions of it appeared under various titles.

Le Moyne, Brevis Narratio eorum qucs in Florida Americce Provincia Gallis acciderunt. Le Moyne was Laudonniere's artist. His narrative forms the Second Part of the Grands Voyages of De Bry (Frankfort, 1591). It is illustrated by numerous drawings made by the writer from memory, and accompanied with descriptive letter-press.

Coppie d'une Lettre venant de la Floride (Paris, 1565). This is a letter from one of the adventurers under Laudonniere. It is reprinted in the Recueil de Pieces sur la Floride of Ternaux.- Compans. Ternaux also prints in the same volume a narrative called Histoire memorable du dernier Voyage faict par le Capitaine Jean Ribaut. It is of no original value, being compiled from Laudonniere and Challeux.

Une Bequete au Roy, faite en forme de Complainte (1566). This is a petition for redress to Charles the Ninth from the relatives of the French massacred in Florida by the Spaniards. It recounts many incidents of that tragedy.

La Reprinse de la Floride par le Cappitaine Gourgue. This is a manuscript in the Bibliotheque Nationale, printed in the Recueil of Ternaux-Compans. It contains a detailed account of the remarkable expedition of Dominique de Gourgues against the Spaniards in Florida in 1567-68.

Charlevoix, in his Histoire de la Nouvelle France, speaks of another narrative of this expedition in manuscript, preserved in the Gourgues family. A copy of it, made in 1831 by the Vicomte de Gourgues, has been placed at the writer's disposal.

Popeliniere, De Thou, Wytfleit, D'Aubigne De Laet, Brantome, Lescarbot, Champlain, and other writers of the sixteenth and seventeenth centuries, have told or touched upon the story of the Huguenots in Florida; but they all draw their information from one or more of the sources named above.

Lettres et Papiers d' Estat du Sieur de Forguevaulx (Bibliotheque Nationale). These include the correspondence of the French and Spanish courts concerning the massacre of the Huguenots. They are printed by Gaffarel in his Histoire de le Floride Francaise.

The Spanish authorities are the following—Barcia (Cardenas y Cano), Ensayo Cronologico para la Historia General de la Florida (Madrid, 1723). This annalist had access to original documents of great interest. Some of them are used as material for his narrative, others are copied entire. Of these, the most remarkable is that of

Solis de las Meras, Memorial de todas las Jornadas de la Conquista de la Florida.

Francisco Lopez de Mendoza Grajales, Relacion de la Jornada de Pedro Menendez de Aviles en la Florida (Documentos Ineditos del Archivo de Indias, III. 441). A French translation of this journal will be found in the Recueil de Pieces sur let Floride of Ternaux-Compans. Mendoza was chaplain of the expedition commanded by Menendez de Aviles, and, like Solfs, he was an eye-witness of the events which he relates.

Pedro Menendez de Aviles, Siete Cartas escritas al Rey, Anos de 1565 y 1566, MSS. These are the despatches of the Adelantado Menendez to Philip the Second. They were procured for the writer, together with other documents, from the archives of Seville, and their contents are now for the first time made public. They consist of seventy-two closely written foolscap pages, and are of the highest interest and value as regards the present subject, confirming and amplifying the statements of Solis and Mendoza, and giving new and curious information with respect to the designs of Spain upon the continent of North America.

It is unnecessary to specify the authorities for the introductory and subordinate portions of the narrative.

The writer is indebted to Mr. Buckingham Smith, for procuring copies of documents from the archives of Spain; to Mr. Bancroft, the historian of the United States, for the use of the Vicomte de Gourgues's copy of the journal describing the expedition of his ancestor against the Spaniards; and to Mr. Charles Russell Lowell, of the Boston Athenaeum, and Mr. John Langdon Sibley, Librarian of Harvard College, for obliging aid in consulting books and papers.

CHAPTER I.
1512-1561.
EARLY SPANISH ADVENTURE

Towards the close of the fifteenth century, Spain achieved her final triumph over the infidels of Granada, and made her name glorious through all generations by the discovery of America. The religious zeal and romantic daring which a long course of Moorish wars had called forth were now exalted to redoubled fervor. Every ship from the New World came freighted with marvels which put the fictions of chivalry to shame; and to the Spaniard of that day America was a region of wonder and mystery, of vague and magnificent promise. Thither adventurers hastened, thirsting for glory and for gold, and often mingling the enthusiasm of the crusader and the valor of the knight-errant with the bigotry of inquisitors and the rapacity of pirates. They roamed over land and sea; they climbed unknown mountains, surveyed unknown oceans, pierced the sultry intricacies of tropical forests; while from year to year and from day to day new wonders were unfolded, new islands and archipelagoes, new regions of gold and pearl, and barbaric empires of more than Oriental wealth. The extravagance of hope and the fever of adventure knew no bounds. Nor is it surprising that amid such waking marvels the imagination should run wild in romantic dreams; that between the possible and the impossible the line of distinction should be but faintly drawn, and that men should be found ready to stake life and honor in pursuit of the most insane fantasies.

Such a man was the veteran cavalier Juan Ponce de Leon. Greedy of honors and of riches, he embarked at Porto Rico with three brigantines, bent on schemes of discovery. But that which gave the chief stimulus to his enterprise was a story, current among the Indians of Cuba and Hispaniola, that on the island of Bimini, said to be one of the Bahamas, there was a fountain of such virtue, that, bathing in its waters, old men resumed their youth. 1 It was said, moreover, that on a neighboring shore might be found a river gifted with the same beneficent property, and believed by some to be no other than the Jordan. 2 Ponce de Leon found the island of Bimini, but not the fountain. Farther westward, in the latitude of thirty degrees and eight minutes, he approached an unknown land, which he named Florida, and, steering southward, explored its coast as far as the extreme point of the peninsula, when, after some farther explorations, he retraced his course to Porto Rico.

Ponce de Leon had not regained his youth, but his active spirit was unsubdued.

Nine years later he attempted to plant a colony in Florida; the Indians attacked him fiercely; he was mortally wounded, and died soon afterwards in Cuba. 3

The voyages of Garay and Vasquez de Ayllon threw new light on the discoveries of Ponce, and the general outline of the coasts of Florida became known to the Spaniards. 4 Meanwhile, Cortes had conquered Mexico, and the fame of that iniquitous but magnificent exploit rang through all Spain. Many an impatient cavalier burned to achieve a kindred fortune. To the excited fancy of the Spaniards the unknown land of Florida seemed the seat of surpassing wealth, and Pamphilo de Narvaez essayed to possess himself of its fancied treasures. Landing on its shores, and proclaiming destruction to the Indians unless they acknowledged the sovereignty of the Pope and the Emperor, he advanced into the forests with three hundred men. Nothing could exceed their sufferings. Nowhere could they find the gold they came to seek. The village of Appalache, where they hoped to gain a rich booty, offered nothing but a few mean wigwams. The horses gave out, and the famished soldiers fed upon their flesh. The men sickened, and the Indians unceasingly harassed their march. At length, after two hundred and eighty leagues 5 of wandering, they found themselves on the northern shore of the Gulf of Mexico, and desperately put to sea in such crazy boats as their skill and means could construct. Cold, disease, famine, thirst, and the fury of the waves, melted them away. Narvaez himself perished, and of his wretched followers no more than four escaped, reaching by land, after years of vicissitude, the Christian settlements of New Spain. 6

The interior of the vast country then comprehended under the name of Florida still remained unexplored. The Spanish voyager, as his caravel ploughed the adjacent seas, might give full scope to his imagination, and dream that beyond the long, low margin of forest which bounded his horizon lay hid a rich harvest for some future conqueror; perhaps a second Mexico with its royal palace and sacred pyramids, or another Cuzco with its temple of the Sun, encircled with a frieze of gold. Haunted by such visions, the ocean chivalry of Spain could not long stand idle.

Hernando de Soto was the companion of Pizarro in the conquest of Peru. He had come to America a needy adventurer, with no other fortune than his sword and target. But his exploits had given him fame and fortune, and he appeared at court with the retinue of a nobleman. 7 Still, his active energies could not endure repose, and his avarice and ambition goaded him to fresh enterprises. He asked and obtained permission to conquer Florida. While this design was in agitation, Cabeca de Vaca, one of those who had survived the expedition of Narvaez, appeared in Spain, and for purposes of his own spread abroad the mischievous falsehood, that Florida was the richest country yet discovered. De Soto's plans were embraced with enthusiasm. Nobles and gentlemen contended for the privilege of joining his standard; and, setting sail with an ample armament, he landed at the bay of Espiritu Santo, now Tampa Bay, in Florida, with six hundred and twenty chosen men, a band as gallant and well appointed, as eager in purpose and audacious in hope, as ever trod the shores of the New World. The clangor of trumpets, the neighing of horses, the fluttering of pennons, the glittering of helmet and lance, startled the ancient forest with unwonted greeting. Amid this pomp of chivalry, religion was not forgotten. The sacred vessels and vestments with bread and wine for the Eucharist were carefully provided; and De Soto himself declared that the enterprise was undertaken for God alone, and seemed to be the object of His especial care. These devout marauders could not neglect the spiritual welfare of the Indians whom they had come to plunder; and besides fetters to bind, and bloodhounds to hunt them, they brought priests and monks for the saving of their souls.

The adventurers began their march. Their story has been often told. For month after month and year after year, the procession of priests and cavaliers, crossbowmen, arquebusiers, and Indian captives laden with the baggage, still wandered on through wild and boundless wastes, lured hither and thither by the ignis fatuus of their hopes. They traversed great portions of Georgia, Alabama, and Mississippi, everywhere inflicting and enduring misery, but never approaching their phantom El Dorado. At length, in the third year of their journeying, they reached the banks of the Mississippi, a hundred and thirty-two years before its second discovery by Marquette. One of their number describes the great river as almost half a league wide, deep, rapid, and constantly rolling down trees and drift-wood on its turbid current.

The Spaniards crossed over at a point above the mouth of the Arkansas. They advanced westward, but found no treasures,— nothing indeed but hardships, and an Indian enemy, furious, writes one of their officers, "as mad dogs." They heard of a country towards the north where maize could not be cultivated because the vast herds of wild cattle devoured it. They penetrated so far that they entered the range of the roving prairie tribes; for, one day, as they pushed their way with difficulty across great plains covered with tall, rank grass, they met a band of savages who dwelt in lodges of skins sewed together, subsisting on game alone, and wandering perpetually from place to place. Finding neither gold nor the South Sea, for both of which they had hoped, they returned to the banks of the Mississippi.

De Soto, says one of those who accompanied him, was a "stern man, and of few words." Even in the midst of reverses, his will had been law to his followers, and he had sustained himself through the depths of disappointment with the energy of a stubborn pride. But his hour was come. He fell into deep dejection, followed by an attack of fever, and soon after died miserably. To preserve his body from the Indians, his followers sank it at midnight in the river, and the sullen waters of the Mississippi buried his ambition and his hopes.

The adventurers were now, with few exceptions, disgusted with the enterprise, and longed only to escape from the scene of their miseries. After a vain attempt to reach Mexico by land, they again turned back to the Mississippi, and labored, with all the resources which their desperate necessity could suggest, to construct vessels in which they might make their way to some Christian settlement. Their condition was most forlorn. Few of their horses remained alive; their baggage had been destroyed at the burning of the Indian town of Mavila, and many of the soldiers were without armor and without weapons. In place of the gallant array which, more than three years before, had left the harbor of Espiritu Santo, a company of sickly and starving men were laboring among the swampy forests of the Mississippi, some clad in skins, and some in mats woven from a kind of wild vine.

Seven brigantines were finished and launched; and, trusting their lives on board these frail vessels, they descended the Mississippi, running the gantlet between hostile tribes, who fiercely attacked them. Reaching the Gulf, though not without the loss of eleven of their number, they made sail for the Spanish settlement on the river Panuco, where they arrived safely, and where the inhabitants met them with a cordial welcome. Three hundred and eleven men thus escaped with life, leaving behind them the bones of their comrades strewn broadcast through the wilderness.

De Soto's fate proved an insufficient warning, for those were still found who begged a fresh commission for the conquest of Florida; but the Emperor would not hear them. A more pacific enterprise was undertaken by Cancello, a Dominican monk, who with several brother ecclesiastics undertook to convert the natives to the true faith, but was murdered in the attempt. Nine years later, a plan was formed for the colonization of Florida, and Guido de las Bazares sailed to explore the coasts, and find a spot suitable for the establishment. 8 After his return, a squadron, commanded by Angel de Villafane, and freighted with supplies and men, put to sea from San Juan d'Ulloa; but the elements were adverse, and the result was a total failure. Not a Spaniard had yet gained foothold in Florida.

That name, as the Spaniards of that day understood it, comprehended the whole country extending from the Atlantic on the east to the longitude of New Mexico on the west, and from the Gulf of Mexico and the River of Palms indefinitely northward towards the polar sea. This vast territory was claimed by Spain in right of the discoveries of Columbus, the grant of the Pope, and the various expeditions mentioned above. England claimed it in right of the discoveries of Cabot; while France could advance no better title than might be derived from the voyage of Verazzano and vague traditions of earlier visits of Breton adventurers.

With restless jealousy Spain watched the domain which she could not occupy, and on France especially she kept an eye of deep distrust. When, in 1541, Cartier and Roberval essayed to plant a colony in the part of ancient Spanish Florida now called Canada, she sent spies and fitted out caravels to watch that abortive enterprise. Her fears proved just. Canada, indeed, was long to remain a solitude; but, despite the Papal bounty gifting Spain with exclusive ownership of a hemisphere, France and Heresy at length took root in the sultry forests of modern Florida.

CHAPTER II
1550-1558.
VILLEGAGNON

In the middle of the sixteenth century, Spain was the incubus of Europe. Gloomy and portentous, she chilled the world with her baneful shadow. Her old feudal liberties were gone, absorbed in the despotism of Madrid. A tyranny of monks and inquisitors, with their swarms of spies and informers, their racks, their dungeons, and their fagots, crushed all freedom of thought or speech; and, while the Dominican held his reign of terror and force, the deeper Jesuit guided the mind from infancy into those narrow depths of bigotry from which it was never to escape. Commercial despotism was joined to political and religious despotism. The hands of the government were on every branch of industry. Perverse regulations, uncertain and ruinous taxes, monopolies, encouragements, prohibitions, restrictions, cramped the national energy. Mistress of the Indies, Spain swarmed with beggars. Yet, verging to decay, she had an ominous and appalling strength. Her condition was that of an athletic man penetrated with disease, which had not yet unstrung the thews and sinews formed in his days of vigor. Philip the Second could command the service of warriors and statesmen developed in the years that were past. The gathered energies of ruined feudalism were wielded by a single hand. The mysterious King, in his den in the Escorial, dreary and silent, and bent like a scribe over his papers, was the type and the champion of arbitrary power. More than the Pope himself, he was the head of Catholicity. In doctrine and in deed, the inexorable bigotry of Madrid was ever in advance of Rome.

Not so with France. She was full of life,—a discordant and struggling vitality. Her monks and priests, unlike those of Spain, were rarely either fanatics or bigots; yet not the less did they ply the rack and the fagot, and howl for heretic blood. Their all was at stake: their vast power, their bloated wealth, were wrapped up in the ancient faith. Men were burned, and women buried alive. All was in vain. To the utmost bounds of France, the leaven of the Reform was working. The Huguenots, fugitives from torture and death, found an asylum at Geneva, their city of refuge, gathering around Calvin, their great high-priest. Thence intrepid colporteurs, their lives in their hands, bore the Bible and the psalm-book to city, hamlet, and castle, to feed the rising flame. The scattered churches, pressed by a common danger, began to organize. An ecclesiastical republic spread its ramifications through France, and grew underground to a vigorous life,—pacific at the outset, for the great body of its members were the quiet bourgeoisie, by habit, as by faith, averse to violence. Yet a potent fraction of the warlike noblesse were also of the new faith; and above them all, preeminent in character as in station, stood Gaspar de Coligny, Admiral of France.

The old palace of the Louvre, reared by the "Roi Chevalier" on the site of those dreary feudal towers which of old had guarded the banks of the Seine, held within its sculptured masonry the worthless brood of Valois. Corruption and intrigue ran riot at the court. Factious nobles, bishops, and cardinals, with no God but pleasure and ambition, contended around the throne or the sickbed of the futile King. Catherine de Medicis, with her stately form, her mean spirit, her bad heart, and her fathomless depths of duplicity, strove by every subtle art to hold the balance of power among them. The bold, pitiless, insatiable Guise, and his brother the Cardinal of Lorraine, the incarnation of falsehood, rested their ambition on the Catholic party. Their army was a legion of priests, and the black swarms of countless monasteries, who by the distribution of alms held in pay the rabble of cities and starving peasants on the lands of impoverished nobles. Montmorency, Conde, and Navarre leaned towards the Reform,—doubtful and inconstant chiefs, whose faith weighed light against their interests. Yet, amid vacillation, selfishness, weakness, treachery, one great man was like a tower of trust, and this was Gaspar de Coligny.

Firm in his convictions, steeled by perils and endurance, calm, sagacious, resolute, grave even to severity, a valiant and redoubted soldier, Coligny looked abroad on the gathering storm and read its danger in advance. He saw a strange depravity of manners; bribery and violence overriding justice; discontented nobles, and peasants ground down with taxes. In the midst of this rottenness, the Calvinistic churches, patient and stern, were fast gathering to themselves the better life of the nation. Among and around them tossed the surges of clerical hate. Luxurious priests and libertine monks saw their disorders rebuked by the grave virtues of the Protestant zealots. Their broad lands, their rich endowments, their vessels of silver and of gold, their dominion over souls,—in itself a revenue,—were all imperiled by the growing heresy. Nor was the Reform less exacting, less intolerant, or, when its hour came, less aggressive than the ancient faith. The storm was thickening, and it must burst soon.

When the Emperor Charles the Fifth beleaguered Algiers, his camps were deluged by a blinding tempest, and at its height the infidels made a furious sally. A hundred Knights of Malta, on foot, wearing over their armor surcoats of crimson blazoned with the white cross, bore the brunt of the assault. Conspicuous among them was Nicolas Durand de Villegagnon. A Moorish cavalier, rushing upon him, pierced his arm with a lance, and wheeled to repeat the blow; but the knight leaped on the infidel, stabbed him with his dagger, flung him from his horse, and mounted in his place. Again, a Moslem host landed in Malta and beset the Cite Notable. The garrison was weak, disheartened, and without a leader. Villegagnon with six followers, all friends of his own, passed under cover of night through the infidel leaguer, climbed the walls by ropes lowered from above, took command, repaired the shattered towers, aiding with his own hands in the work, and animated the garrison to a resistance so stubborn that the besiegers lost heart and betook themselves to their galleys. No less was he an able and accomplished mariner, prominent among that chivalry of the sea who held the perilous verge of Christendom against the Mussuhuan. He claimed other laurels than those of the sword. He was a scholar, a linguist, a controversialist, potent with the tongue and with the pen, commanding in presence, eloquent and persuasive in discourse. Yet this Crichton of France had proved himself an associate nowise desirable. His sleepless intellect was matched with a spirit as restless, vain, unstable, and ambitious, as it was enterprising and bold. Addicted to dissent, and enamoured of polemics, he entered those forbidden fields of inquiry and controversy to which the Reform invited him. Undaunted by his monastic vows, he battled for heresy with tongue and pen, and in the ear of Protestants professed himself a Protestant. As a Commander of his Order, he quarreled with the Grand Master, a domineering Spaniard; and, as Vice-Admiral of Brittany, he was deep in a feud with the Governor of Brest. Disgusted at home, his fancy crossed the seas. He aspired to build for France and himself an empire amid the tropical splendors of Brazil. Few could match him in the gift of persuasion; and the intrepid seamen whose skill and valor had run the gantlet of the English fleet, and borne Mary Stuart of Scotland in safety to her espousals with the Dauphin, might well be intrusted with a charge of moment so far inferior. Henry the Second was still on the throne. The lance of Montgomery had not yet rid France of that infliction. To win a share in the rich domain of the New World, of which Portuguese and Spanish arrogance claimed the monopoly, was the end held by Villegagnon before the eyes of the King. Of the Huguenots, he said not a word. For Coligny he had another language. He spoke of an asylum for persecuted religion, a Geneva in the wilderness, far from priests and monks and Francis of Guise. The Admiral gave him a ready ear; if, indeed, he himself had not first conceived the plan. Yet to the King, an active burner of Huguenots, Coligny too urged it as an enterprise, not for the Faith, but for France. In secret, Geneva was made privy to it, and Calvin himself embraced it with zeal. The enterprise, in fact, had a double character, political as well as religious. It was the reply of France, the most emphatic she had yet made, to the Papal bull which gave all the western hemisphere to Portugal and Spain; and, as if to point her answer, she sent, not Frenchmen only, but Protestant Frenchmen, to plant the fleur-de-lis on the shores of the New World.

Two vessels were made ready, in the name of the King. The body of the emigration was Huguenot, mingled with young nobles, restless, idle, and poor, with reckless artisans, and piratical sailors from the Norman and Breton seaports. They put to sea from Havre on the twelfth of July, 1555, and early in November saw the shores of Brazil. Entering the harbor of Rio Janeiro, then called Ganabara, Villegagnon landed men and stores on an island, built huts, and threw up earthworks. In anticipation of future triumphs, the whole continent, by a strange perversion of language, was called Antarctic France, while the fort received the name of Coligny.

Villegagnon signalized his new-born Protestantism by an intolerable solicitude for the manners and morals of his followers. The whip and the pillory requited the least offence. The wild and discordant crew, starved and flogged for a season into submission, conspired at length to rid themselves of him; but while they debated whether to poison him, blow him up, or murder him and his officers in their sleep, three Scotch soldiers, probably Calvinists, revealed the plot, and the vigorous hand of the commandant crushed it in the bud.

But how was the colony to subsist? Their island was too small for culture, while the mainland was infested with hostile tribes, and threatened by the Portuguese, who regarded the French occupancy as a violation of their domain.

Meanwhile, in France, Huguenot influence, aided by ardent letters sent home by Villegagnon in the returning ships, was urging on the work. Nor were the Catholic chiefs averse to an enterprise which, by colonizing heresy, might tend to relieve France of its presence. Another embarkation was prepared, in the name of Henry the Second, under Bois-Lecomte, a nephew of Villegagnon. Most of the emigrants were Huguenots. Geneva sent a large deputation, and among them several ministers, full of zeal for their land of promise and their new church in the wilderness. There were five young women, also, with a matron to watch over them. Soldiers, emigrants, and sailors, two hundred and ninety in all, were embarked in three vessels; and, to the sound of cannon, drums, fifes, and trumpets, they unfurled their sails at Honfleur. They were no sooner on the high seas than the piratical character of the Norman sailors, in no way exceptional at that day, began to declare itself. They hailed every vessel weaker than themselves, pretended to be short of provisions, and demanded leave to buy them; then, boarding the stranger, plundered her from stem to stern. After a passage of four months, on the ninth of March, 1557, they entered the port of Ganabara, and saw the fleur-de-lis floating above the walls of Fort Coligny. Amid salutes of cannon, the boats, crowded with sea-worn emigrants, moved towards the landing. It was an edifying scene when Villegagnon, in the picturesque attire which marked the warlike nobles of the period, came down to the shore to greet the sombre ministers of Calvin. With hands uplifted and eyes raised to heaven, he bade them welcome to the new asylum of the faithful; then launched into a long harangue full of zeal and unction. His discourse finished, he led the way to the dining-hall. If the redundancy of spiritual aliment had surpassed their expectations, the ministers were little prepared for the meagre provision which awaited their temporal cravings; for, with appetites whetted by the sea, they found themselves seated at a board whereof, as one of them complains the choicest dish was a dried fish, and the only beverage rain-water. They found their consolation in the inward graces of the commandant, whom they likened to the Apostle Paul.

For a time all was ardor and hope. Men of birth and station, and the ministers themselves, labored with pick and shovel to finish the fort. Every day exhortations, sermons, prayers, followed in close succession, and Villegagnon was always present, kneeling on a velvet cushion brought after him by a page. Soon, however, he fell into sharp controversy with the ministers upon points of faith. Among the emigrants was a student of the Sorbonne, one Cointac, between whom and the ministers arose a fierce and unintermitted war of words. Is it lawful to mix water with the wine of the Eucharist? May the sacramental bread be made of meal of Indian corn? These and similar points of dispute filled the fort with wranglings, begetting cliques, factions, and feuds without number. Villegagnon took part with the student, and between them they devised a new doctrine, abhorrent alike to Geneva and to Rome. The advent of this nondescript heresy was the signal of redoubled strife. The dogmatic stiffness of the Geneva ministers chafed Villegagnon to fury. He felt himself, too, in a false position. On one side he depended on the Protestant, Coligny; on the other, he feared the Court. There were Catholics in the colony who might report him as an open heretic. On this point his doubts were set at rest; for a ship from France brought him a letter from the Cardinal of Lorraine, couched, it is said, in terms which restored him forthwith to the bosom of the Church. Villegagnon now affirmed that he had been deceived in Calvin, and pronounced him a "frightful heretic." He became despotic beyond measure, and would bear no opposition. The ministers, reduced nearly to starvation, found themselves under a tyranny worse than that from which they had fled.

At length he drove them from the fort, and forced them to bivouac on the mainland, at the risk of being butchered by Indians, until a vessel loading with Brazil-wood in the harbor should be ready to carry them back to France. Having rid himself of the ministers, he caused three of the more zealous Calvinists to be seized, dragged to the edge of a rock, and thrown into the sea. A fourth, equally obnoxious, but who, being a tailor, could ill be spared, was permitted to live on condition of recantation. Then, mustering the colonists, he warned them to shun the heresies of Luther and Calvin; threatened that all who openly professed those detestable doctrines should share the fate of their three comrades; and, his harangue over, feasted the whole assembly, in token, says the narrator, of joy and triumph.

Meanwhile, in their crazy vessel, the banished ministers drifted slowly on their way. Storms fell upon them, their provisions failed, their water-casks were empty, and, tossing in the wilderness of waves, or rocking on the long swells of subsiding gales, they sank almost to despair. In their famine they chewed the Brazil-wood with which the vessel was laden, devoured every scrap of leather, singed and ate the horn of lanterns, hunted rats through the hold, and sold them to each other at enormous prices. At length, stretched on the deck, sick, listless, attenuated, and scarcely able to move a limb, they descried across the waste of sea the faint, cloud-like line that marked the coast of Brittany. Their perils were not past; for, if we may believe one of them, Jean de Lery, they bore a sealed letter from Villegagnon to the magistrates of the first French port at which they might arrive. It denounced them as heretics, worthy to be burned. Happily, the magistrates leaned to the Reform, and the malice of the commandant failed of its victims.

Villegagnon himself soon sailed for France, leaving the wretched colony to its fate. He presently entered the lists against Calvin, and engaged him in a hot controversial war, in which, according to some of his contemporaries, the knight often worsted the theologian at his own weapons. Before the year 1558 was closed, Ganabara fell a prey to the Portuguese. They set upon it in force, battered down the fort, and slew the feeble garrison, or drove them to a miserable refuge among the Indians. Spain and Portugal made good their claim to the vast domain, the mighty vegetation, and undeveloped riches of "Antarctic France."

CHAPTER III.
1562, 1563.
JEAN RIBAUT

In the year 1562 a cloud of black and deadly portent was thickening over France. Surely and swiftly she glided towards the abyss of the religious wars. None could pierce the future, perhaps none dared to contemplate it: the wild rage of fanaticism and hate, friend grappling with friend, brother with brother, father with son; altars profaned, hearth-stones made desolate, the robes of Justice herself bedrenched with murder. In the gloom without lay Spain, imminent and terrible. As on the hill by the field of Dreux, her veteran bands of pikemen, dark masses of organized ferocity, stood biding their time while the battle surged below, and then swept downward to the slaughter,—so did Spain watch and wait to trample and crush the hope of humanity.

In these days of fear, a second Huguenot colony sailed for the New World. The calm, stern man who represented and led the Protestantism of France felt to his inmost heart the peril of the time. He would fain build up a city of refuge for the persecuted sect. Yet Gaspar de Coligny, too high in power and rank to be openly assailed, was forced to act with caution. He must act, too, in the name of the Crown, and in virtue of his office of Admiral of France. A nobleman and a soldier,—for the Admiral of France was no seaman,—he shared the ideas and habits of his class; nor is there reason to believe him to have been in advance of his time in a knowledge of the principles of successful colonization. His scheme promised a military colony, not a free commonwealth. The Huguenot party was already a political as well as a religious party. At its foundation lay the religious element, represented by Geneva, the martyrs, and the devoted fugitives who sang the psalms of Marot among rocks and caverns. Joined to these were numbers on whom the faith sat lightly, whose hope was in commotion and change. Of the latter, in great part, was the Huguenot noblesse, from Conde, who aspired to the crown,

"Ce petit homme tant joli,

Qui toujours chante, toujours rit,"

to the younger son of the impoverished seigneur whose patrimony was his sword. More than this, the restless, the factious, and the discontented, began to link their fortunes to a party whose triumph would involve confiscation of the wealth of the only rich class in France. An element of the great revolution was already mingling in the strife of religions.

America was still a land of wonder. The ancient spell still hung unbroken over the wild, vast world of mystery beyond the sea,—a land of romance, adventure, and gold.

Fifty-eight years later the Puritans landed on the sands of Massachusetts Bay. The illusion was gone,—the ignis fatuus of adventure, the dream of wealth. The rugged wilderness offered only a stern and hard won independence. In their own hearts, and not in the promptings of a great leader or the patronage of an equivocal government, their enterprise found its birth and its achievement. They were of the boldest and most earnest of their sect. There were such among the French disciples of Calvin; but no Mayflower ever sailed from a port of France. Coligny's colonists were of a different stamp, and widely different was their fate.

An excellent seaman and stanch Protestant, Jean Ribaut of Dieppe, commanded the expedition. Under him, besides sailors, were a band of veteran soldiers, and a few young nobles. Embarked in two of those antiquated craft whose high poops and tub-like porportions are preserved in the old engravings of De Bry, they sailed from Havre on the eighteenth of February, 1562. They crossed the Atlantic, and on the thirtieth of April, in the latitude of twenty-nine and a half degrees, saw the long, low line where the wilderness of waves met the wilderness of woods. It was the coast of Florida. They soon descried a jutting point, which they called French Cape, perhaps one of the headlands of Matanzas Inlet. They turned their prows northward, coasting the fringes of that waste of verdure which rolled in shadowy undulation far to the unknown West.

On the next morning, the first of May, they found themselves off the mouth of a great river. Riding at anchor on a sunny sea, they lowered their boats, crossed the bar that obstructed the entrance, and floated on a basin of deep and sheltered water, "boyling and roaring," says Ribaut, "through the multitude of all kind of fish." Indians were running along the beach, and out upon the sand-bars, beckoning them to land. They pushed their boats ashore and disembarked,—sailors, soldiers, and eager young nobles. Corselet and morion, arquebuse and halberd, flashed in the sun that flickered through innumerable leaves, as, kneeling on the ground, they gave thanks to God, who had guided their voyage to an issue full of promise. The Indians, seated gravely under the neighboring trees, looked on in silent respect, thinking that they worshipped the sun. "They be all naked and of a goodly stature, mightie, and as well shapen and proportioned of body as any people in ye world; and the fore part of their body and armes be painted with pretie deuised workes, of Azure, red, and blacke, so well and so properly as the best Painter of Europe could not amende it." With their squaws and children, they presently drew near, and, strewing the earth with laurel boughs, sat down among the Frenchmen. Their visitors were much pleased with them, and Ribaut gave the chief, whom he calls the king, a robe of blue cloth, worked in yellow with the regal fleur-de-lis.

But Ribaut and his followers, just escaped from the dull prison of their ships, were intent on admiring the wild scenes around them. Never had they known a fairer May-day. The quaint old narrative is exuberant with delight. The tranquil air, the warm sun, woods fresh with young verdure, meadows bright with flowers; the palm, the cypress, the pine, the magnolia; the grazing deer; herons, curlews, bitterns, woodcock, and unknown water-fowl that waded in the ripple of the beach; cedars bearded from crown to root with long, gray moss; huge oaks smothering in the folds of enormous grapevines;—such were the objects that greeted them in their roamings, till their new-discovered land seemed "the fairest, fruitfullest, and pleasantest of al the world."

They found a tree covered with caterpillars, and hereupon the ancient black-letter says: "Also there be Silke wormes in meruielous number, a great deale fairer and better then be our silk wormes. To bee short, it is a thing vnspeakable to consider the thinges that bee seene there, and shalbe founde more and more in this incomperable lande." 2

Above all, it was plain to their excited fancy that the country was rich in gold and silver, turquoises and pearls. One of these last, "as great as an Acorne at ye least," hung from the neck of an Indian who stood near their boats as they re-embarked. They gathered, too, from the signs of their savage visitors, that the wonderful land of Cibola, with its seven cities and its untold riches, was distant but twenty days' journey by water. In truth, it was two thousand miles westward, and its wealth a fable.

They named the river the River of May. It is now the St. John's. "And on the next morning," says Ribault, "we returned to land againe, accompanied with the Captaines, Gentlemen, and Souldiers, and others of our small troope, carrying with us a Pillour or columne of harde stone, our king's armes graved therein, to plant and set the same in the enterie of the Porte; and being come thither we espied on the south syde of the River a place very fitte for that purpose upon a little hill compassed with Cypres, Bayes, Paulmes, and other trees, with sweete smelling and pleasant shrubbes." Here they set the column, and then, again embarking, held their course northward, happy in that benign decree which locks from mortal eyes the secrets of the future.

Next they anchored near Fernandina, and to a neighboring river, probably the St. Mary's, gave the name of the Seine. Here, as morning broke on the fresh, moist meadows hung with mists, and on broad reaches of inland waters which seemed like lakes, they were tempted to land again, and soon "espied an innumerable number of footesteps of great Hartes and Hindes of a wonderfull greatnesse, the steppes being all fresh and new, and it seemeth that the people doe nourish them like tame Cattell." By two or three weeks of exploration they seem to have gained a clear idea of this rich semi-aquatic region. Ribaut describes it as "a countrie full of hauens, riuers, and Ilands, of such fruitfulnes as cannot with tongue be expressed." Slowly moving northward, they named each river, or inlet supposed to be a river, after some stream of France,—the Loire, the Charente, the Garonne, the Gironde. At length, opening betwixt flat and sandy shores, they saw a commodious haven, and named it Port Royal.

On the twenty-seventh of May they crossed the bar where the war-ships of Dupont crossed three hundred years later, passed Hilton Head, and held their course along the peaceful bosom of Broad River. 10 On the left they saw a stream which they named Libourne, probably Skull Creek; on the right, a wide river, probably the Beaufort. When they landed, all was solitude. The frightened

Indians had fled, but they lured them back with knives, beads, and looking-glasses, and enticed two of them on board their ships. Here, by feeding, clothing, and caressing them, they tried to wean them from their fears, thinking to carry them to France, in obedience to a command of Catherine de Medicis; but the captive warriors moaned and lamented day and night, and at length made their escape.

Ranging the woods, they found them full of game, wild turkeys and partridges, bears and lynxes. Two deer, of unusual size, leaped from the underbrush. Cross-bow and arquebuse were brought to the level; but the Huguenot captain, "moved with the singular fairness and bigness of them," forbade his men to shoot.

Preliminary exploration, not immediate settlement, had been the object of the voyage; but all was still rose-color in the eyes of the voyagers, and many of their number would gladly linger in the New Canaan. Ribaut was more than willing to humor them. He mustered his company on deck, and made them a harangue. He appealed to their courage and their patriotism, told them how, from a mean origin, men rise by enterprise and daring to fame and fortune, and demanded who among them would stay behind and hold Port Royal for the King. The greater part came forward, and "with such a good will and joly corage," writes the commander, "as we had much to do to stay their importunitie." Thirty were chosen, and Albert de Pierria was named to command them.

A fort was begun on a small stream called the Chenonceau, probably Archer's Creek, about six miles from the site of Beaufort. 11 They named it Charlesfort, in honor of the unhappy son of Catherine de Medicis, Charles the Ninth, the future hero of St. Bartholomew. Ammunition and stores were sent on shore, and on the eleventh of June, with his diminished company, Ribaut again embarked and spread his sails for France.

From the beach at Hilton Head, Albert and his companions might watch the receding ships, growing less and less on the vast expanse of blue, dwindling to faint specks, then vanishing on the pale verge of the waters. They were alone in those fearful solitudes. From the north pole to Mexico there was no Christian denizen but they.

The pressing question was how they were to subsist. Their thought was not of subsistence, but of gold. Of the thirty, the greater number were soldiers and sailors, with a few gentlemen; that is to say, men of the sword, born within the pale of nobility, who at home could neither labor nor trade without derogation from their rank. For a time they busied themselves with finishing their fort, and, this done, set forth in quest of adventures.

The Indians had lost fear of them. Ribaut had enjoined upon them to use all kindness and gentleness in their dealing with the men of the woods; and they more than obeyed him. They were soon hand and glove with chiefs, warriors, and squaws; and as with Indians the adage that familiarity breeds contempt holds with peculiar force, they quickly divested themselves of the prestige which had attached at the outset to their supposed character of children of the Sun. Good-will, however, remained, and this the colonists abused to the utmost.

Roaming by river, swamp, and forest, they visited in turn the villages of five petty chiefs, whom they called kings, feasting everywhere on hominy, beans, and game, and loaded with gifts. One of these chiefs, named Audusta, invited them to the grand religious festival of his tribe. When they arrived, they found the village alive with preparation, and troops of women busied in sweeping the great circular area where the ceremonies were to take place. But as the noisy and impertinent guests showed a disposition to undue merriment, the chief shut them all in his wigwam, lest their Gentile eyes should profane the mysteries. Here, immured in darkness, they listened to the howls, yelpings, and lugubrious songs that resounded from without. One of them, however, by some artifice, contrived to escape, hid behind a bush, and saw the whole solemnity,—the procession of the medicinemen and the bedaubed and befeathered warriors; the drumming, dancing, and stamping; the wild lamentation of the women as they gashed the arms of the young girls with sharp mussel-shells, and flung the blood into the air with dismal outcries. A scene of ravenous feasting followed, in which the French, released from durance, were summoned to share.

After the carousal they returned to Charlesfort, where they were soon pinched with hunger. The Indians, never niggardly of food, brought them supplies as long as their own lasted; but the harvest was not yet ripe, and their means did not match their good-will. They told the French of two other kings, Ouade and Couexis, who dwelt towards the south, and were rich beyond belief in maize, beans, and squashes. The mendicant colonists embarked without delay, and, with an Indian guide, steered for the wigwams of these potentates, not by the open sea, but by a perplexing inland navigation, including, as it seems, Calibogue Sound and neighboring waters. Reaching the friendly villages, on or near the Savannah, they were feasted to repletion, and their boat was laden with vegetables and corn. They returned rejoicing; but their joy was short. Their store-house at Charlesfort, taking fire in the night, burned to the ground, and with it their newly acquired stock.

Once more they set out for the realms of King Ouade, and once more returned laden with supplies. Nay, the generous savage assured them that, so long as his cornfields yielded their harvests, his friends should not want.

How long this friendship would have lasted may well be doubted. With the perception that the dependants on their bounty were no demigods, but a crew of idle and helpless beggars, respect would soon have changed to contempt, and contempt to ill-will. But it was not to Indian war-clubs that the infant colony was to owe its ruin. It carried within itself its own destruction. The ill-assorted band of lands-men and sailors, surrounded by that influence of the wilderness which wakens the dormant savage in the breasts of men, soon fell into quarrels. Albert, a rude soldier, with a thousand leagues of ocean betwixt him and responsibility, grew harsh, domineering, and violent beyond endurance. None could question or oppose him without peril of death. He hanged with his own hands a drummer who had fallen under his displeasure, and banished a soldier, named La Chore, to a solitary island, three leagues from the fort, where he left him to starve. For a time his comrades chafed in smothered fury. The crisis came at length. A few of the fiercer spirits leagued together, assailed their tyrant, murdered him, delivered the famished soldier, and called to the command one Nicolas Barre, a man of merit. Barre took the command, and thenceforth there was peace.

Peace, such as it was, with famine, homesickness, and disgust. The rough ramparts and rude buildings of Charlesfort, hatefully familiar to their weary eyes, the sweltering forest, the glassy river, the eternal silence of the lifeless wilds around them, oppressed the senses and the spirits. They dreamed of ease, of home, of pleasures across the sea, of the evening cup on the bench before the cabaret, and dances with kind wenches of Dieppe. But how to escape? A continent was their solitary prison, and the pitiless Atlantic shut them in. Not one of them knew how to build a ship; but Ribaut had left them a forge, with tools and iron, and strong desire supplied the place of skill. Trees were hewn down and the work begun. Had they put forth to maintain themselves at Port Royal the energy and resource which they exerted to escape from it, they might have laid the cornerstone of a solid colony.

All, gentle and simple, labored with equal zeal. They calked the seams with the long moss which hung in profusion from the neighboring trees; the pines supplied them with pitch; the Indians made for them a kind of cordage; and for sails they sewed together their shirts and bedding. At length a brigantine worthy of Robinson Crusoe floated on the waters of the Chenonceau. They laid in what provision they could, gave all that remained of their goods to the Indians, embarked, descended the river, and put to sea. A fair wind filled their patchwork sails and bore them from the hated coast. Day after day they held their course, till at length the breeze died away and a breathless calm fell on the waters. Florida was far behind; France farther yet before.

Floating idly on the glassy waste, the craft lay motionless. Their supplies gave out. Twelve kernels of maize a day were each man's portion; then the maize failed, and they ate their shoes and leather jerkins. The water-barrels were drained, and they tried to slake their thirst with brine. Several died, and the rest, giddy with exhaustion and crazed with thirst, were forced to ceaseless labor, bailing out the water that gushed through every seam. Head-winds set in, increasing to a gale, and the wretched brigantine, with sails close-reefed, tossed among the savage billows at the mercy of the storm. A heavy sea rolled down upon her, and burst the bulwarks on the windward side. The surges broke over her, and, clinging with desperate grip to spars and cordage, the drenched voyagers gave up all for lost. At length she righted. The gale subsided, the wind changed, and the crazy, water-logged vessel again bore slowly towards France.

Gnawed with famine, they counted the leagues of barren ocean that still stretched before, and gazed on each other with haggard wolfish eyes, till a whisper passed from man to man that one, by his death, might ransom all the rest. The lot was cast, and it fell on La Chore, the same wretched man whom Albert had doomed to starvation on a lonely island. They killed him, and with ravenous avidity portioned out his flesh. The hideous repast sustained them till the land rose in sight, when, it is said, in a delirium of joy, they could no longer steer their vessel, but let her drift at the will of the tide. A small English bark bore down upon them, took them all on board, and, after landing the feeblest, carried the rest prisoners to Queen Elizabeth. 12

Thus closed another of those scenes of woe whose lurid clouds are thickly piled around the stormy dawn of American history. It was the opening act of a wild and tragic drama.

CHAPTER IV.
1564.
LAUDONNIERE

ON the twenty-fifth of June, 1564, a French squadron anchored a second time off the mouth of the River of May. There were three vessels, the smallest of sixty tons, the largest of one hundred and twenty, all crowded with men. Rene de Laudonniere held command. He was of a noble race of Poiton, attached to the house of Chatillon, of which Coligny was the head; pious, we are told, and an excellent marine officer. An engraving, purporting to be his likeness, shows us a slender figure, leaning against the mast, booted to the thigh, with slouched hat and plume, slashed doublet, and short cloak. His thin oval face, with curled moustache and close-trimmed beard, wears a somewhat pensive look, as if already shadowed by the destiny that awaited him.

The intervening year since Ribaut's voyage had been a dark year for France. From the peaceful solitude of the River of May, that voyager returned to a land reeking with slaughter. But the carnival of bigotry and hate had found a pause. The Peace of Amboise had been signed. The fierce monk choked down his venom; the soldier sheathed his sword, the assassin his dagger; rival chiefs grasped hands, and masked their rancor under hollow smiles. The king and the queen-mother, helpless amid the storm of factions which threatened their destruction, smiled now on Conde, now on Guise,—gave ear to the Cardinal of Lorraine, or listened in secret to the emissaries of Theodore Beza. Coligny was again strong at Court. He used his opportunity, and solicited with success the means of renewing his enterprise of colonization.

Men were mustered for the work. In name, at least, they were all Huguenots yet now, as before, the staple of the projected colony was unsound,—soldiers, paid out of the royal treasury, hired artisans and tradesmen, with a swarm of volunteers from the young Huguenot nobles, whose restless swords had rusted in their scabbards since the peace. The foundation-stone was forgotten. There were no tillers of the soil. Such, indeed, were rare among the Huegonots; for the dull peasants who guided the plough clung with blind tenacity to the ancient faith. Adventurous gentlemen, reckless soldiers, discontented tradesmen, all keen for novelty and heated with dreams of wealth,—these were they who would build for their country and their religion an empire beyond the sea.

On Thursday, the twenty-second of June, Laudonniere saw the low coast-line of Florida, and entered the harbor of St. Augustine, which he named the River of Dolphins, "because that at mine arrival I saw there a great number of Dolphins which were playing in the mouth thereof." Then he bore northward, following the coast till, on the twenty-fifth, he reached the mouth of the St. John's or River of May. The vessels anchored, the boats were lowered, and he landed with his principal followers on the south shore, near the present village of Mayport. It was the very spot where he had landed with Ribaut two years before. They were scarcely on shore when they saw an Indian chief, "which having espied us cryed very far off, Antipola! Antipola! and being so joyful that he could not containe himselfe, he came to meet us accompanied with two of his sonnes, as faire and mightie persons as might be found in al the world. There was in their trayne a great number of men and women which stil made very much of us, and by signes made us understand how glad they were of our arrival. This good entertainment past, the Paracoussy [chief] prayed me to goe see the pillar which we had erected in the voyage of John Ribault." The Indians, regarding it with mysterious awe, had crowned it with evergreens, and placed baskets full of maize before it as an offering.

The chief then took Laudonniere by the hand, telling him that he was named Satouriona, and pointed out the extent of his dominions, far up the river and along the adjacent coasts. One of his sons, a man "perfect in beautie, wisedome, and honest sobrietie," then gave the French commander a wedge of silver, and received some trifles in return, after which the voyagers went back to their ships. "I prayse God continually," says Laudonniere, "for the great love I have found in these savages."

In the morning the French landed again, and found their new friends on the same spot, to the number of eighty or more, seated under a shelter of boughs, in festal attire of smoke-tanned deer-skins, painted in many colors. The party then rowed up the river, the Indians following them along the shore. As they advanced, coasting the borders of a great marsh that lay upon their left, the

St. John's spread before them in vast sheets of glistening water, almost level with its flat, sedgy shores, the haunt of alligators, and the resort of innumerable birds. Beyond the marsh, some five miles from the mouth of the river, they saw a ridge of high ground abutting on the water, which, flowing beneath in a deep, strong current, had undermined it, and left a steep front of yellowish sand. This was the hill now called St. John's Bluff. Here they landed and entered the woods, where Laudonniere stopped to rest while his lieutenant, Ottigny, with a sergeant and a few soldiers, went to explore the country.

They pushed their way through the thickets till they were stopped by a marsh choked with reeds, at the edge of which, under a great laurel-tree, they had seated themselves to rest, overcome with the summer heat, when five Indians suddenly appeared, peering timidly at them from among the bushes. Some of the men went towards them with signs of friendship, on which, taking heart, they drew near, and one of them, who was evidently a chief, made a long speech, inviting the strangers to their dwellings. The way was across the marsh, through which they carried the lieutenant and two or three of the soldiers on their backs, while the rest circled by a narrow path through the woods. When they reached the lodges, a crowd of Indians came out "to receive our men gallantly, and feast them after their manner." One of them brought a large earthen vessel full of spring water, which was served out to each in turn in a wooden cup. But what most astonished the French was a venerable chief, who assured them that he was the father of five successive generations, and that he had lived two hundred and fifty years. Opposite sat a still more ancient veteran, the father of the first, shrunken to a mere anatomy, and "seeming to be rather a dead carkeis than a living body." "Also," pursues the history, "his age was so great that the good man had lost his sight, and could not speak one onely word but with exceeding great paine." In spite of his dismal condition, the visitors were told that he might expect to live, in the course of nature, thirty or forty years more. As the two patriarchs sat face to face, half hidden with their streaming white hair, Ottigny and his credulous soldiers looked from one to the other, lost in speechless admiration.

One of these veterans made a parting present to his guests of two young eagles, and Ottigny and his followers returned to report what they had seen. Laudonniere was waiting for them on the side of the hill; and now, he says, "I went right to the toppe thereof, where we found nothing else but Cedars, Palme, and Baytrees of so sovereigne odour that Baulme smelleth nothing like in comparison." From this high standpoint they surveyed their Canaan. The unruffled river lay before them, with its marshy islands overgrown with sedge and bulrushes; while on the farther side the flat, green meadows spread mile on mile, veined with countless creeks and belts of torpid water, and bounded leagues away by the verge of the dim pine forest. On the right, the sea glistened along the horizon; and on the left, the St. John's stretched westward between verdant shores, a highway to their fancied Eldorado. "Briefly," writes Laudonniere, "the place is so pleasant that those which are melancholicke would be inforced to change their humour."

On their way back to the ships they stopped for another parley with the chief Satouriona, and Laudonniere eagerly asked where he had got the wedge of silver that he gave him in the morning. The chief told him by signs, that he had taken it in war from a people called Thimagoas, who lived higher up the River, and who were his mortal enemies; on which the French captain had the folly to promise that he would join in an expedition against them. Satouriona was delighted, and declared that, if he kept his word, he should have gold and silver to his heart's content.

Man and nature alike seemed to mark the borders of the River of May as the site of the new colony; for here, around the Indian towns, the harvests of maize, beans, and pumpkins promised abundant food, while the river opened a ready way to the mines of gold and silver and the stores of barbaric wealth which glittered before the dreaming vision of the colonists. Yet, the better to satisfy himself and his men, Laudonniere weighed anchor, and sailed for a time along the neighboring coasts. Returning, confirmed in his first impression, he set out with a party of officers and soldiers to explore the borders of the chosen stream. The day was hot. The sun beat fiercely on the woollen caps and heavy doublets of the men, till at length they gained the shade of one of those deep forests of pine where the dead, hot air is thick with resinous odors, and the earth, carpeted with fallen leaves, gives no sound beneath the foot. Yet, in the stillness, deer leaped up on all sides as they moved along. Then they emerged into sunlight. A meadow was before them, a running brook, and a wall of encircling forests. The men called it the Vale of Laudonniere. The afternoon was spent, and the sun was near its setting, when they reached the bank of the river. They strewed the ground with boughs and leaves, and, stretched on that sylvan couch, slept the sleep of travel-worn and weary men.

They were roused at daybreak by sound of trumpet, and after singing a psalm they set themselves to their task. It was the building of a fort, and the spot they chose was a furlong or more above St. John's Bluff, where close to the water was a wide, flat knoll, raised a few feet above the marsh and the river. 13 Boats came up the stream with laborers, tents, provisions, cannon, and tools. The engineers marked out the work in the form of a triangle; and, from the noble volunteer to the meanest artisan, all lent a hand to complete it. On the river side the defences were a palisade of timber. On the two other sides were a ditch, and a rampart of fascines, earth, and sods. At each angle was a bastion, in one of which was the magazine. Within was a spacious parade, around it were various buildings for lodging and storage, and a large house with covered galleries was built on the side towards the river for Laudonniere and his officers. 14In honor of Charles the Ninth the fort was named Fort Caroline.

Meanwhile Satouriona, "lord of all that country," as the narratives style him, was seized with misgivings on learning these proceedings. The work was scarcely begun, and all was din and confusion around the incipient fort, when the startled Frenchmen saw the neighboring height of St. John's swarming with naked warriors. Laudonniere set his men in array, and for a season, pick and spade were dropped for arquebuse and pike. The savage chief descended to the camp. The artist Le Moyne, who saw him, drew his likeness from memory, a tall, athletic figure, tattooed in token of his rank, plumed, bedecked with strings of beads, and girdled with tinkling pieces of metal which hung from the belt which formed his only garment. He came in regal state, a crowd of warriors around him, and, in advance, a troop of young Indians armed with spears. Twenty musicians followed, blowing hideous discord through pipes of reeds, while he seated himself on the ground "like a monkey," as Le Moyne has it in the grave Latin of his Brevis Narratio. A council followed, in which broken words were aided by signs and pantomime; and a treaty of alliance was made, Laudonniere renewing his rash promise to aid the chief against his enemies. Satouriona, well pleased, ordered his Indians to help the French in their work. They obeyed with alacrity, and in two days the buildings of the fort were all thatched, after the native fashion, with leaves of the palmetto.

These savages belonged to one of the confederacies into which the native tribes of Florida were divided, and with three of which the French came into contact. The first was that of Satouriona; and the second was that of the people called Thimagoas, who, under a chief named Outina, dwelt in forty villages high up the St. John's. The third was that of the chief, cacique, or paracoussy whom the French called King Potanou, and whose dominions lay among the pine barrens, cypress swamps, and fertile hummocks westward and northwestward of this remarkable river. These three confederacies hated each other, and were constantly at war. Their social state was more advanced than that of the wandering hunter tribes. They were an agricultural people, and around all their villages were fields of maize, beans, and pumpkins. The harvest was gathered into a public granary, and they lived on it during three fourths of the year, dispersing in winter to hunt among the forests.

They were exceedingly well formed; the men, or the principal among them, were tattooed on the limbs and body, and in summer were nearly naked. Some wore their straight black hair flowing loose to the waist; others gathered it in a knot at the crown of the head. They danced and sang about the scalps of their enemies, like the tribes of the North; and like them they had their "medicine-men," who combined the functions of physicians, sorcerers, and priests. The most prominent feature of their religion was sun-worship.

Their villages were clusters of large dome-shaped huts, framed with poles and thatched with palmetto leaves. In the midst was the dwelling of the chief, much larger than the rest, and sometimes raised on an artificial mound. They were enclosed with palisades, and, strange to say, some of them were approached by wide avenues, artificially graded, and several hundred yards in length.

Traces of these may still be seen, as may also the mounds in which the Floridians, like the Hurons and various other tribes, collected at stated intervals the bones of their dead.

Social distinctions were sharply defined among them. Their chiefs, whose office was hereditary, sometimes exercised a power almost absolute. Each village had its chief, subordinate to the grand chief of the confederacy. In the language of the French narratives, they were all kings or lords, vassals of the great monarch Satouriona, Outina, or Potanou. All these tribes are now extinct, and it is difficult to ascertain with precision their tribal affinities. There can be no doubt that they were the authors of the aboriginal remains at present found in various parts of Florida.

Having nearly finished the fort, Laudonniere declares that he "would not lose the minute of an houre without employing of the same in some vertuous exercise;" and he therefore sent his lieutenant, Ottigny, to spy out the secrets of the interior, and to learn, above all, "what this Thimagoa might be, whereof the Paracoussy Satouriona had spoken to us so often." As Laudonniere stood pledged to attack the Thimagoas, the chief gave Ottigny two Indian guides, who, says the record, were so eager for the fray that they seemed as if bound to a wedding feast.

The lazy waters of the St. John's, tinged to coffee color by the exudations of the swamps, curled before the prow of Ottigny's sailboat as he advanced into the prolific wilderness which no European eye had ever yet beheld. By his own reckoning, he sailed thirty leagues up the river, which would have brought him to a point not far below Palatka. Here, more than two centuries later, the Bartrams, father and son, guided their skiff and kindled their nightly bivouac-fire; and here, too, roamed Audubon, with his sketch-book and his gun. It was a paradise for the hunter and the naturalist. Earth, air, and water teemed with life, in endless varieties of beauty and ugliness. A half-tropical forest shadowed the low shores, where the palmetto and the cabbage palm mingled with the oak, the maple, the cypress, the liquid-ambar, the laurel, the myrtle, and the broad glistening leaves of the evergreen magnolia. Here was the haunt of bears, wild-cats, lynxes, cougars, and the numberless deer of which they made their prey. In the sedges and the mud the alligator stretched his brutish length; turtles with outstretched necks basked on half-sunken logs; the rattlesnake sunned himself on the sandy bank, and the yet more dangerous moccason lurked under the water-lilies in inlets and sheltered coves. The air and the water were populous as the earth. The river swarmed with fish, from the fierce and restless gar, cased in his horny armor, to the lazy cat-fish in the muddy depths. There were the golden eagle and the white-headed eagle, the gray pelican and the white pelican, the blue heron and the white heron, the egret, the ibis, ducks of various sorts, the whooping crane, the black vulture, and the cormorant; and when at sunset the voyagers drew their boat upon the strand and built their camp-fire under the arches of the woods, the owls whooped around them all night long, and when morning came the sultry mists that wrapped the river were vocal with the clamor of wild turkeys.

When Ottigny was about twenty leagues from Fort Caroline, his two Indian guides, who were always on the watch, descried three canoes, and in great excitement cried, "Thimagoa! Thimagoa!" As they drew near, one of them snatched up a halberd and the other a sword, and in their fury they seemed ready to jump into the water to get at the enemy. To their great disgust, Ottigny permitted the Thimagoas to run their canoes ashore and escape to the woods. Far from keeping Laudonniere's senseless promise to fight them, he wished to make them friends; to which end he now landed with some of his men, placed a few trinkets in their canoes, and withdrew to a distance to watch the result. The fugitives presently returned, step by step, and allowed the French to approach them; on which Ottigny asked, by signs, if they had gold or silver. They replied that they had none, but that if he would give them one of his men they would show him where it was to be found. One of the soldiers boldly offered himself for the venture, and embarked with them. As, however, he failed to return according to agreement, Ottigny, on the next day, followed ten leagues farther up the stream, and at length had the good luck to see him approaching in a canoe. He brought little or no gold, but reported that he had heard of a certain chief, named Mayrra, marvellously rich, who lived three days' journey up the river; and with these welcome tidings Ottigny went back to Fort Caroline.

A fortnight later, an officer named Vasseur went up the river to pursue the adventure. The fever for gold had seized upon the French. As the villages of the Thimagoas lay between them and the imagined treasures, they shrank from a quarrel, and Laudonniere repented already of his promised alliance with Satouriona.

Vasseur was two days' sail from the fort when two Indians hailed him from the shore, inviting him to their dwellings. He accepted their guidance, and presently saw before him the cornfields and palisades of an Indian town. He and his followers were led through the wondering crowd to the lodge of Mollua, the chief, seated in the place of honor, and plentifully regaled with fish and bread. The repast over, Mollua made a speech. He told them that he was one of the forty vassal chiefs of the great Outina, lord of all the Thimagoas, whose warriors wore armor of gold and silver plate. He told them, too, of Potanou, his enemy, "a man cruell in warre;" and of the two kings of the distant Appalachian Mountains,—Onatheaqua and Houstaqua, "great lords and abounding in riches." While thus, with earnest pantomime and broken words, the chief discoursed with his guests, Vasseur, intent and eager, strove to follow his meaning; and no sooner did he hear of these Appalachian treasures than he promised to join Outina in war against the two potentates of the mountains. Mollua, well pleased, promised that each of Outina's vassal chiefs should requite their French allies with a heap of gold and silver two feet high. Thus, while Laudonniere stood pledged to Satouriona, Vasseur made alliance with his mortal enemy.

On his return, he passed a night in the lodge of one of Satouriona's chiefs, who questioned him touching his dealings with the Thimagoas. Vasseur replied that he had set upon them and put them to utter rout. But as the chief, seeming as yet unsatisfied, continued his inquiries, the sergeant Francois de la Caille drew his sword, and, like Falstaff, reenacted his deeds of valor, pursuing and thrusting at the imaginary Thimagoas, as they fled before his fury. The chief, at length convinced, led the party to his lodge, and entertained them with a decoction of the herb called Cassina.

Satouriona, elated by Laudonniere's delusive promises of aid, had summoned his so-called vassals to war. Ten chiefs and some five hundred warriors had mustered at his call, and the forest was alive with their bivouacs. When all was ready, Satouriona reminded the French commander of his pledge, and claimed its fulfilment, but got nothing but evasions in return, He stifled his rage, and prepared to go without his fickle ally.

A fire was kindled near the bank of the river, and two large vessels of water were placed beside it. Here Satouriona took his stand, while his chiefs crouched on the grass around him, and the savage visages of his five hundred warriors filled the outer circle, their long hair garnished with feathers, or covered with the heads and skins of wolves, cougars, bears, or eagles. Satouriona, looking towards the country of his enemy, distorted his features into a wild expression of rage and hate; then muttered to himself; then howled an invocation to his god, the Sun; then besprinkled the assembly with water from one of the vessels, and, turning the other upon the fire, suddenly quenched it. "So," he cried, "may the blood of our enemies be poured out, and their lives extinguished!" and the concourse gave forth an explosion of responsive yells, till the shores resounded with the wolfish din.

The rites over, they set out, and in a few days returned exulting, with thirteen prisoners and a number of scalps. These last were hung on a pole before the royal lodge; and when night came, it brought with it a pandemonium of dancing and whooping, drumming and feasting.

A notable scheme entered the brain of Laudonniere. Resolved, cost what it might, to make a friend of Outina, he conceived it to be a stroke of policy to send back to him two of the prisoners. In the morning he sent a soldier to Satouriona to demand them. The astonished chief gave a fiat refusal, adding that he owed the French no favors, for they had shamefully broken faith with him. On this, Laudonniere, at the head of twenty soldiers, proceeded to the Indian town, placed a guard at the opening of the great lodge, entered with his arquebusiers, and seated himself without ceremony in the highest place. Here, to show his displeasure, he remained in silence for half an hour. At length he spoke, renewing his demand. For some moments Satouriona made no reply; then he coldly observed that the sight of so many armed men had frightened the prisoners away. Laudonniere grew peremptory, when the chief's son, Athore, went out, and presently returned with the two Indians, whom the French led back to Fort Caroline.

Satouriona, says Laudonniere, "was wonderfully offended with his bravado, and bethought himselfe by all meanes how he might be revenged of us." He dissembled for the time, and presently sent three of his followers to the fort with a gift of pumpkins; though under this show of good-will the outrage rankled in his breast, and he never forgave it. The French had been unfortunate in their dealings with the Indians. They had alienated old friends in vain attempts to make new ones.

Vasseur, with the Swiss ensign Arlac, a sergeant, and ten soldiers, went up the river early in September to carry back the two prisoners to Outina. Laudonniere declares that they sailed eighty leagues, which would have carried them far above Lake Monroe; but it is certain that his reckoning is grossly exaggerated. Their boat crawled up the hazy St. John's, no longer a broad lake like expanse, but a narrow and tortuous stream, winding between swampy forests, or through the vast savanna, a verdant sea of brushes and grass. At length they came to a village called Mayarqua, and thence, with the help of their oars, made their way to another cluster of wigwams, apparently on a branch of the main river. Here they found Outina himself, whom, prepossessed with ideas of feudality, they regarded as the suzerain of a host of subordinate lords and princes, ruling over the surrounding swamps and pine barrens. Outina gratefully received the two prisoners whom Laudonniere had sent to propitiate him, feasted the wonderful strangers, and invited them to join him on a raid against his rival, Potanou. Laudonniere had promised to join Satouriona against Outina, and Vasseur now promised to join Outina against Potanon, the hope of finding gold being in both cases the source of this impolitic compliance. Vasseur went back to Fort Caroline with five of the men, and left Arlac with the remaining five to fight the battles of Ontina.

The warriors mustered to the number of some two hundred, and the combined force of white men and red took up their march. The wilderness through which they passed has not yet quite lost its characteristic features,—the bewildering monotony of the pine barrens, with their myriads of bare gray trunks and their canopy of perennial green, through which a scorching sun throws spots and streaks of yellow light, here on an undergrowth of dwarf palmetto, and there on dry sands half hidden by tufted wire-grass, and dotted with the little mounds that mark the burrows of the gopher; or those oases in the desert, the "hummocks," with their wild, redundant vegetation, their entanglement of trees, bushes, and vines, their scent of flowers and song of birds; or the broad sunshine of the savanna, where they waded to the neck in grass; or the deep swamp, where, out of the black and root-encumbered slough, rise the huge buttressed trunks of the Southern cypress, the gray Spanish moss drooping from every bough and twig, wrapping its victims like a drapery of tattered cobwebs, and slowly draining away their life, for even plants devour each other, and play their silent parts in the universal tragedy of nature.

The allies held their way through forest, savanna, and swamp, with Outina's Indians in the front, till they neared the hostile villages, when the modest warriors fell to the rear, and yielded the post of honor to the Frenchmen.

An open country lay before them, with rough fields of maize, beans, and pumpkins, and the palisades of an Indian town. Their approach was seen, and the warriors of Potanon swarmed out to meet them; but the sight of the bearded strangers, the flash and report of the fire-arms, and the fall of their foremost chief, shot through the brain by Arlac, filled them with consternation, and they fled within their defences. Pursuers and pursued entered pell-mell together. The place was pillaged and burned, its inmates captured or killed, and the victors returned triumphant.

CHAPTER V.
1564, 1565.
CONSPIRACY

In the little world of Fort Caroline, a miniature France, cliques and parties, conspiracy and sedition, were fast stirring into life. Hopes had been dashed, and wild expectations had come to naught. The adventurers had found, not conquest and gold, but a dull exile in a petty fort by a hot and sickly river, with hard labor, bad fare, prospective famine, and nothing to break the weary sameness but some passing canoe or floating alligator. Gathered in knots, they nursed each other's wrath, and inveighed against the commandant. Why are we put on half-rations, when he told us that provision should be made for a full year? Where are the reinforcements and supplies that he said should follow us from France? And why is he always closeted with Ottigny, Arlac, and this and that favorite, when we, men of blood as good as theirs, cannot gain his ear for a moment?

The young nobles, of whom there were many, were volunteers, who had paid their own expenses in expectation of a golden harvest, and they chafed in impatience and disgust. The religious element in the colony—unlike the former Huguenot emigration to Brazil—was evidently subordinate. The adventurers thought more of their fortunes than of their faith; yet there were not a few earnest enough in the doctrine of Geneva to complain loudly and bitterly that no ministers had been sent with them. The burden of all grievances was thrown upon Laudonniere, whose greatest errors seem to have arisen from weakness and a lack of judgment,—fatal defects in his position.

The growing discontent was brought to a partial head by one La Roquette, who gave out that, high up the river, he had discovered by magic a mine of gold and silver, which would give each of them a share of ten thousand crowns, besides fifteen hundred thousand for the King. But for Laudonniere, he said, their fortunes would all be made. He found an ally in a gentleman named Genre, one of Laudonniere's confidants, who, while still professing fast adherence to his interests, is charged by him with plotting against his life. "This Genre," he says, "secretly enfourmed the Souldiers that were already suborned by La Roquette, that I would deprive them of this great game, in that I did set them dayly on worke, not sending them on every side to discover the Countreys; therefore that it were a good deede to dispatch mee out of the way, and to choose another Captaine in my place." The soldiers listened too well. They made a flag of an old shirt, which they carried with them to the rampart when they went to their work, at the same time wearing their arms; and, pursues Laudonniere, "these gentle Souldiers did the same for none other ende but to have killed mee and my Lieutenant also, if by chance I had given them any hard speeches." About this time, overheating himself, he fell ill, and was confined to his quarters. On this, Genre made advances to the apothecary, urging him to put arsenic into his medicine; but the apothecary shrugged his shoulders. They next devised a scheme to blow him up by hiding a keg of gunpowder under his bed; but here, too, they failed. Hints of Genre's machinations reaching the ears of Laudonniere, the culprit fled to the woods, whence he wrote repentant letters, with full confession, to his commander.

Two of the ships meanwhile returned to France, the third, the "Breton," remaining at anchor opposite the fort. The malcontents took the opportunity to send home charges against Laudonniere of peculation, favoritism, and tyranny.

On the fourth of September, Captain Bourdet, apparently a private adventurer, had arrived from France with a small vessel. When he returned, about the tenth of November, Laudonniere persuaded him to carry home seven or eight of the malcontent soldiers. Bourdet left some of his sailors in their place. The exchange proved most disastrous. These pirates joined with others whom they had won over, stole Laudonniere's two pinnaces, and set forth on a plundering excursion to the West Indies. They took a small Spanish vessel off the coast of Cuba, but were soon compelled by famine to put into Havana and give themselves up. Here, to make their peace with the authorities, they told all they knew of the position and purposes of their countrymen at Fort Caroline, and thus was forged the thunderbolt soon to be hurled against the wretched little colony.

On a Sunday morning, Francois de la Caille came to Laudonniere's quarters, and, in the name of the whole company, requested him to come to the parade ground. He complied, and issuing forth, his inseparable Ottigny at his side, he saw some thirty of his officers, soldiers, and gentlemen volunteers waiting before the building with fixed and sombre countenances. La Caille, advancing, begged leave to read, in behalf of the rest, a paper which he held in his hand. It opened with protestations of duty and obedience; next came complaints of hard work, starvation, and broken promises, and a request that the petitioners should be allowed to embark in the vessel lying in the river, and cruise along the Spanish Main, in order to procure provisions by purchase "or otherwise." In short, the flower of the company wished to turn buccaneers.

Laudonniere refused, but assured them that, as soon as the defences of the fort should be completed, a search should be begun in earnest for the Appalachian gold mine, and that meanwhile two small vessels then building on the river should be sent along the coast to barter for provisions with the Indians. With this answer they were forced to content themselves; but the fermentation continued, and the plot thickened. Their spokesman, La Caille, however, seeing whither the affair tended, broke with them, and, except Ottigny, Yasseur, and the brave Swiss Arlac, was the only officer who held to his duty.

A severe illness again seized Laudonniere, and confined him to his bed. Improving their advantage, the malcontents gained over nearly all the best soldiers in the fort. The ringleader was one Fourneaux, a man of good birth, but whom Le Moyne calls an avaricious hypocrite. He drew up a paper, to which sixty-six names were signed. La Caille boldly opposed the conspirators, and they resolved to kill him. His room-mate, Le Moyne, who had also refused to sign, received a hint of the design from a friend; upon which he warned La Caille, who escaped to the woods. It was late in the night. Fourneaux, with twenty men armed to the teeth, knocked fiercely at the commandant's door. Forcing an entrance, they wounded a gentleman who opposed them, and crowded around the sick man's bed. Fourneaux, armed with steel cap and cuirass, held his arquebuse to Laudonniere's throat, and demanded leave to go on a cruise among the Spanish islands. The latter kept his presence of mind, and remonstrated with some firmness; on which, with oaths and menaces, they dragged him from his bed, put him in fetters, carried him out to the gate of the fort, placed him in a boat, and rowed him to the ship anchored in the river.

Two other gangs at the same time visited Ottigny and Arlac, whom they disarmed, and ordered to keep their rooms till the night following, on pain of death. Smaller parties were busied, meanwhile, in disarming all the loyal soldiers. The fort was completely in the hands of the conspirators. Fourneaux drew up a commission for his meditated West India cruise, which he required Laudonniere to sign. The sick commandant, imprisoned in the ship with one attendant, at first refused; but receiving a message from the mutineers, that, if he did not comply, they would come on board and cut his throat, he at length yielded.

The buccaneers now bestirred themselves to finish the two small vessels on which the carpenters had been for some time at work. In a fortnight they were ready for sea, armed and provided with the King's cannon, munitions, and stores. Trenchant, an excellent pilot, was forced to join the party. Their favorite object was the plunder of a certain church on one of the Spanish islands, which they proposed to assail during the midnight mass of Christmas, whereby a triple end would be achieved: first, a rich booty; secondly, the punishment of idolatry; thirdly, vengeance on the arch-enemies of their party and their faith. They set sail on the eighth of December, taunting those who remained, calling them greenhorns, and threatening condign punishment if, on their triumphant return, they should be refused free entrance to the fort.

They were no sooner gone than the unfortunate Laudonniere was gladdened in his solitude by the approach of his fast friends Ottigny and Arlac, who conveyed him to the fort and reinstated him. The entire command was reorganized, and new officers appointed. The colony was wofully depleted; but the bad blood had been drawn off, and thenceforth all internal danger was at an end. In finishing the fort, in building two new vessels to replace those of which they had been robbed, and in various intercourse with the tribes far and near, the weeks passed until the twenty-fifth of March, when an Indian came in with the tidings that a vessel was hovering off the coast. Laudonniere sent to reconnoitre. The stranger lay anchored at the mouth of the river. She was a Spanish brigantine, manned by the returning mutineers, starving, downcast, and anxious to make terms. Yet, as their posture seemed not wholly pacific, Landonniere sent down La Caille, with thirty soldiers concealed at the bottom of his little vessel. Seeing only two or three on deck, the pirates allowed her to come alongside; when, to their amazement, they were boarded and taken before they could snatch their arms. Discomfited, woebegone, and drunk, they were landed under a guard. Their story was soon told. Fortune had flattered them at the outset, and on the coast of Cuba they took a brigantine laden with wine and stores. Embarking in her, they next fell in with a caravel, which also they captured. Landing at a village in Jamaica, they plundered and caroused for a week, and had hardly re-embarked when they met a small vessel having on board the governor of the island. She made a desperate fight, but was taken at last, and with her a rich booty. They thought to put the governor to ransom but the astute official deceived them, and, on pretence of negotiating for the sum demanded,—together with "four or six parrots, and as many monkeys of the sort called sanguins, which are very beautiful," and for which his captors had also bargained,— contrived to send instructions to his wife. Hence it happened that at daybreak three armed vessels fell upon them, retook the prize, and captured or killed all the pirates but twenty-six, who, cutting the moorings of their brigantine, fled out to sea. Among these was the ringleader Fourneaux, and also the pilot Trenchant, who, eager to return to Fort Caroline, whence he had been forcibly taken, succeeded during the night in bringing the vessel to the coast of Florida. Great were the wrath and consternation of the pirates when they saw their dilemma; for, having no provisions, they must either starve or seek succor at the fort. They chose the latter course, and bore away for the St. John's. A few casks of Spanish wine yet remained, and nobles and soldiers, fraternizing in the common peril of a halter, joined in a last carouse. As the wine mounted to their heads, in the mirth of drink and desperation, they enacted their own trial. One personated the judge, another the commandant; witnesses were called, with arguments and speeches on either side.

"Say what you like," said one of them, after hearing the counsel for the defence; "but if Laudonniere does not hang us all, I will never call him an honest man."

They had some hope of getting provisions from the Indians at the month of the river, and then putting to sea again; but this was frustrated by La Caille's sudden attack. A court-martial was called near Fort Caroline, and all were found guilty. Fourneaux and three others were sentenced to be hanged.

"Comrades," said one of the condemned, appealing to the soldiers, "will you stand by and see us butchered?"

"These," retorted Laudonniere, "are no comrades of mutineers and rebels."

At the request of his followers, however, he commuted the sentence to shooting.

A file of men, a rattling volley, and the debt of justice was paid. The bodies were hanged on gibbets, at the river's mouth, and order reigned at Fort Caroline.

CHAPTER VI.
1564, 1565.
FAMINE. WAR. SUCCOR.

While the mutiny was brewing, one La Roche Ferriere had been sent out as an agent or emissary among the more distant tribes. Sagacious, bold, and restless, he pushed his way from town to town, and pretended to have reached the mysterious mountains of Appalache. He sent to the fort mantles woven with feathers, quivers covered with choice furs, arrows tipped with gold, wedges of a green stone like beryl or emerald, and other trophies of his wanderings. A gentleman named Grotaut took up the quest, and penetrated to the dominions of Hostaqua, who, it was pretended, could muster three or four thousand warriors, and who promised, with the aid of a hundred arquebusiers, to conquer all the kings of the adjacent mountains, and subject them and their gold mines to the rule of the French. A humbler adventurer was Pierre Gambie, a robust and daring youth, who had been brought up in the household of Coligny, and was now a soldier under Laudonniere. The latter gave him leave to trade with the Indians,—a privilege which he used so well that he grew rich with his traffic, became prime favorite with the chief of the island of Edelano, married his daughter, and, in his absence, reigned in his stead. But, as his sway verged towards despotism, his subjects took offence, and split his head with a hatchet.

During the winter, Indians from the neighborhood of Cape Canaveral brought to the fort two Spaniards, wrecked fifteen years before on the southwestern extremity of the peninsula. They were clothed like the Indians,—in other words, were not clothed at all,—and their uncut hair streamed loose down their backs. They brought strange tales of those among whom they had dwelt. They told of the King of Cabs, on whose domains they had been wrecked, a chief mighty in stature and in power. In one of his villages was a pit, six feet deep and as wide as a hogshead, filled with treasure gathered from Spanish wrecks on adjacent reefs and keys. The monarch was a priest too, and a magician, with power over the elements. Each year he withdrew from the public gaze to hold converse in secret with supernal or infernal powers; and each year he sacrificed to his gods one of the Spaniards whom the fortune of the sea had cast upon his shores. The name of the tribe is preserved in that of the river Caboosa. In close league with him was the mighty Oathcaqua, dwelling near Cape Canaveral, who gave his daughter, a maiden of wondrous beauty, in marriage to his great ally. But as the bride with her bridesmaids was journeying towards Calos, escorted by a chosen band, they were assailed by a wild and warlike race, inhabitants of an island called Sarrope, in the midst of a lake, who put the warriors to flight, bore the maidens captive to their watery fastness, espoused them all, and, we are assured, "loved them above all measure." 15

Outina, taught by Arlac the efficacy of the French fire-arms, begged for ten arquebusiers to aid him on a new raid among the villages of Potanou,—again alluring his greedy allies by the assurance, that, thus reinforced, he would conquer for them a free access to the phantom gold mines of Appalache. Ottigny set forth on this fool's errand with thrice the force demanded. Three hundred Thirnagoas and thirty Frenchmen took up their march through the pine barrens. Outina's conjurer was of the number, and had wellnigh ruined the enterprise. Kneeling on Ottigny's shield, that he might not touch the earth, with hideous grimaces, howlings, and contortions, he wrought himself into a prophetic frenzy, and proclaimed to the astounded warriors that to advance farther would be destruction. 16 Outina was for instant retreat, but Ottigny's sarcasms shamed him into a show of courage. Again they moved forward, and soon encountered Potanou with all his host. 17 The arquebuse did its work,—panic, slaughter, and a plentiful harvest of scalps. But no persuasion could induce Outina to follow up his victory. He went home to dance round his trophies, and the French returned disgusted to Fort Caroline.

And now, in ample measure, the French began to reap the harvest of their folly. Conquest, gold, and military occupation had alone been their aims. Not a rod of ground had been stirred with the spade. Their stores were consumed, and the expected supplies had not come. The Indians, too, were hostile. Satouriona hated them as allies of his enemies; and his tribesmen, robbed and maltreated by the lawless soldiers, exulted in their miseries. Yet in these, their dark and subtle neighbors, was their only hope.

May-day came, the third anniversary of the day when Ribaut and his companions, full of delighted anticipation, had first explored the flowery borders of the St. John's. The contrast was deplorable; for within the precinct of Fort Caroline a homesick, squalid band, dejected and worn, dragged their shrunken limbs about the sun-scorched area, or lay stretched in listless wretchedness under the shade of the barracks. Some were digging roots in the forest, or gathering a kind of sorrel upon the meadows. If they had had any skill in hunting and fishing, the river and the woods would have supplied their needs; but in this point, as in others, they were lamentably unfit for the work they had taken in hand. "Our miserie," says Laudonniere, "was so great that one was found that gathered up all the fish-bones that he could finde, which he dried and beate into powder to make bread thereof. The effects of this hideous famine appeared incontinently among us, for our bones eftsoones beganne to cleave so neere unto the skinne, that the most part of the souldiers had their skinnes pierced thorow with them in many partes of their bodies." Yet, giddy with weakness, they dragged themselves in turn to the top of St. John's Bluff, straining their eyes across the sea to descry the anxiously expected sail.

Had Coligny left them to perish? Or had some new tempest of calamity, let loose upon France, drowned the memory of their exile? In vain the watchman on the hill surveyed the solitude of waters. A deep dejection fell upon them,—a dejection that would have sunk to despair could their eyes have pierced the future.

The Indians had left the neighborhood, but from time to time brought in meagre supplies of fish, which they sold to the famished soldiers at exorbitant prices. Lest they should pay the penalty of their extortion, they would not enter the fort, but lay in their canoes in the river, beyond gunshot, waiting for their customers to come out to them. "Oftentimes," says Laudonniere, "our poor soldiers were constrained to give away the very shirts from their backs to get one fish. If at any time they shewed unto the savages the excessive price which they tooke, these villaines would answere them roughly and churlishly: If thou make so great account of thy marchandise, eat it, and we will eat our fish: then fell they out a laughing, and mocked us with open throat."

The spring wore away, and no relief appeared. One thought now engrossed the colonists, that of return to France. Vasseur's ship, the "Breton," still remained in the river, and they had also the

Spanish brigantine brought by the mutineers. But these vessels were insufficient, and they prepared to build a new one. The energy of reviving hope lent new life to their exhausted frames. Some gathered pitch in the pine forests; some made charcoal; some cut and sawed timber. The maize began to ripen, and this brought some relief; but the Indians, exasperated and greedy, sold it with reluctance, and murdered two half-famished Frenchmen who gathered a handful in the fields.

The colonists applied to Outina, who owed them two victories. The result was a churlish message and a niggardly supply of corn, coupled with an invitation to aid him against an insurgent chief, one Astina, the plunder of whose villages would yield an ample supply. The offer was accepted. Ottigny and Vasseur set out, but were grossly deceived, led against a different enemy, and sent back empty-handed and half-starved.

They returned to the fort, in the words of Laudonniere, "angry and pricked deeply to the quicke for being so mocked," and, joined by all their comrades, fiercely demanded to be led against Outina, to seize him, punish his insolence, and extort from his fears the supplies which could not be looked for from his gratitude. The commandant was forced to comply. Those who could bear the weight of their armor put it on, embarked, to the number of fifty, in two barges, and sailed up the river under Laudonniere himself. Having reached Outina's landing, they marched inland, entered his village, surrounded his mud-plastered palace, seized him amid the yells and howlings of his subjects, and led him prisoner to their boats. Here, anchored in mid-stream, they demanded a supply of corn and beans as the price of his ransom.

The alarm spread. Excited warriors, bedaubed with red, came thronging from all his villages. The forest along the shore was full of them; and the wife of the chief, followed by all the women of the place, uttered moans and outcries from the strand. Yet no ransom was offered, since, reasoning from their own instincts, they never doubted that, after the price was paid, the captive would be put to death.

Laudonniere waited two days, and then descended the river with his prisoner. In a rude chamber of Fort Caroline the sentinel stood his guard, pike in hand, while before him crouched the captive chief, mute, impassive, and brooding on his woes. His old enemy, Satouriona, keen as a hound on the scent of prey, tried, by great offers, to bribe Laudonniere to give Outina into his hands; but the French captain refused, treated his prisoner kindly, and assured him of immediate freedom on payment of the ransom.

Meanwhile his captivity was bringing grievous affliction on his tribesmen; for, despairing of his return, they mustered for the election of a new chief. Party strife ran high. Some were for a boy, his son, and some for an ambitious kinsman. Outina chafed in his prison on learning these dissentions; and, eager to convince his over-hasty subjects that their chief still lived, he was so profuse of promises that he was again embarked and carried up the river.

At no great distance from Lake George, a small affluent of the St. John's gave access by water to a point within six French leagues of Outina's principal town. The two barges, crowded with soldiers, and bearing also the captive Outina, rowed up this little stream. Indians awaited them at the landing, with gifts of bread, beans, and fish, and piteous prayers for their chief, upon whose liberation they promised an ample supply of corn. As they were deaf to all other terms, Laudonniere yielded, released his prisoner, and received in his place two hostages, who were fast bound in the boats. Ottigny and Arlac, with a strong detachment of arquebusiers, went to receive the promised supplies, for which, from the first, full payment in merchandise had been offered. On their arrival at the village, they filed into the great central lodge, within whose dusky precincts were gathered the magnates of the tribe. Council-chamber, forum, banquet-hall, and dancing-hall all in one, the spacious structure could hold half the population. Here the French made their abode. With armor buckled, and arquebuse matches lighted, they watched with anxious eyes the strange, dim scene, half revealed by the daylight that streamed down through the hole at the apex of the roof. Tall, dark forms stalked to and fro, with quivers at their backs, and bows and arrows in their hands, while groups, crouched in the shadow beyond, eyed the hated guests with inscrutable visages, and malignant, sidelong eyes. Corn came in slowly, but warriors mustered fast. The village without was full of them. The French officers grew anxious, and urged the chiefs to greater alacrity in collecting the promised ransom. The answer boded no good: "Our women are afraid when they see the matches of your guns burning. Put them out, and they will bring the corn faster."

Outina was nowhere to be seen. At length they learned that he was in one of the small huts adjacent. Several of the officers went to him, complaining of the slow payment of his ransom. The kindness of his captors at Fort Caroline seemed to have won his heart. He replied, that such was the rage of his subjects that he could no longer control them; that the French were in danger; and that he had seen arrows stuck in the ground by the side of the path, in token that war was declared. The peril was thickening hourly, and Ottigny resolved to regain the boats while there was yet time.

On the twenty-seventh of July, at nine in the morning, he set his men in order. Each shouldering a sack of corn, they marched through the rows of huts that surrounded the great lodge, and out betwixt the overlapping extremities of the palisade that encircled the town. Before them stretched a wide avenue, three or four hundred paces long, flanked by a natural growth of trees,—one of those curious monuments of native industry to which allusion has already been made. Here Ottigny halted and formed his line of march. Arlac, with eight matchlock men, was sent in advance, and flanking parties were thrown into the woods on either side. Ottigny told his soldiers that, if the Indians meant to attack them, they were probably in ambush at the other end of the avenue. He was right. As Arlac's party reached the spot, the whole pack gave tongue at once. The war-whoop rose, and a tempest of stone-headed arrows clattered against the breast-plates of the French, or, scorching like fire, tore through their unprotected limbs. They stood firm, and sent back their shot so steadily that several of the assailants were laid dead, and the rest, two or three hundred in number, gave way as Ottigny came up with his men.

They moved on for a quarter of a mile through a country, as it seems, comparatively open, when again the war-cry pealed in front, and three hundred savages bounded to the assault. Their whoops were echoed from the rear. It was the party whom Arlac had just repulsed, and who, leaping and showering their arrows, were rushing on again with a ferocity restrained only by their lack of courage. There was no panic among the French. The men threw down their bags of corn, and took to their weapons. They blew their matches, and, under two excellent officers, stood well to their work. The Indians, on their part, showed good discipline after their fashion, and were perfectly under the control of their chiefs. With cries that imitated the yell of owls, the scream of cougars, and the howl of wolves, they ran up in successive bands, let fly their arrows, and instantly fell back, giving place to others. At the sight of the leveled arquebuse, they dropped flat on the ground. Whenever the French charged upon them, sword in hand, they fled through the woods like foxes; and whenever the march was resumed, the arrows were showering again upon the flanks and rear of the retiring band. As they fell, the soldiers picked them up and broke them. Thus, beset with swarming savages, the handful of Frenchmen pushed slowly onward, fighting as they went.

The Indians gradually drew off, and the forest was silent again. Two of the French had been killed and twenty-two wounded, several so severely that they were supported to the boats with the utmost difficulty. Of the corn, two bags only had been brought off.

Famine and desperation now reigned at Fort Caroline. The Indians had killed two of the carpenters; hence long delay in the finishing of the new ship. They would not wait, but resolved to put to sea in the "Breton" and the brigantine. The problem was to find food for the voyage; for now, in their extremity, they roasted and ate snakes, a delicacy in which the neighborhood abounded.

On the third of August, Laudonniere, perturbed and oppressed, was walking on the hill, when, looking seaward, he saw a sight that sent a thrill through his exhausted frame. A great ship was standing towards the river's mouth. Then another came in sight, and another, and another. He despatched a messenger with the tidings to the fort below. The languid forms of his sick and despairing men rose and danced for joy, and voices shrill with weakness joined in wild laughter and acclamation, insomuch, he says, "that one would have thought them to bee out of their wittes."

A doubt soon mingled with their joy. Who were the strangers? Were they the friends so long hoped for in vain? or were they Spaniards, their dreaded enemies? They were neither. The foremost ship was a stately one, of seven hundred tons, a great burden at that day. She was named the "Jesus;" and with her were three smaller vessels, the "Solomon," the "Tiger," and the "Swallow." Their commander was "a right worshipful and valiant knight,"—

for so the record styles him,—a pious man and a prudent, to judge him by the orders he gave his crew when, ten months before, he sailed out of Plymouth: "Serve God daily, love one another, preserve your victuals, beware of fire, and keepe good companie." Nor were the crew unworthy the graces of their chief; for the devout chronicler of the voyage ascribes their deliverance from the perils of the sea to "the Almightie God, who never suffereth his Elect to perish."

Who then were they, this chosen band, serenely conscious of a special Providential care? They were the pioneers of that detested traffic destined to inoculate with its infection nations yet unborn, the parent of discord and death, filling half a continent with the tramp of armies and the clash of fratricidal swords. Their chief was Sir John Hawkins, father of the English slave-trade.

He had been to the coast of Guinea, where he bought and kidnapped a cargo of slaves. These he had sold to the jealous Spaniards of Hispaniola, forcing them, with sword, matchlock, and culverin, to grant him free trade, and then to sign testimonials that he had borne himself as became a peaceful merchant. Prospering greatly by this summary commerce, but distressed by the want of water, he had put into the River of May to obtain a supply.

Among the rugged heroes of the British marine, Sir John stood in the front rank, and along with Drake, his relative, is extolled as "a man borne for the honour of the English name.... Neither did the West of England yeeld such an Indian Neptunian paire as were these two Ocean peeres, Hawkins and Drake." So writes the old chronicler, Purchas, and all England was of his thinking. A hardy and skilful seaman, a bold fighter, a loyal friend and a stern enemy, overbearing towards equals, but kind, in his bluff way, to those beneath him, rude in speech, somewhat crafty withal and avaricious, he buffeted his way to riches and fame, and died at last full of years and honor. As for the abject humanity stowed between the reeking decks of the ship "Jesus," they were merely in his eyes so many black cattle tethered for the market. 18

Hawkins came up the river in a pinnace, and landed at Fort Caroline, accompanied, says Laudonniere, "with gentlemen honorably apparelled, yet unarmed." Between the Huguenots and the English Puritans there was a double tie of sympathy. Both hated priests, and both hated Spaniards. Wakening from their apathetic misery, the starveling garrison hailed him as a deliverer. Yet Hawkins secretly rejoiced when he learned their purpose to abandon Florida; for although, not to tempt his cupidity, they hid from him the secret of their Appalachian gold mine, he coveted for his royal mistress the possession of this rich domain. He shook his head, however, when he saw the vessels in which they proposed to embark, and offered them all a free passage to France in his own ships. This, from obvious motives of honor and prudence, Laudonniere declined, upon which Hawkins offered to lend or sell to him one of his smaller vessels.

Laudonniere hesitated, and hereupon arose a great clamor. A mob of soldiers and artisans beset his chamber, threatening loudly to desert him, and take passage with Hawkins, unless the offer were accepted. The commandant accordingly resolved to buy the vessel. The generous slaver, whose reputed avarice nowhere appears in the transaction, desired him to set his own price; and, in place of money, took the cannon of the fort, with other articles now useless to their late owners. He sent them, too, a gift of wine and biscuit, and supplied them with provisions for the voyage, receiving in payment Laudonniere's note; "for which," adds the latter, "untill this present I am indebted to him." With a friendly leave taking, he returned to his ships and stood out to sea, leaving golden opinions among the grateful inmates of Fort Caroline.

Before the English top-sails had sunk beneath the horizon, the colonists bestirred themselves to depart. In a few days their preparations were made. They waited only for a fair wind. It was long in coming, and meanwhile their troubled fortunes assumed a new phase.

On the twenty eighth of August, the two captains Vasseur and Verdier came in with tidings of an approaching squadron. Again the fort was wild with excitement. Friends or foes, French or Spaniards, succor or death,—betwixt these were their hopes and fears divided. On the following morning, they saw seven barges rowing up the river, bristling with weapons, and crowded with men in armor. The sentries on the bluff challenged, and received no answer. One of them fired at the advancing boats, and still there was no response. Laudonniere was almost defenceless. He had given his heavier cannon to Hawkins, and only two field-pieces were left. They were levelled at the foremost boats, and the word to fire was about to be given, when a voice from among the strangers called out that they were French, commanded by Jean Ribaut.

At the eleventh hour, the long looked for succors were come. Ribaut had been commissioned to sail with seven ships for Florida. A disorderly concourse of disbanded soldiers, mixed with artisans and their families, and young nobles weary of a two years' peace, were mustered at the port of Dieppe, and embarked, to the number of three hundred men, bearing with them all things thought necessary to a prosperous colony.

No longer in dread of the Spaniards, the colonists saluted the new-comers with the cannon by which a moment before they had hoped to blow them out of the water. Laudonniere issued from his stronghold to welcome them, and regaled them with what cheer he could. Ribaut was present, conspicuous by his long beard, an astonishment to the Indians; and here, too, were officers, old friends of Laudonniere. Why, then, had they approached in the attitude of enemies? The mystery was soon explained; for they expressed to the commandant their pleasure at finding that the charges made against him had proved false. He begged to know more; on which Ribaut, taking him aside, told him that the returning ships had brought home letters filled with accusations of arrogance, tyranny, cruelty, and a purpose of establishing an independent command,—accusations which he now saw to be unfounded, but which had been the occasion of his unusual and startling precaution. He gave him, too, a letter from Admiral Coligny. In brief but courteous terms, it required him to resign his command, and requested his return to France to clear his name from the imputations cast upon it. Ribaut warmly urged him to remain; but Laudonniere declined his friendly proposals.

Worn in body and mind, mortified and wounded, he soon fell ill again. A peasant woman attended him, who was brought over, he says, to nurse the sick and take charge of the poultry, and of whom Le Moyne also speaks as a servant, but who had been made the occasion of additional charges against him, most offensive to the austere Admiral.

Stores were landed, tents were pitched, women and children were sent on shore, feathered Indians mingled in the throng, and the borders of the River of May swarmed with busy life. "But, lo, how oftentimes misfortune doth search and pursue us, even then when we thinke to be at rest!" exclaims the unhappy Laudonniere. Amidst the light and cheer of renovated hope, a cloud of blackest omen was gathering in the east.

At half-past eleven on the night of Tuesday, the fourth of September, the crew of Ribaut's flag-ship, anchored on the still sea outside the bar, saw a huge hulk, grim with the throats of cannon, drifting towards them through the gloom; and from its stern rolled on the sluggish air the portentous banner of Spain.

CHAPTER VII.
1565.
MENENDEZ.

The monk, the inquisitor, and the Jesuit were lords of Spain,—sovereigns of her sovereign, for they had formed the dark and narrow mind of that tyrannical recluse. They had formed the minds of her people, quenched in blood every spark of rising heresy, and given over a noble nation to a bigotry blind and inexorable as the doom of fate. Linked with pride, ambition, avarice, every passion of a rich, strong nature, potent for good and ill, it made the Spaniard of that day a scourge as dire as ever fell on man.

Day was breaking on the world. Light, hope, and freedom pierced with vitalizing ray the clouds and the miasma that hung so thick over the prostrate Middle Age, once noble and mighty, now a foul image of decay and death. Kindled with new life, the nations gave birth to a progeny of heroes, and the stormy glories of the sixteenth century rose on awakened Europe. But Spain was the citadel of darkness,—a monastic cell, an inquisitorial dungeon, where no ray could pierce. She was the bulwark of the Church, against whose adamantine wall the waves of innovation beat in vain. 19 In every country of Europe the party of freedom and reform was the national party, the party of reaction and absolutism was the Spanish party, leaning on Spain, looking to her for help. Above all, it was so in France; and, while within her bounds there was for a time some semblance of peace, the national and religious rage burst forth on a wilder theatre. Thither it is for us to follow it, where, on the shores of Florida, the Spaniard and the Frenchman, the bigot and the Huguenot, met in the grapple of death.

In a corridor of his palace, Philip the Second was met by a man who had long stood waiting his approach, and who with proud reverence placed a petition in the hand of the pale and sombre King.

The petitioner was Pedro Menendez de Aviles, one of the ablest and most distinguished officers of the Spanish marine. He was born of an ancient Asturian family. His boyhood had been wayward, ungovernable, and fierce. He ran off at eight years of age, and when, after a search of six months, he was found and brought back, he ran off again. This time he was more successful, escaping on board a fleet bound against the Barbary corsairs, where his precocious appetite for blood and blows had reasonable contentment. A few years later, he found means to build a small vessel, in which he cruised against the corsairs and the French, and, though still hardly more than a boy, displayed a singular address and daring. The wonders of the New World now seized his imagination. He made a voyage thither, and the ships under his charge came back freighted with wealth. The war with France was then at its height. As captain-general of the fleet, he was sent with troops to Flanders; and to their prompt arrival was due, it is said, the victory of St. Quentin. Two years later, he commanded the luckless armada which bore back Philip to his native shore. On the way, the King narrowly escaped drowning in a storm off the port of Laredo. This mischance, or his own violence and insubordination, wrought to the prejudice of Menendez. He complained that his services were ill repaid. Philip lent him a favoring ear, and despatched him to the Indies as general of the fleet and army. Here he found means to amass vast riches; and, in 1561, on his return to Spain, charges were brought against him of a nature which his too friendly biographer does not explain. The Council of the Indies arrested him. He was imprisoned and sentenced to a heavy fine; but, gaining his release, hastened to court to throw himself on the royal clemency. His petition was most graciously received. Philip restored his command, but remitted only half his fine, a strong presumption of his guilt.

Menendez kissed the royal hand; he had another petition in reserve. His son had been wrecked near the Bermudas, and he would fain go thither to find tidings of his fate. The pious King bade him trust in God, and promised that he should be despatched without delay to the Bermudas and to Florida, with a commission to make an exact survey of the neighboring seas for the profit of future voyagers; but Menendez was not content with such an errand. He knew, he said, nothing of greater moment to his Majesty than the conquest and settlement of Florida. The climate was healthful, the soil fertile; and, worldly advantages aside, it was peopled by a race sunk in the thickest shades of infidelity. "Such grief," he pursued, "seizes me, when I behold this multitude of wretched Indians, that I should choose the conquest and settling of Florida above all commands, offices, and dignities which your

Majesty might bestow." Those who take this for hypocrisy do not know the Spaniard of the sixteenth century.

The King was edified by his zeal. An enterprise of such spiritual and temporal promise was not to be slighted, and Menendez was empowered to conquer and convert Florida at his own cost. The conquest was to be effected within three years. Menendez was to take with him five hundred men, and supply them with five hundred slaves, besides horses, cattle, sheep, and hogs. Villages were to be built, with forts to defend them, and sixteen ecclesiastics, of whom four should be Jesuits, were to form the nucleus of a Floridan church. The King, on his part, granted Menendez free trade with Hispaniola, Porto Rico, Cuba, and Spain, the office of Adelantado of Florida for life, with the right of naming his successor, and large emoluments to be drawn from the expected conquest.

The compact struck, Menendez hastened to his native Asturias to raise money among his relatives. Scarcely was he gone, when tidings reached Madrid that Florida was already occupied by a colony of French Protestants, and that a reinforcement, under Ribaut, was on the point of sailing thither. A French historian of high authority declares that these advices came from the Catholic party at the French court, in whom every instinct of patriotism was lost in their hatred of Coligny and the Huguenots. Of this there can be little doubt, though information also came about this time from the buccaneer Frenchmen captured in the West Indies.

Foreigners had invaded the territory of Spain. The trespassers, too, were heretics, foes of God, and liegemen of the Devil. Their doom was fixed. But how would France endure an assault, in time of peace, on subjects who had gone forth on an enterprise sanctioned by the Crown, and undertaken in its name and under its commission?

The throne of France, in which the corruption of the nation seemed gathered to a head, was trembling between the two parties of the Catholics and the Huguenots, whose chiefs aimed at royalty. Flattering both, caressing both, playing one against the other, and betraying both, Catherine de Medicis, by a thousand crafty arts and expedients of the moment, sought to retain the crown on the head of her weak and vicious son. Of late her crooked policy had led her towards the Catholic party, in other words the party of Spain; and she had already given ear to the savage Duke of Alva, urging her to the course which, seven years later, led to the carnage of St. Bartholomew. In short, the Spanish policy was in the ascendant, and no thought of the national interest or honor could restrain that basest of courts from abandoning by hundreds to the national enemy those whom it was itself meditating to immolate by thousands. It might protest for form's sake, or to quiet public clamor; but Philip of Spain well knew that it would end in patient submission.

Menendez was summoned back in haste to the Spanish court. His force must be strengthened. Three hundred and ninety-four men were added at the royal charge, and a corresponding number of transport and supply ships. It was a holy war, a crusade, and as such was preached by priest and monk along the western coasts of Spain. All the Biscayan ports flamed with zeal, and adventurers crowded to enroll themselves; since to plunder heretics is good for the soul as well as the purse, and broil and massacre have double attraction when promoted into a means of salvation. It was a fervor, deep and hot, but not of celestial kindling; nor yet that buoyant and inspiring zeal which, when the Middle Age was in its youth and prime, glowed in the souls of Tancred, Godfrey, and St. Louis, and which, when its day was long since past, could still find its home in the great heart of Columbus. A darker spirit urged the new crusade,—born not of hope, but of fear, slavish in its nature, the creature and the tool of despotism; for the typical Spaniard of the sixteenth century was not in strictness a fanatic, he was bigotry incarnate.

Heresy was a plague-spot, an ulcer to be eradicated with fire and the knife, and this foul abomination was infecting the shores which the Vicegerent of Christ had given to the King of Spain, and which the Most Catholic King had given to the Adelantado. Thus would countless heathen tribes be doomed to an eternity of flame, and the Prince of Darkness hold his ancient sway unbroken; and for the Adelantado himself, the vast outlays, the vast debts of his bold Floridan venture would be all in vain, and his fortunes be wrecked past redemption through these tools of Satan. As a Catholic, as a Spaniard, and as an adventurer, his course was clear.

The work assigned him was prodigious. He was invested with power almost absolute, not merely over the peninsula which now retains the name of Florida, but over all North America, from Labrador to Mexico; for this was the Florida of the old Spanish geographers, and the Florida designated in the commission of Menendez. It was a continent which he was to conquer and occupy out of his own purse. The impoverished King contracted with his daring and ambitious subject to win and hold for him the territory of the future United States and British Provinces. His plan, as afterwards exposed at length in his letters to Philip the Second, was, first, to plant a garrison at Port Royal, and next to fortify strongly on Chesapeake Bay, called by him St. Mary's. He believed that adjoining this bay was an arm of the sea, running northward and eastward, and communicating with the Gulf of St. Lawrence, thus making New England, with adjacent districts, an island. His proposed fort on the Chesapeake, securing access by this imaginary passage, to the seas of Newfoundland, would enable the Spaniards to command the fisheries, on which both the French and the English had long encroached, to the great prejudice of Spanish rights. Doubtless, too, these inland waters gave access to the South Sea, and their occupation was necessary to prevent the French from penetrating thither; for that ambitious people, since the time of Cartier, had never abandoned their schemes of seizing this portion of the dominions of the King of Spain. Five hundred soldiers and one hundred sailors must, he urges, take possession, without delay, of Port Royal and the Chesapeake. [20]

Preparation for his enterprise was pushed with furious energy. His whole force, when the several squadrons were united, amounted to two thousand six hundred and forty-six persons, in thirty-four vessels, one of which, the San Pelayo, bearing Menendez himself, was of nine hundred and ninety-six tons burden, and is described as one of the finest ships afloat. [21] There were twelve Franciscans and eight Jesuits, besides other ecclesiastics; and many knights of Galicia, Biscay, and the Asturias took part in the expedition. With a slight exception, the whole was at the Adelantado's charge. Within the first fourteen months, according to his admirer, Barcia, the adventure cost him a million ducats. [22]

Before the close of the year, Sancho do Arciniega was commissioned to join Menendez with an additional force of fifteen hundred men.

Red-hot with a determined purpose, the Adelantado would brook no delay. To him, says the chronicler, every day seemed a year. He was eager to anticipate Ribaut, of whose designs and whose force he seems to have been informed to the minutest particular, but whom he hoped to thwart and ruin by gaining Fort Caroline before him. With eleven ships, therefore, he sailed from Cadiz, on the twenty-ninth of June, 1565, leaving the smaller vessels of his fleet to follow with what speed they might. He touched first at the Canaries, and on the eighth of July left them, steering for Dominica. A minute account of the voyage has come down to us, written by Mendoza, chaplain of the expedition,—a somewhat dull and illiterate person, who busily jots down the incidents of each passing day, and is constantly betraying, with a certain awkward simplicity, how the cares of this world and of the next jostle each other in his thoughts.

On Friday, the twentieth of July, a storm fell upon them with appalling fury. The pilots lost their wits, and the sailors gave themselves up to their terrors. Throughout the night, they beset Mendoza for confession and absolution, a boon not easily granted, for the seas swept the crowded decks with cataracts of foam, and the shriekings of the gale in the rigging overpowered the exhortations of the half-drowned priest. Cannon, cables, spars, water-casks, were thrown overboard, and the chests of the sailors would have followed, had not the latter, in spite of their fright, raised such a howl of remonstrance that the order was revoked. At length day dawned, Plunging, reeling, half under water, quivering with the shock of the seas, whose mountain ridges rolled down upon her before the gale, the ship lay in deadly peril from Friday till Monday noon. Then the storm abated; the sun broke out; and again she held her course.

They reached Dominica on Sunday, the fifth of August. The chaplain tells us how he went on shore to refresh himself; how, while his Italian servant washed his linen at a brook, he strolled along the beach and picked up shells; and how he was scared, first, by a prodigious turtle, and next by a vision of the cannibal natives, which caused his prompt retreat to the boats.

On the tenth, they anchored in the harbor of Porto Rico, where they found two ships of their squadron, from which they had parted in the storm. One of them was the "San Pelayo," with Menendez on board. Mendoza informs us, that in the evening the officers came on board the ship to which he was attached, when he, the chaplain, regaled them with sweetmeats, and that Menendez invited him not only to supper that night, but to dinner the next day, "for the which I thanked him, as reason was," says the gratified churchman.

Here thirty men deserted, and three priests also ran off, of which Mendoza bitterly complains, as increasing his own work. The motives of the clerical truants may perhaps be inferred from a worldly temptation to which the chaplain himself was subjected. "I was offered the service of a chapel where I should have got a peso for every mass I said, the whole year round; but I did not accept it, for fear that what I hear said of the other three would be said of me. Besides, it is not a place where one can hope for any great advancement, and I wished to try whether, in refusing a benefice for the love of the Lord, He will not repay me with some other stroke of fortune before the end of the voyage; for it is my aim to serve God and His blessed Mother."

The original design had been to rendezvous at Havana, but with the Adelantado the advantages of despatch outweighed every other consideration. He resolved to push directly for Florida. Five of his scattered ships had by this time rejoined company, comprising, exclusive of officers, a force of about five hundred soldiers, two hundred sailors, and one hundred colonists. Bearing northward, he advanced by an unknown and dangerous course along the coast of Hayti and through the intricate passes of the Bahamas. On the night of the twenty-sixth, the "San Pelayo" struck three times on the shoals; "but," says the chaplain, "inasmuch as our enterprise was undertaken for the sake of Christ and His blessed Mother, two heavy seas struck her abaft, and set her afloat again."

At length the ships lay becalmed in the Bahama Channel, slumbering on the glassy sea, torpid with the heats of a West Indian August. Menendez called a council of the commanders. There was doubt and indecision. Perhaps Ribaut had already reached the French fort, and then to attack the united force would be an act of desperation. Far better to await their lagging comrades.

But the Adelantado was of another mind; and, even had his enemy arrived, ho was resolved that he should have no time to fortify himself.

"It is God's will," he said, "that our victory should be due, not to our numbers, but to His all-powerful aid. Therefore has He stricken us with tempests, and scattered our ships." And he gave his voice for instant advance.

There was much dispute; even the chaplain remonstrated; but nothing could bend the iron will of Menendez. Nor was a sign of celestial approval wanting. At nine in the evening, a great meteor burst forth in mid-heaven, and, blazing like the sun, rolled westward towards the coast of Florida. The fainting spirits of the crusaders were revived. Diligent preparation was begun. Prayers and masses were said; and, that the temporal arm might not fail, the men were daily practised on deck in shooting at marks, in order, says the chronicle, that the recruits might learn not to be afraid of their guns.

The dead calm continued. "We were all very tired," says the chaplain, "and I above all, with praying to God for a fair wind. To-day, at about two in the afternoon, He took pity on us, and sent us a breeze." Before night they saw land,—the faint line of forest, traced along the watery horizon, that marked the coast of Florida. But where, in all this vast monotony, was the lurking-place of the French? Menendez anchored, and sent a captain with twenty men ashore, who presently found a band of Indians, and gained from them the needed information. He stood northward, till, on the afternoon of Tuesday, the fourth of September, he descried four ships anchored near the mouth of a river. It was the river St. John's, and the ships were four of Ribaut's squadron. The prey was in sight. The Spaniards prepared for battle, and bore down upon the Lutherans; for, with them, all Protestants alike were branded with the name of the arch-heretic. Slowly, before the faint breeze, the ships glided on their way; but while, excited and impatient, the fierce crews watched the decreasing space, and when they were still three leagues from their prize, the air ceased to stir, the sails flapped against the mast, a black cloud with thunder rose above the coast, and the warm rain of the South descended on the breathless sea. It was dark before the wind stirred again and the ships resumed their course. At half-past eleven they reached the French.

The "San Pelayo" slowly moved to windward of Ribaut's flag-ship, the "Trinity," and anchored very near her. The other ships took similar stations. While these preparations were making, a work of two hours, the men labored in silence, and the French, thronging their gangways, looked on in equal silence. "Never, since I came into the world," writes the chaplain, "did I know such a stillness."

It was broken at length by a trumpet from the deck of the "San Pelayo." A French trumpet answered. Then Menendez, "with much courtesy," says his Spanish eulogist, inquired, "Gentlemen, whence does this fleet come?"

"From France," was the reply.

"What are you doing here?" pursued the Adelantado.

"Bringing soldiers and supplies for a fort which the King of France has in this country, and for many others which he soon will have."

"Are you Catholics or Lutherans?"

Many voices cried out together, "Lutherans, of the new religion." Then, in their turn, they demanded who Menendez was, and whence he came.

He answered: "I am Pedro Menendez, General of the fleet of the King of Spain, Don Philip the Second, who have come to this country to hang and behead all Lutherans whom I shall find by land or sea, according to instructions from my King, so precise that I have power to pardon none; and these commands I shall fulfil, as you will see. At daybreak I shall board your ships, and if I find there any Catholic, he shall be well treated; but every heretic shall die."

The French with one voice raised a cry of wrath and defiance.

"If you are a brave man, don't wait till day. Come on now, and see what you will get!"

And they assailed the Adelantado with a shower of scoffs and insults.

Menendez broke into a rage, and gave the order to board. The men slipped the cables, and the sullen black hulk of the "San Pelayo" drifted down upon the "Trinity." The French did not make good their defiance. Indeed, they were incapable of resistance, Ribaut with his soldiers being ashore at Fort Caroline. They cut their cables, left their anchors, made sail, and fled. The Spaniards fired, the French replied. The other Spanish ships had imitated the movement of the "San Pelayo;" "but," writes the chaplain, Mendoza, "these devils are such adroit sailors, and maneuvred so well, that we did not catch one of them." Pursuers and pursued ran out to sea, firing useless volleys at each other.

In the morning Menendez gave over the chase, turned, and, with the "San Pelayo" alone, ran back for the St. John's. But here a welcome was prepared for him. He saw bands of armed men drawn up on the beach, and the smaller vessels of Ribaut's squadron, which had crossed the bar several days before, anchored behind it to oppose his landing. He would not venture an attack, but, steering southward, sailed along the coast till he came to an inlet which he named San Augustine, the same which Laudonniere had named the River of Dolphins.

Here he found three of his ships already debarking their troops, guns, and stores. Two officers, Patiflo and Vicente, had taken possession of the dwelling of the Indian chief Seloy, a huge barn-like structure, strongly framed of entire trunks of trees, and thatched with palmetto leaves. Around it they were throwing up entrenchments of fascines and sand, and gangs of negroes were toiling at the work. Such was the birth of St. Augustine, the oldest town of the United States.

On the eighth, Menendez took formal possession of his domain. Cannon were fired, trumpets sounded, and banners displayed, as he landed in state at the head of his officers and nobles. Mendoza, crucifix in hand, came to meet him, chanting Te Deum laudamus, while the Adelantado and all his company, kneeling, kissed the crucifix, and the assembled Indians gazed in silent wonder.

Meanwhile the tenants of Fort Caroline were not idle. Two or three soldiers, strolling along the beach in the afternoon, had first seen the Spanish ships, and hastily summoned Ribaut. He came down to the mouth of the river, followed by an anxious and excited crowd; but, as they strained their eyes through the darkness, they could see nothing but the flashes of the distant guns. At length the returning light showed, far out at sea, the Adelantado in hot chase of their flying comrades. Pursuers and pursued were soon out of sight. The drums beat to arms. After many hours of suspense, the "San Pelayo" reappeared, hovering about the mouth of the river, then bearing away towards the south. More anxious hours ensued, when three other sail came in sight, and they recognized three of their own returning ships. Communication was opened, a boat's crew landed, and they learned from Cosette, one of the French captains, that, confiding in the speed of his ship, he had followed the Spaniards to St. Augustine, reconnoitred their position, and seen them land their negroes and intrench themselves.

Laudonniere lay sick in bed in his chamber at Fort Caroline when Ribaut entered, and with him La Grange, Sainte Marie, Ottigny, Yonville, and other officers. At the bedside of the displaced commandant, they held their council of war. Three plans were proposed: first, to remain where they were and fortify themselves; next, to push overland for St. Augustine and attack the invaders in their intrenchments; and, finally, to embark and assail them by sea. The first plan would leave their ships a prey to the Spaniards; and so, too, in all likelihood, would the second, besides the uncertainties of an overland march through an unknown wilderness. By sea, the distance was short and the route explored. By a sudden blow they could capture or destroy the Spanish ships, and master the troops on shore before reinforcements could arrive, and before they had time to complete their defences.

Such were the views of Ribaut, with which, not unnaturally, Laudonniere finds fault, and Le Moyne echoes the censures of his chief. And yet the plan seems as well conceived as it was bold, lacking nothing but success. The Spaniards, stricken with terror, owed their safety to the elements, or, as they say, to the special interposition of the Holy Virgin. Menendez was a leader fit to stand with Cortes and Pizarro; but he was matched with a man as cool, skilful, prompt, and daring as himself. The traces that have come down to us indicate in Ribaut one far above the common stamp,—"a distinguished man, of many high qualities," as even the fault-finding Le Moyne calls him; devout after the best spirit of the Reform; and with a human heart under his steel breastplate.

La Grange and other officers took part with Landonniere, and opposed the plan of an attack by sea; but Ribaut's conviction was unshaken, and the order was given. All his own soldiers fit for duty embarked in haste, and with them went La Caille, Arlac, and, as it seems, Ottigny, with the best of Laudonniere's men. Even Le Moyne, though wounded in the fight with Outina's warriors, went on board to bear his part in the fray, and would have sailed with the rest had not Ottigny, seeing his disabled condition, ordered him back to the fort.

On the tenth, the ships, crowded with troops, set sail. Ribaut was gone, and with him the bone and sinew of the colony. The miserable remnant watched his receding sails with dreary foreboding,—a fore-boding which seemed but too just, when, on the next day, a storm, more violent than the Indians had ever known, howled through the forest and lashed the ocean into fury. Most forlorn was the plight of these exiles, left, it might be, the prey of a band of ferocious bigots more terrible than the fiercest hordes of the wilderness; and when night closed on the stormy river and the gloomy waste of pines, what dreams of terror may not have haunted the helpless women who crouched under the hovels of Fort Caroline!

The fort was in a ruinous state, with the palisade on the water side broken down, and three breaches in the rampart. In the driving rain, urged by the sick Laudonniere, the men, bedrenched and disheartened, labored as they could to strengthen their defences. Their muster-roll shows but a beggarly array. "Now," says Laudonniere, "let them which have bene bold to say that I had men ynough left me, so that I had meanes to defend my selfe, give care a little now vnto mee, and if they have eyes in their heads, let them see what men I had." Of Ribaut's followers left at the fort, only nine or ten had weapons, while only two or three knew how to use them. Four of them were boys, who kept Ribaut's dogs, and another was his cook. Besides these, he had left a brewer, an old crossbow-maker, two shoemakers, a player on the spinet, four valets, a carpenter of threescore,—Challeux, no doubt, who has left us the story of his woes,—with a crowd of women, children, and eighty-six camp-followers. To these were added the remnant of Laudonniere's men, of whom seventeen could bear arms, the rest being sick or disabled by wounds received in the fight with Outina.

Laudonniere divided his force, such as it was, into two watches, over which he placed two officers, Saint Cler and La Vigne, gave them lanterns for going the rounds, and an hour-glass for setting the time; while he himself, giddy with weakness and fever, was every night at the guard-room.

It was the night of the nineteenth of September, the season of tempests; floods of rain drenched the sentries on the rampart, and, as day dawned on the dripping barracks and deluged parade, the storm increased in violence. What enemy could venture out on such a night? La Vigne, who had the watch, took pity on the sentries and on himself, dismissed them, and went to his quarters. He little knew what human energies, urged by ambition, avarice, bigotry, and desperation, will dare and do.

To return to the Spaniards at St. Augustine. On the morning of the eleventh, the crew of one of their smaller vessels, lying outside the bar, with Menendez himself on board, saw through the twilight of early dawn two of Ribaut's ships close upon them. Not a breath of air was stirring. There was no escape, and the Spaniards fell on their knees in supplication to Our Lady of Utrera, explaining to her that the heretics were upon them, and begging her to send them a little wind. "Forthwith," says Mendoza, "one would have said that Our Lady herself came down upon the vessel." A wind sprang up, and the Spaniards found refuge behind the bar. The returning day showed to their astonished eyes all the ships of Ribaut, their decks black with men, hovering off the entrance of the port; but Heaven had them in its charge, and again they experienced its protecting care. The breeze sent by Our Lady of Utrera rose to a gale, then to a furious tempest; and the grateful Adelantado saw through rack and mist the ships of his enemy tossed wildly among the raging waters as they struggled to gain an offing. With exultation in his heart, the skilful seaman read their danger, and saw them in his mind's eye dashed to utter wreck among the sand-bars and breakers of the lee shore.

A bold thought seized him. He would march overland with five hundred men, and attack Fort Caroline while its defenders were absent. First he ordered a mass, and then he called a council. Doubtless it was in that great Indian lodge of Seloy, where he had made his headquarters; and here, in this dim and smoky abode, nobles, officers, and priests gathered at his summons. There were fears and doubts and murmurings, but Menendez was desperate; not with the mad desperation that strikes wildly and at random, but the still white heat that melts and burns and seethes with a steady, unquenchable fierceness. "Comrades," he said, "the time has come to show our courage and our zeal. This is God's war, and we must not flinch. It is a war with Lutherans, and we must wage it with blood and fire."

But his hearers gave no response. They had not a million of ducats at stake, and were not ready for a cast so desperate. A clamor of remonstrance rose from the circle. Many voices, that of Mendoza among the rest, urged waiting till their main forces should arrive. The excitement spread to the men without, and the swarthy, black-bearded crowd broke into tumults mounting almost to mutiny, while an officer was heard to say that he would not go on such a hare-brained errand to be butchered like a beast. But nothing could move the Adelantado. His appeals or his threats did their work at last; the confusion was quelled, and preparation was made for the march.

On the morning of the seventeenth, five hundred arquebusiers and pikemen were drawn up before the camp. To each was given six pounds of biscuit and a canteen filled with wine. Two Indians and a renegade Frenchman, called Francois Jean, were to guide them, and twenty Biscayan axemen moved to the front to clear the way. Through floods of driving rain, a hoarse voice shouted the word of command, and the sullen march began.

With dismal misgiving, Mendoza watched the last files as they vanished in the tempestuous forest. Two days of suspense ensued, when a messenger came back with a letter from the Adelantado, announcing that he had nearly reached the French fort, and that on the morrow, September the twentieth, at sunrise, he hoped to assault it. "May the Divine Majesty deign to protect us, for He knows that we have need of it," writes the scared chaplain; "the Adelantado's great zeal and courage make us hope he will succeed, but, for the good of his Majesty's service, he ought to be a little less ardent in pursuing his schemes."

Meanwhile the five hundred pushed their march, now toiling across the inundated savanrias, waist-deep in bulrushes and mud; now filing through the open forest to the moan and roar of the storm-racked pines: now hacking their way through palmetto thickets; and now turning from their path to shun some pool, quagmire, cypress swamp, or "hummock," matted with impenetrable bushes, brambles, and vines. As they bent before the tempest, the water trickling from the rusty head-piece crept clammy and cold betwixt the armor and the skin; and when they made their wretched bivouac, their bed was the spongy soil, and the exhaustless clouds their tent.

The night of Wednesday, the nineteenth, found their vanguard in a deep forest of pines, less than a mile from Fort Caroline, and near the low hills which extended in its rear, and formed a continuation of St. John's Bluff. All around was one great morass. In pitchy darkness, knee-deep in weeds and water, half starved, worn with toil and lack of sleep, drenched to the skin, their provisions spoiled, their ammunition wet, and their spirit chilled out of them, they stood in shivering groups, cursing the enterprise and the author of it. Menendez heard Fernando Perez, an ensign, say aloud to his comrades: "This Asturian Corito, who knows no more of war on shore than an ass, has betrayed us all. By God, if my advice had been followed, he would have had his deserts, the day he set out on this cursed journey!"

The Adelantado pretended not to hear.

Two hours before dawn he called his officers about him. All night, he said, he had been praying to God and the Virgin.

"Senores, what shall we resolve on? Our ammunition and provisions are gone. Our case is desperate." And he urged a bold rush on the fort.

But men and officers alike were disheartened and disgusted. They listened coldly and sullenly; many were for returning at every risk; none were in the mood for fight. Menendez put forth all his eloquence, till at length the dashed spirits of his followers were so far revived that they consented to follow him.

All fell on their knees in the marsh; then, rising, they formed their ranks and began to advance, guided by the renegade Frenchman, whose hands, to make sure of him, were tied behind his back. Groping and stumbling in the dark among trees, roots, and underbrush, buffeted by wind and rain, and lashed in the face by the recoiling boughs which they could not see, they soon lost their way, fell into confusion, and came to a stand, in a mood more savagely desponding than before. But soon a glimmer of returning day came to their aid, and showed them the dusky sky, and the dark columns of the surrounding pines. Menendez ordered the men forward on pain of death. They obeyed, and presently, emerging from the forest, could dimly discern the ridge of a low hill, behind which, the Frenchman told them, was the fort. Menendez, with a few officers and men, cautiously mounted to the top. Beneath lay Fort Caroline, three bow-shots distant; but the rain, the imperfect light, and a cluster of intervening houses prevented his seeing clearly, and he sent two officers to reconnoiter. As they descended, they met a solitary Frenchman. They knocked him down with a sheathed sword, wounded him, took him prisoner, kept him for a time, and then stabbed him as they returned towards the top of the hill. Here, clutching their weapons, all the gang stood in fierce expectancy.

"Santiago!" cried Menendez. "At them! God is with us! Victory!" And, shouting their hoarse war-cries, the Spaniards rushed down the slope like starved wolves.

Not a sentry was on the rampart. La Vigne, the officer of the guard, had just gone to his quarters; but a trumpeter, who chanced to remain, saw, through sheets of rain, the swarm of assailants sweeping down the hill. He blew the alarm, and at the summons a few half-naked soldiers ran wildly out of the barracks. It was too late. Through the breaches and over the ramparts the Spaniards came pouring in, with shouts of "Santiago! Santiago!"

Sick men leaped from their beds. Women and children, blind with fright, darted shrieking from the houses. A fierce, gaunt visage, the thrust of a pike, or blow of a rusty halberd,—such was the greeting that met all alike. Laudonniere snatched his sword and target, and ran towards the principal breach, calling to his soldiers. A rush of Spaniards met him; his men were cut down around him; and he, with a soldier named Bartholomew, was forced back into the yard of his house. Here stood a tent, and, as the pursuers stumbled among the cords, he escaped behind Ottigny's house, sprang through the breach in the western rampart, and fled for the woods.

Le Moyne had been one of the guard. Scarcely had he thrown himself into a hammock which was slung in his room, when a savage shout, and a wild uproar of shrieks, outcries, and the clash of weapons, brought him to his feet. He rushed by two Spaniards in the doorway, ran behind the guard-house, leaped through an embrasure into the ditch, and escaped to the forest.

Challeux, the carpenter, was going betimes to his work, a chisel in his hand. He was old, but pike and partisan brandished at his back gave wings to his flight. In the ecstasy of his terror, he leaped upward, clutched the top of the palisade, and threw himself over with the agility of a boy. He ran up the hill, no one pursuing, and, as he neared the edge of the forest, turned and looked back. From the high ground where he stood, he could see the butchery, the fury of the conquerors, and the agonizing gestures of the victims. He turned again in horror, and plunged into the woods. As he tore his way through the briers and thickets, he met several fugitives escaped like himself. Others presently came up, haggard and wild, like men broken loose from the jaws of death. They gathered together and consulted. One of them, known as Master Robert, in great repute for his knowledge of the Bible, was for returning and surrendering to the Spaniards. "They are men," he said; "perhaps, when their fury is over, they will spare our lives; and, even if they kill us, it will only be a few moments' pain. Better so, than to starve here in the woods, or be torn to pieces by wild beasts."

The greater part of the naked and despairing company assented, but Challeux was of a different mind. The old Huguenot quoted Scripture, and called the names of prophets and apostles to witness, that, in the direst extremity, God would not abandon those who rested their faith in Him. Six of the fugitives, however, still held to their desperate purpose. Issuing from the woods, they descended towards the fort, and, as with beating hearts their comrades watched the result, a troop of Spaniards rushed out, hewed them down with swords and halberds, and dragged their bodies to the brink of the river, where the victims of the massacre were already flung in heaps.

Le Moyne, with a soldier named Grandehemin, whom he had met in his flight, toiled all day through the woods and marshes, in the hope of reaching the small vessels anchored behind the bar. Night found them in a morass. No vessel could be seen, and the soldier, in despair, broke into angry upbraidings against his companion,—saying that he would go back and give himself up. Le

Moyne at first opposed him, then yielded. But when they drew near the fort, and heard the uproar of savage revelry that rose from within, the artist's heart failed him. He embraced his companion, and the soldier advanced alone. A party of Spaniards came out to meet him. He kneeled, and begged for his life. He was answered by a death-blow; and the horrified Le Moyne, from his hiding-place in the thicket, saw his limbs hacked apart, stuck on pikes, and borne off in triumph.

Meanwhile, Menendez, mustering his followers, had offered thanks to God for their victory; and this pious butcher wept with emotion as he recounted the favors which Heaven had showered upon their enterprise. His admiring historian gives it in proof of his humanity, that, after the rage of the assault was spent, he ordered that women, infants, and boys under fifteen should thenceforth be spared. Of these, by his own account, there were about fifty. Writing in October to the King, he says that they cause him great anxiety, since he fears the anger of God should he now put them to death in cold blood, while, on the other hand, he is in dread lest the venom of their heresy should infect his men.

A hundred and forty-two persons were slain in and around the fort, and their bodies lay heaped together on the bank of the river. Nearly opposite was anchored a small vessel, called the "Pearl," commanded by Jacques Ribaut, son of the Admiral. The ferocious soldiery, maddened with victory and drunk with blood, crowded to the water's edge, shouting insults to those on board, mangling the corpses, tearing out their eyes, and throwing them towards the vessel from the points of their daggers. Thus did the Most Catholic Philip champion the cause of Heaven in the New World.

It was currently believed in France, and, though no eye-witness attests it, there is reason to think it true, that among those murdered at Fort Caroline there were some who died a death of peculiar ignominy. Menendez, it is affirmed, hanged his prisoners on trees, and placed over them the inscription, "I do this, not as to Frenchmen, but as to Lutherans."

The Spaniards gained a great booty in armor, clothing, and provisions. "Nevertheless," says the devout Mendoza, after closing his inventory of the plunder, "the greatest profit of this victory is the triumph which our Lord has granted us, whereby His holy

Gospel will be introduced into this country, a thing so needful for saving so many souls from perdition." Again he writes in his journal, "We owe to God and His Mother, more than to human strength, this victory over the adversaries of the holy Catholic religion."

To whatever influence, celestial or other, the exploit may best be ascribed, the victors were not yet quite content with their success. Two small French vessels, besides that of Jacques Ribaut, still lay within range of the fort. When the storm had a little abated, the cannon were turned on them. One of them was sunk, but Ribaut, with the others, escaped down the river, at the mouth of which several light craft, including that bought from the English, had been anchored since the arrival of his father's squadron.

While this was passing, the wretched fugitives were flying from the scene of massacre through a tempest, of whose persistent violence all the narratives speak with wonder. Exhausted, starved, half naked,—for most of them had escaped in their shirts,—they pushed their toilsome way amid the ceaseless wrath of the elements. A few sought refuge in Indian villages; but these, it is said, were afterwards killed by the Spaniards. The greater number attempted to reach the vessels at the mouth of the river. Among the latter was Le Moyne, who, notwithstanding his former failure, was toiling through the mazes of tangled forests, when he met a Belgian soldier, with the woman described as Laudonniere's maid-servant, who was wounded in the breast; and, urging their flight towards the vessels, they fell in with other fugitives, including Laudonniere himself. As they struggled through the salt marsh, the rank sedge cut their naked limbs, and the tide rose to their waists. Presently they descried others, toiling like themselves through the matted vegetation, and recognized Challeux and his companions, also in quest of the vessels. The old man still, as he tells us, held fast to his chisel, which had done good service in cutting poles to aid the party to cross the deep creeks that channelled the morass. The united band, twenty-six in all, were cheered at length by the sight of a moving sail. It was the vessel of Captain Mallard, who, informed of the massacre, was standing along shore in the hope of picking up some of the fugitives. He saw their signals, and sent boats to their rescue; but such was their exhaustion, that, had not the sailors, wading to their armpits among the rushes, borne them out on their shoulders, few could have escaped. Laudonniere was so feeble that nothing but the support of a soldier, who held him upright in his arms, had saved him from drowning in the marsh.

On gaining the friendly decks, the fugitives counselled together. One and all, they sickened for the sight of France.

After waiting a few days, and saving a few more stragglers from the marsh, they prepared to sail. Young Ribaut, though ignorant of his father's fate, assented with something more than willingness; indeed, his behavior throughout had been stamped with weakness and poltroonery. On the twenty-fifth of September they put to sea in two vessels; and, after a voyage the privations of which were fatal to many of them, they arrived, one party at Rochelle, the other at Swansea, in Wales.

CHAPTER VIII
1565.
MASSACRE OF THE HERETICS.

In suspense and fear, hourly looking seaward for the dreaded fleet of Jean Ribaut, the chaplain Mendoza and his brother priests held watch and ward at St. Augustine in the Adelantado's absence. Besides the celestial guardians whom they ceased not to invoke, they had as protectors Bartholomew Menendez, the brother of the Adelantado, and about a hundred soldiers. Day and night they toiled to throw up earthworks and strengthen their position.

A week elapsed, when they saw a man running towards them, shouting as he ran.

Mendoza went to meet him.

"Victory! victory!" gasped the breathless messenger. "The French fort is ours!" And he flung his arms about the chaplain's neck.'

"To-day," writes the priest in his journal, "Monday, the twenty-fourth, came our good general himself, with fifty soldiers, very tired, Like all those who were with him. As soon as they told me he was coming, I ran to my lodging, took a new cassock, the best I had, put on my surplice, and went out to meet him with a crucifix in my hand; whereupon he, like a gentleman and a good Christian, kneeled down with all his followers, and gave the Lord a thousand thanks for the great favors he had received from Him."

In solemn procession, with four priests in front chanting Te Deum, the victors entered St. Augustine in triumph.

On the twenty-eighth, when the weary Adelantado was taking his siesta under the sylvan roof of Seloy, a troop of Indians came in with news that quickly roused him from his slumbers. They had seen a French vessel wrecked on the coast towards the south. Those who escaped from her were four or six leagues off, on the banks of a river or arm of the sea, which they could not cross.

Menendez instantly sent forty or fifty men in boats to reconnoitre. Next, he called the chaplain,—for he would fain have him at his elbow to countenance the deeds he meditated,—and, with him twelve soldiers and two Indian guides, embarked in another boat. They rowed along the channel between Anastasia Island and the main shore; then they landed, struck across the island on foot, traversed plains and marshes, reached the sea towards night, and searched along shore till ten o'clock to find their comrades who had gone before. At length, with mutual joy, the two parties met, and bivouacked together on the sands. Not far distant they could see lights. These were the camp-fires of the shipwrecked French.

To relate with precision the fortunes of these unhappy men is impossible; for henceforward the French narratives are no longer the narratives of eye-witnesses.

It has been seen how, when on the point of assailing the Spaniards at St. Augustine, Jean Ribaut was thwarted by a gale, which they hailed as a divine interposition. The gale rose to a tempest of strange fury. Within a few days, all the French ships were cast on shore, between Matanzas Inlet and Cape Canaveral. According to a letter of Menendez, many of those on board were lost; but others affirm that all escaped but a captain, La Grange, an officer of high merit, who was washed from a floating mast. One of the ships was wrecked at a point farther northward than the rest, and it was her company whose campfires were seen by the Spaniards at their bivouac on the sands of Anastasia Island. They were endeavoring to reach Fort Caroline, of the fate of which they knew nothing, while Ribaut with the remainder was farther southward, struggling through the wilderness towards the same goal. What befell the latter will appear hereafter. Of the fate of the former party there is no French record. What we know of it is due to three Spanish eye-witnesses, Mendoza, Doctor Soils de las Meras, and Menendez himself. Soils was a priest, and brother-in-law to Menendez. Like Mendoza, he minutely describes what he saw, and, like him, was a red-hot zealot, lavishing applause on the darkest deeds of his chief. But the principal witness, though not the most minute or most trustworthy, is Menendez, in his long despatches sent from Florida to the King, and now first brought to light from the archives of Seville,—a cool record of unsurpassed atrocities, inscribed on the back with the royal indorsement, "Say to him that he has done well."

When the Adelantado saw the French fires in the distance, he lay close in his bivouac, and sent two soldiers to reconnoitre. At two o'clock in the morning they came back, and reported that it was impossible to get at the enemy, since they were on the farther side of an arm of the sea (Matanzas Inlet). Menendez, however, gave orders to march, and before daybreak reached the hither bank, where he hid his men in a bushy hollow. Thence, as it grew light, they could discern the enemy, many of whom were searching along the sands and shallows for shell-fish, for they were famishing. A thought struck Menendez, an inspiration, says Mendoza, of the Holy Spirit. He put on the clothes of a sailor, entered a boat which had been brought to the spot, and rowed towards the shipwrecked men, the better to learn their condition. A Frenchman swam out to meet him. Menendez demanded what men they were.

"Followers of Ribaut, Viceroy of the King of France," answered the swimmer.

"Are you Catholics or Lutherans?"

"All Lutherans."

A brief dialogue ensued, during which the Adelantado declared his name and character, and the Frenchman gave an account of the designs of Ribaut, and of the disaster that had thwarted them. He then swam back to his companions, but soon returned, and asked safe conduct for his captain and four other gentlemen, who wished to hold conference with the Spanish general. Menendez gave his word for their safety, and, returning to the shore, sent his boat to bring them over. On their landing, he met them very courteously. His followers were kept at a distance, so disposed behind hills and among bushes as to give an exaggerated idea of their force,—a precaution the more needful, as they were only about sixty in number, while the French, says Solfs, were above two hundred. Menendez, however, declares that they did not exceed a hundred and forty. The French officer told him the story of their shipwreck, and begged him to lend them a boat to aid them in crossing the rivers which lay between them and a fort of their King, whither they were making their way.

Then came again the ominous question,

- 84 -

"Are you Catholics or Lutherans?"

"We are Lutherans."

"Gentlemen," pursued Menendez, "your fort is taken, and all in it are put to the sword." And, in proof of his declaration, he caused articles plundered from Fort Caroline to be shown to the unhappy petitioners. He then left them, and went to breakfast with his officers, first ordering food to be placed before them. Having breakfasted, he returned to them.

"Are you convinced now," he asked, "that what I have told you is true?"

The French captain assented, and implored him to lend them ships in which to return home. Menendez answered that he would do so willingly if they were Catholics, and if he had ships to spare, but he had none. The supplicants then expressed the hope that at least they and their followers would be allowed to remain with the Spaniards till ships could be sent to their relief, since there was peace between the two nations, whose kings were friends and brothers.

"All Catholics," retorted the Spaniard, "I will befriend; but as you are of the New Sect, I hold you as enemies, and wage deadly war against you; and this I will do with all cruelty [crueldad] in this country, where I command as Viceroy and Captain-General for my King. I am here to plant the Holy Gospel, that the Indians may be enlightened and come to the knowledge of the Holy Catholic faith of our Lord Jesus Christ, as the Roman Church teaches it. If you will give up your arms and banners, and place yourselves at my mercy, you may do so, and I will act towards you as God shall give me grace. Do as you will, for other than this you can have neither truce nor friendship with me."

Such were the Adelantado's words, as reported by a bystanders his admiring brother-in-law and that they contain an implied assurance of mercy has been held, not only by Protestants, but by Catholics and Spaniards. The report of Menendez himself is more brief, and sufficiently equivocal:—

"I answered, that they could give up their arms and place themselves under my mercy,—that I should do with them what our

Lord should order; and from that I did not depart, nor would I, unless God our Lord should otherwise inspire."

One of the Frenchmen recrossed to consult with his companions. In two hours he returned, and offered fifty thousand ducats to secure their lives; but Menendez, says his brother-in-law, would give no pledges. On the other hand, expressions in his own despatches point to the inference that a virtual pledge was given, at least to certain individuals.

The starving French saw no resource but to yield themselves to his mercy. The boat was again sent across the river. It returned laden with banners, arquebuses, swords, targets, and helmets. The Adelantado ordered twenty soldiers to bring over the prisoners, ten at a time. He then took the French officers aside behind a ridge of sand, two gunshots from the bank. Here, with courtesy on his lips and murder at his heart, he said:

"Gentlemen, I have but few men, and you are so many that, if you were free, it would be easy for you to take your satisfaction on us for the people we killed when we took your fort. Therefore it is necessary that you should go to my camp, four leagues from this place, with your hands tied."

Accordingly, as each party landed, they were led out of sight behind the sand-hill, and their hands tied behind their backs with the match-cords of the arquebuses, though not before each had been supplied with food. The whole day passed before all were brought together, bound and helpless, under the eye of the inexorable Adelantado. But now Mendoza interposed. "I was a priest," he says, "and had the bowels of a man." He asked that if there were Christians—that is to say, Catholics—among the prisoners, they should be set apart. Twelve Breton sailors professed themselves to be such; and these, together with four carpenters and calkers, "of whom," writes Menendez, "I was in great need," were put on board the boat and sent to St. Augustine. The rest were ordered to march thither by land.

The Adelantado walked in advance till he came to a lonely spot, not far distant, deep among the bush-covered hills. Here he stopped, and with his cane drew a line in the sand. The sun was set when the captive Huguenots, with their escort, reached the fatal goal thus marked out. And now let the curtain drop; for here, in the name of Heaven, the hounds of hell were turned loose, and the savage soldiery, like wolves in a sheepfold, rioted in slaughter. Of all that wretched company, not one was left alive.

"I had their hands tied behind their backs," writes the chief criminal, "and themselves put to the knife. It appeared to me that, by thus chastising them, God our Lord and your Majesty were served; whereby in future this evil sect will leave us more free to plant the Gospel in these parts."

Again Menendez returned triumphant to St. Augustine, and behind him marched his band of butchers, steeped in blood to the elbows, but still unsated. Great as had been his success, he still had cause for anxiety. There was ill news of his fleet. Some of the ships were lost, others scattered, or lagging tardily on their way. Of his whole force, less than a half had reached Florida, and of these a large part were still at Fort Caroline. Ribaut could not be far off; and, whatever might be the condition of his shipwrecked company, their numbers would make them formidable, unless taken at advantage. Urged by fear and fortified by fanaticism, Menendez had well begun his work of slaughter; but rest for him there was none,—a darker deed was behind.

On the tenth of October, Indians came with the tidings that, at the spot where the first party of the shipwrecked French had been found, there was now another party still larger. This murder-loving race looked with great respect on Menendez for his wholesale butchery of the night before,—an exploit rarely equalled in their own annals of massacre. On his part, he doubted not that Ribaut was at hand. Marching with a hundred and fifty men, he crossed the bush-covered sands of Anastasia Island, followed the strand between the thickets and the sea, reached the inlet at midnight, and again, like a savage, ambushed himself on the bank. Day broke, and he could plainly see the French on the farther side. They had made a raft, which lay in the water ready for crossing. Menendez and his men showed themselves, when, forthwith, the French displayed their banners, sounded drums and trumpets, and set their sick and starving ranks in array of battle. But the Adelantado, regardless of this warlike show, ordered his men to seat themselves at breakfast, while he with three officers walked unconcernedly along the shore. His coolness had its effect. The French blew a trumpet of parley, and showed a white flag. The Spaniards replied. A Frenchman came out upon the raft, and, shouting across the water, asked that a Spanish envoy should be sent over.

"You have a raft," was the reply; "come yourselves."

An Indian canoe lay under the bank on the Spanish side. A French sailor swam to it, paddled back unmolested, and presently returned, bringing with him La Caille, Ribaut's sergeant-major. He told Menendez that the French were three hundred and fifty in all, and were on their way to Fort Caroline; and, like the officers of the former party, he begged for boats to aid them in crossing the river.

"My brother," said Menendez, "go and tell your general, that, if he wishes to speak with me, he may come with four or six companions, and that I pledge my word he shall go back safe."

La Caille returned; and Ribaut, with eight gentlemen, soon came over in the canoe. Menendez met them courteously, caused wine and preserved fruits to be placed before them,—he had come well provisioned on his errand of blood,—and next led Ribaut to the reeking Golgotha, where, in heaps upon the sand, lay the corpses of his slaughtered followers. Ribaut was prepared for the spectacle,—La Caille had already seen it,—but he would not believe that Fort Caroline was taken till a part of the plunder was shown him. Then, mastering his despair, he turned to the conqueror. "What has befallen us," he said, "may one day befall you." And, urging that the kings of France and Spain were brothers and close friends, he begged, in the name of that friendship, that the Spaniard would aid him in conveying his followers home. Menendez gave him the same equivocal answer that he had given the former party, and Ribaut returned to consult with his officers. After three hours of absence, he came back in the canoe, and told the Adelantado that some of his people were ready to surrender at discretion, but that many refused.

"They can do as they please," was the reply. In behalf of those who surrendered, Ribaut offered a ransom of a hundred thousand ducats. "It would much grieve me," said Menendez, "not to accept it; for I have great need of it."

Ribaut was much encouraged. Menendez could scarcely forego such a prize, and he thought, says the Spanish narrator, that the lives of his followers would now be safe. He asked to be allowed the night for deliberation, and at sunset recrossed the river. In the morning he reappeared among the Spaniards, and reported that two hundred of his men had retreated from the spot, but that the remaining hundred and fifty would surrender. At the same time he gave into the hands of Menendez the royal standard and other flags, with his sword, dagger, helmet, buckler, and the official seal given him by Coligny. Menendez directed an officer to enter the boat and bring over the French by tens. He next led Ribaut among the bushes behind the neighboring sand-hill, and ordered his hands to be bound fast. Then the scales fell from the prisoner's eyes. Face to face his fate rose up before him. He saw his followers and himself entrapped,—the dupes of words artfully framed to lure them to their ruin. The day wore on; and, as band after band of prisoners was brought over, they were led behind the sand-hill out of sight from the farther shore, and bound like their general. At length the transit was finished. With bloodshot eyes and weapons bared, the Spaniards closed around their victims.

"Are you Catholics or Lutherans? and is there any one among you who will go to confession?"

Ribaut answered, "I and all here are of the Reformed Faith."

And he recited the Psalm, "Domine, memento mei."

"We are of earth," he continued, "and to earth we must return; twenty years more or less can matter little;" and, turning to the Adelantado, he bade him do his will.

The stony-hearted bigot gave the signal; and those who will may paint to themselves the horrors of the scene.

A few, however, were spared. "I saved," writes Menendez, "the lives of two young gentlemen of about eighteen years of age, as well as of three others, the fifer, the drummer, and the trumpeter; and I caused Juan Ribao [Ribaut] with all the rest to be put to the knife, judging this to be necessary for the service of God our Lord and of your Majesty. And I consider it great good fortune that he [Juan Ribao] should be dead, for the King of France could effect more with him and five hundred ducats than with other men and five thousand; and he would do more in one year than another in ten, for he was the most experienced sailor and naval commander known, and of great skill in this navigation of the Indies and the coast of Florida. He was, besides, greatly liked in England, in which kingdom his reputation was such that he was appointed Captain-General of all the English fleet against the French Catholics in the war between England and France some years ago."

Such is the sum of the Spanish accounts,—the self-damning testimony of the author and abettors of the crime; a picture of lurid and awful coloring; and yet there is reason to believe that the truth was darker still. Among those who were spared was one Christophe le Breton, who was carried to Spain, escaped to France, and told his story to Challeux. Among those struck down in the butchery was a sailor of Dieppe, stunned and left for dead under a heap of corpses. In the night he revived, contrived to draw his knife, cut the cords that bound his hands, and made his way to an Indian village. The Indians, not without reluctance, abandoned him to the Spaniards, who sold him as a slave; but, on his way in fetters to Portugal, the ship was taken by the Huguenots, the sailor set free, and his story published in the narrative of Le Moyne. When the massacre was known in France, the friends and relatives of the victims sent to the King, Charles the Ninth, a vehement petition for redress; and their memorial recounts many incidents of the tragedy. From these three sources is to be drawn the French version of the story. The following is its substance.

Famished and desperate, the followers of Ribaut were toiling northward to seek refuge at Fort Caroline, when they found the Spaniards in their path. Some were filled with dismay; others, in their misery, almost hailed them as deliverers. La Caille, the sergeant-major, crossed the river. Menendez met him with a face of friendship, and protested that he would spare the lives of the shipwrecked men, sealing the promise with an oath, a kiss, and many signs of the cross. He even gave it in writing, under seal. Still, there were many among the French who would not place themselves in his power. The most credulous crossed the river in a boat. As each successive party landed, their hands were bound fast at their backs; and thus, except a few who were set apart, they were all driven towards the fort, like cattle to the shambles, with curses and scurrilous abuse. Then, at sound of drums and trumpets, the Spaniards fell upon them, striking them down with swords, pikes, and halberds. Ribaut vainly called on the Adelantado to remember his oath. By his order, a soldier plunged a dagger into the French

- 90 -

commander's heart; and Ottigny, who stood near, met a similar fate. Ribaut's beard was cut off, and portions of it sent in a letter to Philip the Second. His head was hewn into four parts, one of which was displayed on the point of a lance at each corner of Fort St. Augustine. Great fires were kindled, and the bodies of the murdered burned to ashes.

Such is the sum of the French accounts. The charge of breach of faith contained in them was believed by Catholics as well as Protestants; and it was as a defence against this charge that the narrative of the Adelantado's brother-in-law was published. That Ribaut, a man whose good sense and courage were both reputed high, should have submitted himself and his men to Menendez without positive assurance of safety, is scarcely credible; nor is it lack of charity to believe that a bigot so savage in heart and so perverted in conscience would act on the maxim, current among certain casuists of the day, that faith ought not to be kept with heretics.

It was night when the Adelantado again entered St. Augustine. There were some who blamed his cruelty; but many applauded. "Even if the French had been Catholics,"—such was their language,—"he would have done right, for, with the little provision we have, they would all have starved; besides, there were so many of them that they would have cut our throats."

And now Menendez again addressed himself to the despatch, already begun, in which he recounts to the King his labors and his triumphs, a deliberate and business-like document, mingling narratives of butchery with recommendations for promotions, commissary details, and petitions for supplies,—enlarging, too, on the vast schemes of encroachment which his successful generalship had brought to naught. The French, he says, had planned a military and naval depot at Los Martires, whence they would make a descent upon Havana, and another at the Bay of Ponce de Leon, whence they could threaten Vera Cruz. They had long been encroaching on Spanish rights at Newfoundland, from which a great arm of the sea—doubtless meaning the St. Lawrence—would give them access to the Moluccas and other parts of the East Indies. He adds, in a later despatch, that by this passage they may reach the mines of Zacatecas and St. Martin, as well as every part of the South Sea. And, as already mentioned, he urges immediate occupation of Chesapeake Bay, which, by its supposed water communication with the St. Lawrence, would enable Spain to vindicate her rights, control the fisheries of Newfoundland, and thwart her rival in vast designs of commercial and territorial aggrandizement. Thus did France and Spain dispute the possession of North America long before England became a party to the strife. 24

Some twenty days after Menendez returned to St. Augustine, the Indians, enamoured of carnage, and exulting to see their invaders mowed down, came to tell him that on the coast southward, near Cape Canaveral, a great number of Frenchmen were intrenching themselves. They were those of Ribaut's party who had refused to surrender. Having retreated to the spot where their ships had been cast ashore, they were trying to build a vessel from the fragments of the wrecks.

In all haste Menendez despatched messengers to Fort Caroline, named by him San Mateo, ordering a reinforcement of a hundred and fifty men. In a few days they came. He added some of his own soldiers, and, with a united force of two hundred and fifty, set out, as he tells us, on the second of November. A part of his force went by sea, while the rest pushed southward along the shore with such merciless energy that several men dropped dead with wading night and day through the loose sands. When, from behind their frail defences, the French saw the Spanish pikes and partisans glittering into view, they fled in a panic, and took refuge among the hills. Menendez sent a trumpet to summon them, pledging his honor for their safety. The commander and several others told the messenger that they would sooner be eaten by the savages than trust themselves to Spaniards; and, escaping, they fled to the Indian towns. The rest surrendered; and Menendez kept his word. The comparative number of his own men made his prisoners no longer dangerous. They were led back to St. Augustine, where, as the Spanish writer affirms, they were well treated. Those of good birth sat at the Adelantado's table, eating the bread of a homicide crimsoned with the slaughter of their comrades. The priests essayed their pious efforts, and, under the gloomy menace of the Inquisition, some of the heretics renounced their errors. The fate of the captives may be gathered from the endorsement, in the handwriting of the King, on one of the despatches of Menendez.

"Say to him," writes Philip the Second, "that, as to those he has killed, he has done well; and as to those he has saved, they shall be sent to the galleys."

CHAPTER IX.
1565-1567.
CHARLES IX. AND PHILLIP II.

The state of international relations in the sixteenth century is hardly conceivable at this day. The Puritans of England and the Huguenots of France regarded Spain as their natural enemy, and on the high seas and in the British Channel they joined hands with godless freebooters to rifle her ships, kill her sailors, or throw them alive into the sea. Spain on her side seized English Protestant sailors who ventured into her ports, and burned them as heretics, or consigned them to a living death in the dungeons of the Inquisition. Yet in the latter half of the century these mutual outrages went on for years while the nations professed to be at peace. There was complaint, protest, and occasional menace, but no redress, and no declaration of war.

Contemporary writers of good authority have said that, when the news of the massacres in Florida reached the court of France, Charles the Ninth and Catherine de Medicis submitted to the insult in silence; but documents lately brought to light show that a demand for redress was made, though not insisted on. A cry of horror and execration had risen from the Huguenots and many even of the Catholics had echoed it; yet the perpetrators of the crime, and not its victims, were the first to make complaint. Philip the Second resented the expeditions of Ribaut and Laudonniere as an invasion of the American domains of Spain, and ordered D'Alava, his ambassador at Paris, to denounce them to the French King. Charles, thus put on the defensive, replied, that the country in question belonged to France, having been discovered by Frenchmen a hundred years before, and named by them Terre des Bretons. This alludes to the tradition that the Bretons and Basques visited the northern coasts of America before the voyage of Columbus. In several maps of the sixteenth century the region of New England and the neighboring states and provinces is set down as Terre des Bretons, or Tierra de los Bretones, and this name was assumed by Charles to extend to the Gulf of Mexico, as the name of Florida was assumed by the Spaniards to extend to the Gulf of St. Lawrence, and even beyond it. Philip spurned the claim, asserted the Spanish right to all Florida, and asked whether or not the followers of Ribaut and Laudonniere had gone thither by authority of their King. The Queen Mother, Catherine de Medicis, replied in her son's behalf, that certain Frenchmen had gone to a country called Terre aux Bretons, discovered by French subjects, and that in so doing they had been warned not to encroach on lands belonging to the King of Spain. And she added, with some spirit, that the Kings of France were not in the habit of permitting themselves to be threatened.

Philip persisted in his attitude of injured innocence; and Forquevaulx, French ambassador at Madrid, reported that, as a reward for murdering French subjects, Menendez was to receive the title of Marquis of Florida. A demand soon followed from Philip, that Admiral Coligny should be punished for planting a French colony on Spanish ground, and thus causing the disasters that ensued. It was at this time that the first full account of the massacres reached the French court, and the Queen Mother, greatly moved, complained to the Spanish ambassador, saying that she could not persuade herself that his master would refuse reparation. The ambassador replied by again throwing the blame on Coligny and the Huguenots; and Catherine de Medicis returned that, Huguenots or not, the King of Spain had no right to take upon himself the punishment of French subjects. Forquevaulx was instructed to demand redress at Madrid; but Philip only answered that he was very sorry for what had happened, and again insisted that Coligny should be punished as the true cause of it.

Forquevaulx, an old soldier, remonstrated with firmness, declared that no deeds so execrable had ever been committed within his memory, and demanded that Menendez and his followers should be chastised as they deserved. The King said that he was sorry that the sufferers chanced to be Frenchmen, but, as they were pirates also, they ought to be treated as such. The ambassador replied, that they were no pirates, since they bore the commission of the Admiral of France, who in naval affairs represented the King; and Philip closed the conversation by saying that he would speak on the subject with the Duke of Alva. This was equivalent to refusal, for the views of the Duke were well known; "and so, Madame," writes the ambassador to the Queen

Mother, "there is no hope that any reparation will be made for the aforesaid massacre."

On this, Charles wrote to Forquevaulx "It is my will that you renew your complaint, and insist urgently that, for the sake of the union and friendship between the two crowns, reparation be made for the wrong done me and the cruelties committed on my subjects, to which I cannot submit without too great loss of reputation." And, jointly with his mother, he ordered the ambassador to demand once more that Menendez and his men should be punished, adding, that he trusts that Philip will grant justice to the King of France, his brother-in-law and friend, rather than pardon a gang of brigands. "On this demand," concludes Charles, "the Sieur de Forquevaulx will not fail to insist, be the answer what it may, in order that the King of Spain shall understand that his Majesty of France has no less spirit than his predecessors to repel an insult." The ambassador fulfilled his commission, and Philip replied by referring him to the Duke of Alva. "I have no hope," reports Forquevaulx, "that the Duke will give any satisfaction as to the massacre, for it was he who advised it from the first." A year passed, and then he reported that Menendez had returned from Florida, that the King had given him a warm welcome, and that his fame as a naval commander was such that he was regarded as a sort of Neptune.

In spite of their brave words, Charles and the Queen Mother tamely resigned themselves to the affront, for they would not quarrel with Spain. To have done so would have been to throw themselves into the arms of the Protestant party, adopt the principle of toleration, and save France from the disgrace and blight of her later years. France was not so fortunate. The enterprise of Florida was a national enterprise, undertaken at the national charge, with the royal commission, and under the royal standard; and it had been crushed in time of peace by a power professing the closest friendship. Yet Huguenot influence had prompted and Huguenot hands executed it. That influence had now ebbed low; Coligny's power had waned; Charles, after long vacillation, was leaning more and more towards the Guises and the Catholics, and fast subsiding into the deathly embrace of Spain, for whom, at last, on the bloody eve of St. Bartholomew, he was to become the assassin of his own best subjects.

In vain the relatives of the slain petitioned him for redress; and had the honor of the nation rested in the keeping of its King, the blood of hundreds of murdered Frenchmen would have cried from the ground in vain. But it was not to be so. Injured humanity found an avenger, and outraged France a champion. Her chivalrous annals may be searched in vain for a deed of more romantic daring than the vengeance of Dominique de Gourgues.

CHAPTER X.
1567-1583.
DOMINIQUE DE GOURGUES.

There was a gentleman of Mont-de-Marsan, Dominique de Gourgues, a soldier of ancient birth and high renown. It is not certain that he was a Huguenot. The Spanish annalist calls him a "terrible heretic;" but the French Jesuit, Charlevoix, anxious that the faithful should share the glory of his exploits, affirms that, like his ancestors before him, he was a good Catholic. If so, his faith sat lightly upon him; and, Catholic or heretic, he hated the Spaniards with a mortal hate. Fighting in the Italian wars,—for from boyhood he was wedded to the sword,—he had been taken prisoner by them near Siena, where he had signalized himself by a fiery and determined bravery. With brutal insult, they chained him to the oar as a galley slave. After he had long endured this ignominy the Turks captured the vessel and carried her to Constantinople. It was but a change of tyrants but, soon after, while she was on a cruise, Gourgues still at the oar, a galley of the knights of Malta hove in sight, bore down on her, recaptured her, and set the prisoner free. For several years after, his restless spirit found employment in voyages to Africa, Brazil, and regions yet more remote. His naval repute rose high, but his grudge against the Spaniards still rankled within him; and when, returned from his rovings, he learned the tidings from Florida, his hot Gascon blood boiled with fury.

The honor of France had been foully stained, and there was none to wipe away the shame. The faction-ridden King was dumb. The nobles who surrounded him were in the Spanish interest. Then, since they proved recreant, he, Dominique de Gourgues, a simple gentleman, would take upon him to avenge the wrong, and restore the dimmed lustre of the French name. He sold his inheritance, borrowed money from his brother, who held a high post in Guienne, and equipped three small vessels, navigable by sail or oar. On board he placed a hundred arquebusiers and eighty sailors, prepared to fight on land, if need were. The noted Blaise de Montluc, then lieutenant for the King in Guienne, gave him a commission to make war on the negroes of Benin,—that is, to kidnap them as slaves, an adventure then held honorable.

His true design was locked within his own breast. He mustered his followers,—not a few of whom were of rank equal to his own, feasted them, and, on the twenty-second of August, 1567, sailed from the mouth of the Charente. Off Cape Finisterre, so violent a storm buffeted his ships that his men clamored to return; but Gourgues's spirit prevailed. He bore away for Africa, and, landing at the Rio del Oro, refreshed and cheered them as he best might. Thence he sailed to Cape Blanco, where the jealous Portuguese, who had a fort in the neighborhoods set upon him three negro chiefs. Gourgues beat them off, and remained master of the harbor; whence, however, he soon voyaged onward to Cape Verd, and, steering westward, made for the West Indies. Here, advancing from island to island, he came to Hispaniola, where, between the fury of a hurricane at sea and the jealousy of the Spaniards on shore, he was in no small jeopardy,—"the Spaniards", exclaims the indignant journalist, "who think that this New World was made for nobody but them, and that no other living man has a right to move or breathe here!" Gourgues landed, however, obtained the water of which he was in need, and steered for Cape San Antonio, at the western end of Cuba. There he gathered his followers about him, and addressed them with his fiery Gascon eloquence. For the first time, he told them his true purpose, inveighed against Spanish cruelty, and painted, with angry rhetoric, the butcheries of Fort Caroline and St. Augustine.

"What disgrace," he cried, "if such an insult should pass unpunished! What glory to us if we avenge it! To this I have devoted my fortune. I relied on you. I thought you jealous enough of your country's glory to sacrifice life itself in a cause like this. Was I deceived? I will show you the way; I will be always at your head; I will bear the brunt of the danger. Will you refuse to follow me?"

At first his startled hearers listened in silence; but soon the passions of that adventurous age rose responsive to his words. The combustible French nature burst into flame. The enthusiasm of the soldiers rose to such a pitch that Gourgues had much ado to make them wait till the moon was full before tempting the perils of the Bahama Channel. His time came at length. The moon rode high above the lonely sea, and, silvered in its light, the ships of the avenger held their course.

Meanwhile, it had fared ill with the Spaniards in Florida; the good-will of the Indians had vanished. The French had been obtrusive and vexatious guests; but their worst trespasses had been mercy and tenderness compared to the daily outrage of the new-comers. Friendship had changed to aversion, aversion to hatred, and hatred to open war. The forest paths were beset; stragglers were cut off; and woe to the Spaniard who should venture after nightfall beyond call of the outposts.

Menendez, however, had strengthened himself in his new conquest. St. Augustine was well fortified; Fort Caroline, now Fort San Mateo, was repaired; and two redoubts, or small forts, were thrown up to guard the mouth of the River of May,—one of them near the present lighthouse at Mayport, and the other across the river on Fort George Island. Thence, on an afternoon in early spring, the Spaniards saw three sail steering northward. They suspected no enemy, and their batteries boomed a salute. Gourgues's ships replied, then stood out to sea, and were lost in the shades of evening.

They kept their course all night, and, as day broke, anchored at the mouth of a river, the St. Mary's, or the Santilla, by their reckoning fifteen leagues north of the River of May. Here, as it grew light, Gourgues saw the borders of the sea thronged with savages, armed and plumed for war. They, too, had mistaken the strangers for Spaniards, and mustered to meet their tyrants at the landing. But in the French ships there was a trumpeter who had been long in Florida, and knew the Indians well. He went towards them in a boat, with many gestures of friendship; and no sooner was he recognized, than the naked crowd, with yelps of delight, danced for joy along the sands. Why had he ever left them? they asked; and why had he not returned before? The intercourse thus auspiciously begun was actively kept up. Gourgues told the principal chief,—who was no other than Satouriona, once the ally of the French,—that he had come to visit them, make friendship with them, and bring them presents. At this last announcement, so grateful to Indian ears the dancing was renewed with double zeal. The next morning was named for a grand council, and Satouriona sent runners to summon all Indians within call; while Gourgues, for safety, brought his vessels within the mouth of the river.

Morning came, and the woods were thronged with warriors. Gourgues and his soldiers landed with martial pomp. In token of mutual confidence, the French laid aside their arquebuses, and the Indians their bows and arrows. Satouriona came to meet the strangers, and seated their commander at his side, on a wooden stool, draped and cushioned with the gray Spanish moss. Two old Indians cleared the spot of brambles, weeds, and grass; and, when their task was finished, the tribesmen took their places, ring within ring, standing, sitting, and crouching on the ground,—a dusky concourse, plumed in festal array, waiting with grave visages and intent eyes. Gourgues was about to speak, when the chief, who, says the narrator, had not learned French manners, anticipated him, and broke into a vehement harangue, denouncing the cruelty of the Spaniards.

Since the French fort was taken, he said, the Indians had not had one happy day. The Spaniards drove them from their cabins, stole their corn, ravished their wives and daughters, and killed their children; and all this they had endured because they loved the French. There was a French boy who had escaped from the massacre at the fort; they had found him in the woods and though the Spaniards, who wished to kill him, demanded that they should give him up, they had kept him for his friends.

"Look!" pursued the chief, "here he is! "—and he brought forward a youth of sixteen, named Pierre Debre, who became at once of the greatest service to the French, his knowledge of the Indian language making him an excellent interpreter.

Delighted as he was at this outburst against the Spaniards, Gourgues did not see fit to display the full extent of his satisfaction. He thanked the Indians for their good-will, exhorted them to continue in it, and pronounced an ill-merited eulogy on the greatness and goodness of his King. As for the Spaniards, he said, their day of reckoning was at hand; and, if the Indians had been abused for their love of the French, the French would be their avengers. Here Satouriona forgot his dignity, and leaped up for joy.

"What!" he cried, "will you fight the Spaniards?"

"I came here," replied Gourgues, "only to reconnoitre the country and make friends with you, and then go back to bring more soldiers; but, when I hear what you are suffering from them, I wish to fall upon them this very day, and rescue you from their tyranny." All around the ring a clamor of applauding voices greeted his words.

"But you will do your part," pursued the Frenchman; "you will not leave us all the honor."

"We will go," replied Satouriona, "and die with you, if need be."

"Then, if we fight, we ought to fight at once. How soon can you have your warriors ready to march?"

The chief asked three days for preparation. Gourgues cautioned him to secrecy, lest the Spaniards should take alarm.

"Never fear," was the answer; "we hate them more than you do."

Then came a distribution of gifts,—knives, hatchets, mirrors, bells, and beads,—while the warrior rabble crowded to receive them, with eager faces and outstretched arms. The distribution over, Gourgues asked the chiefs if there was any other matter in which he could serve them. On this, pointing to his shirt, they expressed a peculiar admiration for that garment, and begged each to have one, to be worn at feasts and councils during life, and in their graves after death. Gourgues complied; and his grateful confederates were soon stalking about him, fluttering in the spoils of his wardrobe.

To learn the strength and position of the Spaniards, Gourgues now sent out three scouts; and with them went Olotoraca, Satourioria's nephew, a young brave of great renown.

The chief, eager to prove his good faith, gave as hostages his only surviving son and his favorite wife. They were sent on board the ships, while the Indians dispersed to their encampments, with leaping, stamping, dancing, and whoops of jubilation.

The day appointed came, and with it the savage army, hideous in war-paint, and plumed for battle. The woods rang back their songs and yells, as with frantic gesticulation they brandished their war-clubs and vaunted their deeds of prowess. Then they drank the black drink, endowed with mystic virtues against hardship and danger; and Gourgues himself pretended to swallow the nauseous decoction. 25

These ceremonies consumed the day. It was evening before the allies filed off into their forests, and took the path for the Spanish forts. The French, on their part, were to repair by sea to the rendezvous. Gourgues mustered and addressed his men. It was needless: their ardor was at fever height. They broke in upon his words, and demanded to be led at once against the enemy. Francois Bourdelais, with twenty sailors, was left with the ships, and Gourgues affectionately bade him farewell.

"If I am slain in this most just enterprise," he said, "I leave all in your charge, and pray you to carry back my soldiers to France."

There were many embracings among the excited Frenchmen,— many sympathetic tears from those who were to stay behind,— many messages left with them for wives, children, friends, and mistresses; and then this valiant band pushed their boats from shore. It was a hare-brained venture, for, as young Debre had assured them, the Spaniards on the River of May were four hundred in number, secure behind their ramparts.

Hour after hour the sailors pulled at the oar. They glided slowly by the sombre shores in the shimmering moonlight, to the sound of the surf and the moaning pine-trees. In the gray of the morning, they came to the mouth of a river, probably the Nassau; and here a northeast wind set in with a violence that almost wrecked their boats. Their Indian allies were waiting on the bank, but for a while the gale delayed their crossing. The bolder French would lose no time, rowed through the tossing waves, and, landing safely, left their boats, and pushed into the forest. Gourgues took the lead, in breastplate and back-piece. At his side marched the young chief Olotoraca, with a French pike in his hand; and the files of arquebuse-men and armed sailors followed close behind. They plunged through swamps, hewed their way through brambly thickets and the matted intricacies of the forests, and, at five in the afternoon, almost spent with fatigue and hunger, came to a river or inlet of the sea, not far from the first Spanish fort. Here they found three hundred Indians waiting for them.

Tired as he was, Gourgues would not rest. He wished to attack at daybreak, and with ten arquebusiers and his Indian guide he set out to reconnoitre. Night closed upon him. It was a vain task to struggle on, in pitchy darkness, among trunks of trees, fallen logs, tangled vines, and swollen streams. Gourgues returned, anxious and gloomy. An Indian chief approached him, read through the darkness his perturbed look, and offered to lead him by a better path along the margin of the sea. Gourgues joyfully assented, and ordered all his men to march. The Indians, better skilled in woodcraft, chose the shorter course through the forest.

The French forgot their weariness, and pressed on with speed. At dawn they and their allies met on the bank of a stream, probably Sister Creek, beyond which, and very near, was the fort. But the tide was in, and they tried in vain to cross. Greatly vexed,—for he had hoped to take the enemy asleep,—Gourgues withdrew his soldiers into the forest, where they were no sooner ensconced than a drenching rain fell, and they had much ado to keep their gun-matches burning. The light grew fast. Gourgues plainly saw the fort, the defences of which seemed slight and unfinished. He even saw the Spaniards at work within. A feverish interval elapsed, till at length the tide was out,—so far, at least, that the stream was fordable. A little higher up, a clump of trees lay between it and the fort. Behind this friendly screen the passage was begun. Each man tied his powder-flask to his steel cap, held his arquebuse above his head with one hand, and grasped his sword with the other. The channel was a bed of oysters. The sharp shells cut their feet as they waded through. But the farther bank was gained. They emerged from the water, drenched, lacerated, and bleeding, but with unabated mettle. Gourgues set them in array under cover of the trees. They stood with kindling eyes, and hearts throbbing, but not with fear. Gourgues pointed to the Spanish fort, seen by glimpses through the boughs. "Look I" he said, "there are the robbers who have stolen this land from our King; there are the murderers who have butchered our countrymen!" With voices eager, fierce, but half suppressed, they demanded to be led on.

Gourgues gave the word. Cazenove, his lientenant, with thirty men, pushed for the fort gate; he himself, with the main body, for the glacis. It was near noon; the Spaniards had just finished their meal, and, says the narrative, "were still picking their teeth," when a startled cry rang in their ears:—"To arms! to arms! The French are coming! The French are coming!"

It was the voice of a cannoneer who had that moment mounted the rampart and seen the assailants advancing in unbroken ranks, with heads lowered and weapons at the charge. He fired his cannon among them. He even had time to load and fire again, when the light-limbed Olotoraca bounded forward, ran up the glacis, leaped the unfinished ditch, and drove his pike through the Spaniard from breast to back. Gourgues was now on the glacis, when he heard Cazenove shouting from the gate that the Spaniards were escaping on that side. He turned and led his men thither at a run. In a moment, the fugitives, sixty in all, were enclosed between his party and that of his lieutenant. The Indians, too, came leaping to the spot. Not a Spaniard escaped. All were cut down but a few, reserved by Gourgues for a more inglorious end.

Meanwhile the Spaniards in the other fort, on the opposite shore, cannonaded the victors without ceasing. The latter turned four captured guns against them. One of Gourgues's boats, a very large one, had been brought along-shore, and, entering it with eighty soldiers, he pushed for the farther bank. With loud yells, the Indians leaped into the river, which is here about three fourths of a mile wide. Each held his bow and arrows aloft in one hand, while he swam with the other. A panic seized the garrison as they saw the savage multitude. They broke out of the fort and fled into the forest. But the French had already landed; and, throwing themselves in the path of the fugitives, they greeted them with a storm of lead. The terrified wretches recoiled; but flight was vain. The Indian whoop rang behind them, and war-clubs and arrows finished the work. Gourgues's utmost efforts saved but fifteen, not out of mercy, but from a refinement of vengeance.

The next day was Quasimodo Sunday, or the Sunday after Easter. Gourgues and his men remained quiet, making ladders for the assault on Fort San Mateo. Meanwhile the whole forest was in arms, and, far and near, the Indians were wild with excitement. They beset the Spanish fort till not a soldier could venture out. The garrison, aware of their danger, though ignorant of its extent, devised an expedient to gain information; and one of them, painted and feathered like an Indian, ventured within Gourgues's outposts. He himself chanced to be at hand, and by his side walked his constant attendant, Olotoraca. The keen-eyed young savage pierced the cheat at a glance. The spy was seized, and, being examined, declared that there were two hundred and sixty Spaniards in San Mateo, and that they believed the French to be two thousand, and were so frightened that they did not know what they were doing.

Gourgues, well pleased, pushed on to attack them. On Monday evening he sent forward the Indians to ambush themselves on both sides of the fort. In the morning he followed with his Frenchmen; and, as the glittering ranks came into view, defiling between the forest and the river, the Spaniards opened on them with culverins from a projecting bastion. The French took cover in the woods with which the hills below and behind the fort were densely overgrown. Here, himself unseen, Gourgues could survey whole extent of the defences, and he presently descried a strong party of Spaniards issuing from their works, crossing the ditch, and advancing to reconnoitre.

On this, he sent Cazenove, with a detachment, to station himself at a point well hidden by trees on the flank of the Spaniards, who, with strange infatuation, continued their advance. Gourgues and his followers pushed on through the thickets to meet them. As the Spaniards reached the edge of the open ground, a deadly fire blazed in their faces, and, before the smoke cleared, the French were among them, sword in hand. The survivors would have fled; but Cazenove's detachment fell upon their rear, and all were killed or taken.

When their comrades in the fort beheld their fate, a panic seized them. Conscious of their own deeds, perpetrated on this very spot, they could hope no mercy, and their terror multiplied immeasurably the numbers of their enemy. They abandoned the fort in a body, and fled into the woods most remote from the French. But here a deadlier foe awaited them; for a host of Indians leaped up from ambush. Then rose those hideous war-cries which have curdled the boldest blood and blanched the manliest cheek. The forest warriors, with savage ecstasy, wreaked their long arrears of vengeance, while the French hastened to the spot, and lent their swords to the slaughter. A few prisoners were saved alive; the rest were slain; and thus did the Spaniards make bloody atonement for the butchery of Fort Caroline.

But Gourgues's vengeance was not yet appeased. Hard by the fort, the trees were pointed out to him on which Menendez had hanged his captives, and placed over them the inscription, "Not as to Frenchmen, but as to Lutherans."

Gourgues ordered the Spanish prisoners to be led thither.

"Did you think," he sternly said, as the pallid wretches stood ranged before him, "that so vile a treachery, so detestable a cruelty, against a King so potent and a nation so generous, would go unpunished? I, one of the humblest gentlemen among my King's subjects, have charged myself with avenging it. Even if the Most Christian and the Most Catholic Kings had been enemies, at deadly war, such perfidy and extreme cruelty would still have been unpardonable. Now that they are friends and close allies, there is no name vile enough to brand your deeds, no punishment sharp enough to requite them. But though you cannot suffer as you deserve, you shall suffer all that an enemy can honorably inflict, that your example may teach others to observe the peace and alliance which you have so perfidiously violated."

They were hanged where the French had hung before them; and over them was nailed the inscription, burned with a hot iron on a tablet of pine, "Not as to Spaniards, but as to Traitors, Robbers, and Murderers."

Gourgues's mission was fulfilled. To occupy the country had never been his intention; nor was it possible, for the Spaniards were still in force at St. Augustine. His was a whirlwind visitation,—to ravage, ruin, and vanish. He harangued the Indians, and exhorted them to demolish the fort. They fell to the work with eagerness, and in less than a day not one stone was left on another.

Gourgues returned to the forts at the mouth of the river, destroyed them also, and took up his march for his ships. It was a triumphal procession. The Indians thronged around the victors with gifts of fish and game; and an old woman declared that she was now ready to die, since she had seen the French once more.

The ships were ready for sea. Gourgues bade his disconsolate allies farewell, and nothing would content them but a promise to return soon. Before embarking, he addressed his own men:—"My friends, let us give thanks to God for the success He has granted us. It is He who saved us from tempests; it is He who inclined the hearts of the Indians towards us; it is He who blinded the understanding of the Spaniards. They were four to one, in forts well armed and provisioned. Our right was our only strength; and yet we have conquered. Not to our own swords, but to God only, we owe our victory. Then let us thank Him, my friends; let us never forget His favors; and let us pray that He may continue them, saving us from dangers, and guiding us safely home. Let us pray, too, that He may so dispose the hearts of men that our perils and toils may find favor in the eyes of our King and of all France, since all we have done was done for the King's service and for the honor of our country."

Thus Spaniards and Frenchmen alike laid their reeking swords on God's altar.

Gourgues sailed on the third of May, and, gazing back along their foaming wake, the adventurers looked their last on the scene of their exploits. Their success had cost its price. A few of their number had fallen, and hardships still awaited the survivors. Gourgues, however, reached Rochelle on the day of Pentecost, and the Huguenot citizens greeted him with all honor. At court it fared worse with him. The King, still obsequious to Spain, looked on him coldly and askance. The Spanish minister demanded his head. It was hinted to him that he was not safe, and he withdrew to Ronen, where he found asylum among his friends. His fortune was gone; debts contracted for his expedition weighed heavily on him; and for years he lived in obscurity, almost in misery.

At length his prospects brightened. Elizabeth of England learned his merits and his misfortunes, and invited him to enter her service. The King, who, says the Jesuit historian, had always at heart been delighted with his achievement, openly restored him to favor; while, some years later, Don Antonio tendered him command of his fleet, to defend his right to the crown of Portugal against Philip the Second. Gourgues, happy once more to cross swords with the Spaniards, gladly embraced this offer; but in 1583, on his way to join the Portuguese prince, he died at Tours of a sudden illness. The French mourned the loss of the man who had wiped a blot from the national scutcheon, and respected his memory as that of one of the best captains of his time. And, in truth, if a zealous patriotism, a fiery valor, and skilful leadership are worthy of honor, then is such a tribute due to Dominique de Gourgues, slave-catcher and half-pirate as he was, like other naval heroes of that wild age.

Romantic as was his exploit, it lacked the fullness of poetic justice, since the chief offender escaped him. While Gourgues was sailing towards Florida, Menendez was in Spain, high in favor at court, where he told to approving ears how he had butchered the heretics. Borgia, the sainted General of the Jesuits, was his fast friend; and two years later, when he returned to America, the Pope, Paul the Fifth, regarding him as an instrument for the conversion of the Indians, wrote him a letter with his benediction. He re-established his power in Florida, rebuilt Fort San Mateo, and taught the Indians that death or flight was the only refuge from Spanish tyranny. They murdered his missionaries and spurned their doctrine. "The Devil is the best thing in the world," they cried; "we adore him; he makes men brave." Even the Jesuits despaired, and abandoned Florida in disgust.

Menendez was summoned home, where fresh honors awaited him from the Crown, though, according to the somewhat doubtful assertion of the heretical Grotius, his deeds had left a stain upon his name among the people. He was given command of the armada of three hundred sail and twenty thousand men, which, in 1574, was gathered at Santander against England and Flanders. But now, at the height of his fortunes, his career was abruptly closed. He died suddenly, at the age of fifty-five. Grotius affirms that he killed himself; but, in his eagerness to point the moral of his story, he seems to have overstepped the bounds of historic truth. The Spanish bigot was rarely a suicide; for the rites of Christian burial and repose in consecrated ground were denied to the remains of the self-murderer. There is positive evidence, too, in a codicil to the will of Menendez, dated at Santander on the fifteenth of September, 1574, that he was on that day seriously ill, though, as the instrument declares, "of sound mind." There is reason, then, to believe that this pious cut-throat died a natural death, crowned with honors, and soothed by the consolations of his religion.

It was he who crushed French Protestantism in America. To plant religious freedom on this western soil was not the mission of France. It was for her to rear in northern forests the banner of absolutism and of Rome; while among the rocks of Massachusetts

England and Calvin fronted her in dogged opposition, long before the ice-crusted pines of Plymouth had listened to the rugged psalmody of the Puritan, the solitudes of Western New York and the stern wilderness of Lake Huron were trodden by the iron heel of the soldier and the sandalled foot of the Franciscan friar. France was the true pioneer of the Great West. They who bore the fleur-de-lis were always in the van, patient, daring, indomitable. And foremost on this bright roll of forest chivalry stands the half-forgotten name of Samuel de Champlain.

Part 2
SAMUEL DE CHAMPLAIN AND HIS ASSOCIATES;

WITH A VIEW OF EARLIER FRENCH ADVENTURE IN AMERICA, AND THE LEGENDS OF THE NORTHERN COASTS.

SAMUEL DE CHAMPLAIN.

CHAPTER I.
1488-1543.
EARLY FRENCH ADVENTURE IN NORTH AMERICA.

When America was first made known to Europe, the part assumed by France on the borders of that new world was peculiar, and is little recognized. While the Spaniard roamed sea and land, burning for achievement, red-hot with bigotry and avarice, and while England, with soberer steps and a less dazzling result, followed in the path of discovery and gold-hunting, it was from France that those barbarous shores first learned to serve the ends of peaceful commercial industry.

A French writer, however, advances a more ambitious claim. In the year 1488, four years before the first voyage of Columbus, America, he maintains, was found by Frenchmen. Cousin, a navigator of Dieppe, being at sea off the African coast, was forced westward, it is said, by winds and currents to within sight of an unknown shore, where he presently descried the mouth of a great river. On board his ship was one Pinzon, whose conduct became so mutinous that, on his return to Dieppe, Cousin made complaint to the magistracy, who thereupon dismissed the offender from the maritime service of the town. Pinzon went to Spain, became known to Columbus, told him the discovery, and joined him on his voyage of 1492.

To leave this cloudland of tradition, and approach the confines of recorded history. The Normans, offspring of an ancestry of conquerors,—the Bretons, that stubborn, hardy, unchanging race, who, among Druid monuments changeless as themselves, still cling with Celtic obstinacy to the thoughts and habits of the past,—the Basques, that primeval people, older than history,—all frequented from a very early date the cod-banks of Newfoundland. There is some reason to believe that this fishery existed before the voyage of Cabot, in 1497; there is strong evidence that it began as early as the year 1504; and it is well established that, in 1517, fifty Castilian, French, and Portuguese vessels were engaged in it at once; while in 1527, on the third of August, eleven sail of Norman, one of

Breton, and two of Portuguese fishermen were to be found in the Bay of St. John.

From this time forth, the Newfoundland fishery was never abandoned. French, English, Spanish, and Portuguese made resort to the Banks, always jealous, often quarrelling, but still drawing up treasure from those exhaustless mines, and bearing home bountiful provision against the season of Lent.

On this dim verge of the known world there were other perils than those of the waves. The rocks and shores of those sequestered seas had, so thought the voyagers, other tenants than the seal, the walrus, and the screaming sea-fowl, the bears which stole away their fish before their eyes, and the wild natives dressed in seal-skins. Griffius—so ran the story—infested the mountains of Labrador. Two islands, north of Newfoundland, were given over to the fiends from whom they derived their name, the Isles of Demons. An old map pictures their occupants at length,—devils rampant, with wings, horns, and tail. The passing voyager heard the din of their infernal orgies, and woe to the sailor or the fisherman who ventured alone into the haunted woods. "True it is," writes the old cosmographer Thevet, "and I myself have heard it, not from one, but from a great number of the sailors and pilots with whom I have made many voyages, that, when they passed this way, they heard in the air, on the tops and about the masts, a great clamor of men's voices, confused and inarticulate, such as you may hear from the crowd at a fair or market-place whereupon they well knew that the Isle of Demons was not far off." And he adds, that he himself, when among the Indians, had seen them so tormented by these infernal persecutors, that they would fall into his arms for relief; on which, repeating a passage of the Gospel of St. John, he had driven the imps of darkness to a speedy exodus. They are comely to look upon, he further tells us; yet, by reason of their malice, that island is of late abandoned, and all who dwelt there have fled for refuge to the main.

While French fishermen plied their trade along these gloomy coasts, the French government spent it's energies on a different field. The vitality of the kingdom was wasted in Italian wars. Milan and Naples offered a more tempting prize than the wilds of Baccalaos. Eager for glory and for plunder, a swarm of restless nobles followed their knight-errant King, the would-be paladin, who, misshapen in body and fantastic in mind, had yet the power to raise a storm which the lapse of generations could not quell. Under Charles the Eighth and his successor, war and intrigue ruled the day; and in the whirl of Italian politics there was no leisure to think of a new world.

Yet private enterprise was not quite benumbed. In 1506, one Denis of Honfleur explored the Gulf of St. Lawrence; 2 two years later, Aubert of Dieppe followed on his track; and in 1518, the Baron de Lery made an abortive attempt at settlement on Sable Island, where the cattle left by him remained and multiplied.

The crown passed at length to Francis of Angouleme. There were in his nature seeds of nobleness,—seeds destined to bear little fruit. Chivalry and honor were always on his lips; but Francis the First, a forsworn gentleman, a despotic king, vainglorious, selfish, sunk in debaucheries, was but the type of an era which retained the forms of the Middle Age without its soul, and added to a still prevailing barbarism the pestilential vices which hung fog-like around the dawn of civilization. Yet he esteemed arts and letters, and, still more, coveted the eclat which they could give. The light which was beginning to pierce the feudal darkness gathered its rays around his throne. Italy was rewarding the robbers who preyed on her with the treasures of her knowledge and her culture; and Italian genius, of whatever stamp, found ready patronage at the hands of Francis. Among artists, philosophers, and men of letters enrolled in his service stands the humbler name of a Florentine navigator, John Verrazzano.

He was born of an ancient family, which could boast names eminent in Florentine history, and of which the last survivor died in 1819. He has been called a pirate, and he was such in the same sense in which Drake, Hawkins, and other valiant sea-rovers of his own and later times, merited the name; that is to say, he would plunder and kill a Spaniard on the high seas without waiting for a declaration of war.

The wealth of the Indies was pouring into the coffers of Charles the Fifth, and the exploits of Cortes had given new lustre to his crown. Francis the First begrudged his hated rival the glories and profits of the New World. He would fain have his share of the prize; and Verrazzano, with four ships, was despatched to seek out a passage westward to the rich kingdom of Cathay.

Some doubt has of late been cast on the reality of this voyage of Verrazzano, and evidence, mainly negative in kind, has been adduced to prove the story of it a fabrication; but the difficulties of incredulity appear greater than those of belief, and no ordinary degree of scepticism is required to reject the evidence that the narrative is essentially true.

Towards the end of the year 1523, his four ships sailed from Dieppe; but a storm fell upon him, and, with two of the vessels, he ran back in distress to a port of Brittany. What became of the other two does not appear. Neither is it clear why, after a preliminary cruise against the Spaniards, he pursued his voyage with one vessel alone, a caravel called the "Dauphine." With her he made for Madeira, and, on the seventeenth of January, 1524, set sail from a barren islet in its neighborhood, and bore away for the unknown world. In forty-nine days they neared a low shore, not far from the site of Wilmington in North Carolina, "a newe land," exclaims the voyager, "never before seen of any man, either auncient or moderne." Verrazzano steered southward in search of a harbor, and, finding none, turned northward again. Presently he sent a boat ashore. The inhabitants, who had fled at first, soon came down to the strand in wonder and admiration, pointing out a landing-place, and making gestures of friendship. "These people," says Verrazzano, "goe altogether naked, except only certain skinnes of beastes like unto marterns [martens], which they fasten onto a narrowe girdle made of grasse. They are of colour russet, and not much unlike the Saracens, their hayre blacke, thicke, and not very long, which they tye togeather in a knot behinde, and weare it like a taile."

He describes the shore as consisting of small low hillocks of fine sand, intersected by creeks and inlets, and beyond these a country "full of Palme [pine?] trees, Bay trees, and high Cypresse trees, and many other sortes of trees, vnknowne in Europe, which yeeld most sweete sauours, farre from the shore." Still advancing northward, Verrazzano sent a boat for a supply of water. The surf ran high, and the crew could not land; but an adventurous young sailor jumped overboard and swam shoreward with a gift of beads and trinkets for the Indians, who stood watching him. His heart failed as he drew near; he flung his gift among them, turned, and struck out for the boat. The surf dashed him back, flinging him with violence on the beach among the recipients of his bounty, who seized him by the arms and legs, and, while he called lustily for aid, answered him with outcries designed to allay his terrors. Next they kindled a great fire,—doubtless to roast and devour him before the eyes of his comrades, gazing in horror from their boat. On the contrary, they carefully warmed him, and were trying to dry his clothes, when, recovering from his bewilderment, he betrayed a strong desire to escape to his friends; whereupon, "with great love, clapping him fast about, with many embracings," they led him to the shore, and stood watching till he had reached the boat.

It only remained to requite this kindness, and an opportunity soon occurred; for, coasting the shores of Virginia or Maryland, a party went on shore and found an old woman, a young girl, and several children, hiding with great terror in the grass. Having, by various blandishments, gained their confidence, they carried off one of the children as a curiosity, and, since the girl was comely, would fain have taken her also, but desisted by reason of her continual screaming.

Verrazzano's next resting-place was the Bay of New York. Rowing up in his boat through the Narrows, under the steep heights of Staten Island, he saw the harbor within dotted with canoes of the feathered natives, coming from the shore to welcome him. But what most engaged the eyes of the white men were the fancied signs of mineral wealth in the neighboring hills.

Following the shores of Long Island, they came to an island, which may have been Block Island, and thence to a harbor, which was probably that of Newport. Here they stayed fifteen days, most courteously received by the inhabitants. Among others appeared two chiefs, gorgeously arrayed in painted deer-skins,—kings, as Verrazzano calls them, with attendant gentlemen; while a party of squaws in a canoe, kept by their jealous lords at a safe distance from the caravel, figure in the narrative as the queen and her maids. The Indian wardrobe had been taxed to its utmost to do the strangers honor,—copper bracelets, lynx-skins, raccoon-skins, and faces bedaubed with gaudy colors.

Again they spread their sails, and on the fifth of May bade farewell to the primitive hospitalities of Newport, steered along the rugged coasts of New England, and surveyed, ill pleased, the surf-beaten rocks, the pine-tree and the fir, the shadows and the gloom of mighty forests. Here man and nature alike were savage and repellent. Perhaps some plundering straggler from the fishing-banks, some manstealer like the Portuguese Cortereal, or some kidnapper of children and ravisher of squaws like themselves, had warned the denizens of the woods to beware of the worshippers of Christ. Their only intercourse was in the way of trade. From the brink of the rocks which overhung the sea the Indians would let down a cord to the boat below, demand fish-hooks, knives, and steel, in barter for their furs, and, their bargain made, salute the voyagers with unseemly gestures of derision and scorn. The French once ventured ashore; but a war-whoop and a shower of arrows sent them back to their boats.

Verrazzano coasted the seaboard of Maine, and sailed northward as far as Newfoundland, whence, provisions failing, he steered for France. He had not found a passage to Cathay, but he had explored the American coast from the thirty-fourth degree to the fiftieth, and at various points had penetrated several leagues into the country. On the eighth of July, he wrote from Dieppe to the King the earliest description known to exist of the shores of the United States.

Great was the joy that hailed his arrival, and great were the hopes of emolument and wealth from the new-found shores. The merchants of Lyons were in a flush of expectation. For himself, he was earnest to return, plant a colony, and bring the heathen tribes within the pale of the Church. But the time was inauspicious. The year of his voyage was to France a year of disasters,—defeat in Italy, the loss of Milan, the death of the heroic Bayard; and, while Verrazzano was writing his narrative at Dieppe, the traitor Bourbon was invading Provence. Preparation, too, was soon on foot for the expedition which, a few months later, ended in the captivity of Francis on the field of Pavia. Without a king, without an army, without money, convulsed within, and threatened from without, France after that humiliation was in no condition to renew her Transatlantic enterprise.

Henceforth few traces remain of the fortunes of Verrazzano. Ramusio affirms, that, on another voyage, he was killed and eaten by savages, in sight of his followers; and a late writer hazards the conjecture that this voyage, if made at all, was made in the service of Henry the Eighth of England. But a Spanish writer affirms that, in 1527, he was hanged at Puerto del Pico as a pirate, and this assertion is fully confirmed by authentic documents recently brought to light.

The fickle-minded King, always ardent at the outset of an enterprise and always flagging before its close, divided, moreover, between the smiles of his mistresses and the assaults of his enemies, might probably have dismissed the New World from his thoughts. But among the favorites of his youth was a high-spirited young noble, Philippe de BrionChabot, the partner of his joustings and tennis-playing, his gaming and gallantries. He still stood high in the royal favor, and, after the treacherous escape of Francis from captivity, held the office of Admiral of France. When the kingdom had rallied in some measure from its calamities, he conceived the purpose of following up the path which Verrazzano had opened.

The ancient town of St. Malo—thrust out like a buttress into the sea, strange and grim of aspect, breathing war front its walls and battlements of ragged stone, a stronghold of privateers, the home of a race whose intractable and defiant independence neither time nor change has subdued—has been for centuries a nursery of hardy mariners. Among the earliest and most eminent on its list stands the name of Jacques Cartier. His portrait hangs in the town-hall of St. Malo,—bold, keen features bespeaking a spirit not apt to quail before the wrath of man or of the elements. In him Chabot found a fit agent of his design, if, indeed, its suggestion is not due to the Breton navigator.

Sailing from St. Malo on the twentieth of April, 1534, Cartier steered for Newfoundland, passed through the Straits of Belle Isle, entered the Gulf of Chaleurs, planted a cross at Gaspe, and, never doubting that he was on the high road to Cathay, advanced up the St. Lawrence till he saw the shores of Anticosti. But autumnal storms were gathering. The voyagers took counsel together, turned their prows eastward, and bore away for France, carrying thither, as a sample of the natural products of the New World, two young

Indians, lured into their clutches by an act of villanous treachery. The voyage was a mere reconnoissance.

The spirit of discovery was awakened. A passage to India could be found, and a new France built up beyond the Atlantic. Mingled with such views of interest and ambition was another motive scarcely less potent. The heresy of Luther was convulsing Germany, and the deeper heresy of Calvin infecting France. Devout Catholics, kindling with redoubled zeal, would fain requite the Church for her losses in the Old World by winning to her fold the infidels of the New. But, in pursuing an end at once so pious and so politic, Francis the First was setting at naught the supreme Pontiff himself, since, by the preposterous bull of Alexander the Sixth, all America had been given to the Spaniards.

In October, 1534, Cartier received from Chabot another commission, and, in spite of secret but bitter opposition from jealous traders of St. Malo, he prepared for a second voyage. Three vessels, the largest not above a hundred and twenty tons, were placed at his disposal, and Claude de Pontbriand, Charles de la Pommeraye, and other gentlemen of birth, enrolled themselves for the adventure. On the sixteenth of May, 1535, officers and sailors assembled in the cathedral of St. Malo, where, after confession and mass, they received the parting blessing of the bishop. Three days later they set sail. The dingy walls of the rude old seaport, and the white rocks that line the neighboring shores of Brittany, faded from their sight, and soon they were tossing in a furious tempest. The scattered ships escaped the danger, and, reuniting at the Straits of Belle Isle, steered westward along the coast of Labrador, till they reached a small bay opposite the island of Anticosti. Cartier called it the Bay of St. Lawrence,—a name afterwards extended to the entire gulf, and to the great river above.

To ascend this great river, and tempt the hazards of its intricate navigation with no better pilots than the two young Indians kidnapped the year before, was a venture of no light risk. But skill or fortune prevailed; and, on the first of September, the voyagers reached in safety the gorge of the gloomy Saguenay, with its towering cliffs and sullen depth of waters. Passing the Isle aux Coudres, and the lofty promontory of Cape Tourmente, they came to anchor in a quiet channel between the northern shore and the margin of a richly wooded island, where the trees were so thickly hung with grapes that Cartier named it the Island of Bacchus.

Indians came swarming from the shores, paddled their canoes about the ships, and clambered to the decks to gaze in bewilderment at the novel scene, and listen to the story of their travelled countrymen, marvellous in their ears as a visit to another planet. Cartier received them kindly, listened to the long harangue of the great chief Donnacona, regaled him with bread and wine; and, when relieved at length of his guests, set forth in a boat to explore the river above.

As he drew near the opening of the channel, the Hochelaga again spread before him the broad expanse of its waters. A mighty promontory, rugged and bare, thrust its scarped front into the surging current. Here, clothed in the majesty of solitude, breathing the stern poetry of the wilderness, rose the cliffs now rich with heroic memories, where the fiery Count Frontenac cast defiance at his foes, where Wolfe, Montcalm, and Montgomery fell. As yet, all was a nameless barbarism, and a cluster of wigwams held the site of the rock-built city of Quebec. Its name was Stadacone, and it owned the sway of the royal Donnacona.

Cartier set out to visit this greasy potentate; ascended the river St. Charles, by him called the St. Croix, landed, crossed the meadows, climbed the rocks, threaded the forest, and emerged upon a squalid hamlet of bark cabins. When, having satisfied their curiosity, he and his party were rowing for the ships, a friendly interruption met them at the mouth of the St. Charles. An old chief harangued them from the bank, men, boys, and children screeched welcome from the meadow, and a troop of hilarious squaws danced knee-deep in the water. The gift of a few strings of beads completed their delight and redoubled their agility; and, from the distance of a mile, their shrill songs of jubilation still reached the ears of the receding Frenchmen.

The hamlet of Stadacone, with its king, Donnacona, and its naked lords and princes, was not the metropolis of this forest state, since a town far greater—so the Indians averred—stood by the brink of the river, many days' journey above. It was called Hochelaga, and the great river itself, with a wide reach of adjacent country, had borrowed its name. Thither, with his two young

Indians as guides, Cartier resolved to go; but misgivings seized the guides as the time drew near, while Donnacona and his tribesmen, jealous of the plan, set themselves to thwart it. The Breton captain turned a deaf ear to their dissuasions; on which, failing to touch his reason, they appealed to his fears.

One morning, as the ships still lay at anchor, the French beheld three Indian devils descending in a canoe towards them, dressed in black and white dog-skins, with faces black as ink, and horns long as a man's arm. Thus arrayed, they drifted by, while the principal fiend, with fixed eyes, as of one piercing the secrets of futurity, uttered in a loud voice a long harangue. Then they paddled for the shore; and no sooner did they reach it than each fell flat like a dead man in the bottom of the canoe. Aid, however, was at hand; for Donnacona and his tribesmen, rushing pell-mell from the adjacent woods, raised the swooning masqueraders, and, with shrill clamors, bore them in their arms within the sheltering thickets. Here, for a full half-hour, the French could hear them haranguing in solemn conclave. Then the two young Indians whom Cartier had brought back from France came out of the bushes, enacting a pantomime of amazement and terror, clasping their hands, and calling on Christ and the Virgin; whereupon Cartier, shouting from the vessel, asked what was the matter. They replied, that the god Coudonagny had sent to warn the French against all attempts to ascend the great river, since, should they persist, snows, tempests, and drifting ice would requite their rashness with inevitable ruin. The French replied that Coudonagny was a fool; that he could not hurt those who believed in Christ; and that they might tell this to his three messengers. The assembled Indians, with little reverence for their deity, pretended great contentment at this assurance, and danced for joy along the beach.

Cartier now made ready to depart. And, first, he caused the two larger vessels to be towed for safe harborage within the mouth of the St. Charles. With the smallest, a galleon of forty tons, and two open boats, carrying in all fifty sailors, besides Pontbriand, La Pommeraye, and other gentlemen, he set out for Hochelaga.

Slowly gliding on their way by walls of verdure brightened in the autumnal sun, they saw forests festooned with grape-vines, and waters alive with wild-fowl; they heard the song of the blackbird, the thrush, and, as they fondly thought, the nightingale. The galleon grounded; they left her, and, advancing with the boats alone, on the second of October neared the goal of their hopes, the mysterious Hochelaga.

Just below where now are seen the quays and storehouses of Montreal, a thousand Indians thronged the shore, wild with delight, dancing, singing, crowding about the strangers, and showering into the boats their gifts of fish and maize; and, as it grew dark, fires lighted up the night, while, far and near, the French could see the excited savages leaping and rejoicing by the blaze.

At dawn of day, marshalled and accoutred, they marched for Hochelaga. An Indian path led them through the forest which covered the site of Montreal. The morning air was chill and sharp, the leaves were changing hue, and beneath the oaks the ground was thickly strewn with acorns. They soon met an Indian chief with a party of tribesmen, or, as the old narrative has it, "one of the principal lords of the said city," attended with a numerous retinue. Greeting them after the concise courtesy of the forest, he led them to a fire kindled by the side of the path for their comfort and refreshment, seated them on the ground, and made them a long harangue, receiving in requital of his eloquence two hatchets, two knives, and a crucifix, the last of which he was invited to kiss. This done, they resumed their march, and presently came upon open fields, covered far and near with the ripened maize, its leaves rustling, and its yellow grains gleaming between the parting husks. Before them, wrapped in forests painted by the early frosts, rose the ridgy back of the Mountain of Montreal, and below, encompassed with its corn-fields, lay the Indian town. Nothing was visible but its encircling palisades. They were of trunks of trees, set in a triple row. The outer and inner ranges inclined till they met and crossed near the summit, while the upright row between them, aided by transverse braces, gave to the whole an abundant strength. Within were galleries for the defenders, rude ladders to mount them, and magazines of stones to throw down on the heads of assailants. It was a mode of fortification practised by all the tribes speaking dialects of the Iroquois.

The voyagers entered the narrow portal. Within, they saw some fifty of those large oblong dwellings so familiar in after years to the eyes of the Jesuit apostles in Iroquois and Huron forests. They were about fifty yards in length, and twelve or fifteen wide, framed of sapling poles closely covered with sheets of bark, and each containing several fires and several families. In the midst of the town was an open area, or public square, a stone's throw in width. Here Cartier and his followers stopped, while the surrounding houses of bark disgorged their inmates,—swarms of children, and young women and old, their infants in their arms. They crowded about the visitors, crying for delight, touching their beards, feeling their faces, and holding up the screeching infants to be touched in turn. The marvellous visitors, strange in hue, strange in attire, with moustached lip and bearded chin, with arquebuse, halberd, helmet, and cuirass, seemed rather demigods than men.

Due time having been allowed for this exuberance of feminine rapture, the warriors interposed, banished the women and children to a distance, and squatted on the ground around the French, row within row of swarthy forms and eager faces, "as if," says Cartier, "we were going to act a play." Then appeared a troop of women, each bringing a mat, with which they carpeted the bare earth for the behoof of their guests. The latter being seated, the chief of the nation was borne before them on a deerskin by a number of his tribesmen, a bedridden old savage, paralyzed and helpless, squalid as the rest in his attire, and distinguished only by a red fillet, inwrought with the dyed quills of the Canada porcupine, encircling his lank black hair. They placed him on the ground at Cartier's feet and made signs of welcome for him, while he pointed feebly to his powerless limbs, and implored the healing touch from the hand of the French chief. Cartier complied, and received in acknowledgment the red fillet of his grateful patient. Then from surrounding dwellings appeared a woeful throng, the sick, the lame, the blind, the maimed, the decrepit, brought or led forth and placed on the earth before the perplexed commander, "as if," he says, "a god had come down to cure them." His skill in medicine being far behind the emergency, he pronounced over his petitioners a portion of the Gospel of St. John, made the sign of the cross, and uttered a prayer, not for their bodies only, but for their miserable souls. Next he read the passion of the Saviour, to which, though comprehending not a word, his audience listened with grave attention. Then came a distribution of presents. The squaws and children were recalled, and, with the warriors, placed in separate groups. Knives and hatchets were given to the men, and beads to the women, while pewter rings and images of the Agnus

Dei were flung among the troop of children, whence ensued a vigorous scramble in the square of Hochelaga. Now the French trumpeters pressed their trumpets to their lips, and blew a blast that filled the air with warlike din and the hearts of the hearers with amazement and delight. Bidding their hosts farewells the visitors formed their ranks and defiled through the gate once more, despite the efforts of a crowd of women, who, with clamorous hospitality, beset them with gifts of fish, beans, corn, and other viands of uninviting aspect, which the Frenchmen courteously declined.

A troop of Indians followed, and guided them to the top of the neighboring mountain. Cartier called it Mont Royal, Montreal; and hence the name of the busy city which now holds the site of the vanished Iloclielaga. Stadacone and Hochelaga, Quebec and Montreal, in the sixteenth century as in the nineteenth, were the centres of Canadian population.

From the summit, that noble prospect met his eye which at this day is the delight of tourists, but strangely changed, since, first of white men, the Breton voyager gazed upon it. Tower and dome and spire, congregated roofs, white sail, and gliding steamer, animate its vast expanse with varied life. Cartier saw a different scene. East, west, and south, the mantling forest was over all, and the broad blue ribbon of the great river glistened amid a realm of verdure. Beyond, to the bounds of Mexico, stretched a leafy desert, and the vast hive of industry, the mighty battle-ground of later centuries, lay sunk in savage torpor, wrapped in illimitable woods.

The French re-embarked, bade farewell to Hochelaga, retraced their lonely course down the St. Lawrence, and reached Stadacone in safety. On the bank of the St. Charles, their companions had built in their absence a fort of palisades, and the ships, hauled up the little stream, lay moored before it. Here the self-exiled company were soon besieged by the rigors of the Canadian winter. The rocks, the shores, the pine-trees, the solid floor of the frozen river, all alike were blanketed in snow beneath the keen cold rays of the dazzling sun. The drifts rose above the sides of their ships; masts, spars, and cordage were thick with glittering incrustations and sparkling rows of icicles; a frosty armor, four inches thick, encased the bulwarks. Yet, in the bitterest weather, the neighboring Indians, "hardy," says the journal, "as so many beasts," came daily to the fort, wading, half naked, waist-deep through the snow. At length, their friendship began to abate; their visits grew less frequent, and during December had wholly ceased, when a calamity fell upon the French.

A malignant scurvy broke out among them. Man after man went down before the hideous disease, till twenty-five were dead, and only three or four were left in health. The sound were too few to attend the sick, and the wretched sufferers lay in helpless despair, dreaming of the sun and the vines of France. The ground, hard as flint, defied their feeble efforts, and, unable to bury their dead, they hid them in snow-drifts. Cartier appealed to the saints; but they turned a deaf ear. Then he nailed against a tree an image of the Virgin, and on a Sunday summoned forth his woe-begone followers, who, haggard, reeling, bloated with their maladies, moved in procession to the spot, and, kneeling in the snow, sang litanies and psalms of David. That day died Philippe Rougemont, of Amboise, aged twenty-two years. The Holy Virgin deigned no other response.

There was fear that the Indians, learning their misery, might finish the work that scurvy had begun. None of them, therefore, were allowed to approach the fort; and when a party of savages lingered within hearing, Cartier forced his invalid garrison to beat with sticks and stones against the walls, that their dangerous neighbors, deluded by the clatter, might think them engaged in hard labor. These objects of their fear proved, however, the instruments of their salvation. Cartier, walking one day near the river, met an Indian, who not long before had been prostrate, like many of his fellows, with the scurvy, but who was now, to all appearance, in high health and spirits. What agency had wrought this marvellous recovery? According to the Indian, it was a certain evergreen, called by him ameda, a decoction of the leaves of which was sovereign against the disease. The experiment was tried. The sick men drank copiously of the healing draught,—so copiously indeed that in six days they drank a tree as large as a French oak. Thus vigorously assailed, the distemper relaxed its hold, and health and hope began to revisit the hapless company.

When this winter of misery had worn away, and the ships were thawed from their icy fetters, Cartier prepared to return. He had made notable discoveries; but these were as nothing to the tales of wonder that had reached his ear,—of a land of gold and rubies, of a nation white like the French, of men who lived without food, and of others to whom Nature had granted but one leg. Should he stake his credit on these marvels? It were better that they who had recounted them to him should, with their own lips, recount them also to the King, and to this end he resolved that Donnacona and his chiefs should go with him to court. He lured them therefore to the fort, and led them into an ambuscade of sailors, who, seizing the astonished guests, hurried them on board the ships. Having accomplished this treachery, the voyagers proceeded to plant the emblem of Christianity. The cross was raised, the fleur-de-lis planted near it, and, spreading their sails, they steered for home. It was the sixteenth of July, 1536, when Cartier again cast anchor under the walls of St. Malo.

A rigorous climate, a savage people, a fatal disease, and a soil barren of gold were the allurements of New France. Nor were the times auspicious for a renewal of the enterprise. Charles the Fifth, flushed with his African triumphs, challenged the Most Christian King to single combat. The war flamed forth with renewed fury, and ten years elapsed before a hollow truce varnished the hate of the royal rivals with a thin pretence of courtesy. Peace returned; but Francis the First was sinking to his ignominious grave, under the scourge of his favorite goddess, and Chabot, patron of the former voyages, was in disgrace.

Meanwhile the ominous adventure of New France had found a champion in the person of Jean Francois de la Roque, Sieur de Roberval, a nobleman of Picardy. Though a man of high account in his own province, his past honors paled before the splendor of the titles said to have been now conferred on him, Lord of Norembega, Viceroy and Lieutenant-General in Canada, Hochelaga, Saguenay, Newfoundland, Belle Isle, Carpunt, Labrador, the Great Bay, and Baccalaos. To this windy gift of ink and parchment was added a solid grant from the royal treasury, with which five vessels were procured and equipped; and to Cartier was given the post of Captain-General. "We have resolved," says Francis, "to send him again to the lands of Canada and Hochelaga, which form the extremity of Asia towards the west." His commission declares the objects of the enterprise to be discovery, settlement, and the conversion of the Indians, who are described as "men without knowledge of God or use of reason,"—a pious design, held doubtless in full sincerity by the royal profligate, now, in his decline, a fervent champion of the Faith and a strenuous tormentor of heretics. The machinery of conversion was of a character somewhat questionable, since Cartier and Roberval were empowered to ransack the prisons for thieves, robbers, and other malefactors, to complete their crews and strengthen the colony. "Whereas," says the King, "we have undertaken this voyage for the honor of God our Creator, desiring with all our heart to do that which shall be agreeable to Him, it is our will to perform a compassionate and meritorious work towards criminals and malefactors, to the end that they may acknowledge the Creator, return thanks to Him, and mend their lives. Therefore we have resolved to cause to be delivered to our aforesaid lieutenant (Roberval), such and so many of the aforesaid criminals and malefactors detained in our prisons as may seem to him useful and necessary to be carried to the aforesaid countries." Of the expected profits of the voyage the adventurers were to have one third and the King another, while the remainder was to be reserved towards defraying expenses.

With respect to Donnacona and his tribesmen, basely kidnapped at Stadacone, their souls had been better cared for than their bodies; for, having been duly baptized, they all died within a year or two, to the great detriment, as it proved, of the expedition.

Meanwhile, from beyond the Pyrenees, the Most Catholic King, with alarmed and jealous eye, watched the preparations of his Most Christian enemy. America, in his eyes, was one vast province of Spain, to be vigilantly guarded against the intruding foreigner. To what end were men mustered, and ships fitted out in the Breton seaports? Was it for colonization, and if so, where? Was it in Southern Florida, or on the frozen shores of Baccalaos, of which Breton cod-fishers claimed the discovery? Or would the French build forts on the Bahamas, whence they could waylay the gold ships in the Bahama Channel? Or was the expedition destined against the Spanish settlements of the islands or the Main? Reinforcements were despatched in haste, and a spy was sent to France, who, passing from port to port, Quimper, St. Malo, Brest, Morlaix, came back freighted with exaggerated tales of preparation. The Council of the Indies was called. "The French are bound for Baccalaos,"—such was the substance of their report; "your Majesty will do well to send two caravels to watch their movements, and a force to take possession of the said country. And since there is no other money to pay for it, the gold from Peru, now at Panama, might be used to that end." The Cardinal of Seville thought lightly of the danger, and prophesied that the French would reap nothing from their enterprise but disappointment and loss. The King of Portugal, sole acknowledged partner with Spain in the ownership of the New World, was invited by the Spanish ambassador to take part in an expedition against the encroaching French. "They can do no harm at Baccalaos," was the cold reply; "and so," adds the indignant ambassador, "this King would say if they should come and take him here at Lisbon; such is the softness they show here on the one hand, while, on the other, they wish to give law to the whole world."

The five ships, occasions of this turmoil and alarm, had lain at St. Malo waiting for cannon and munitions from Normandy and Champagne. They waited in vain, and as the King's orders were stringent against delay, it was resolved that Cartier should sail at once, leaving Roberval to follow with additional ships when the expected supplies arrived.

On the twenty-third of May, 1541, the Breton captain again spread his canvas for New France, and, passing in safety the tempestuous Atlantic, the fog-banks of Newfoundland, the island rocks clouded with screaming sea-fowl, and the forests breathing piny odors from the shore, cast anchor again beneath the cliffs of Quebec. Canoes came out from shore filled with feathered savages inquiring for their kidnapped chiefs. "Donnacona," replied Cartier, "is dead;" but he added the politic falsehood, that the others had married in France, and lived in state, like great lords. The Indians pretended to be satisfied; but it was soon apparent that they looked askance on the perfidious strangers.

Cartier pursued his course, sailed three leagues and a half up the St. Lawrence, and anchored off the mouth of the River of Cap Rouge. It was late in August, and the leafy landscape sweltered in the sun. The Frenchmen landed, picked up quartz crystals on the shore and thought them diamonds, climbed the steep promontory, drank at the spring near the top, looked abroad on the wooded slopes beyond the little river, waded through the tall grass of the meadow, found a quarry of slate, and gathered scales of a yellow mineral which glistened like gold, then returned to their boats, crossed to the south shore of the St. Lawrence, and, languid with the heat, rested in the shade of forests laced with an entanglement of grape-vines.

Now their task began, and while some cleared off the woods and sowed turnip-seed, others cut a zigzag road up the height, and others built two forts, one at the summit, and one on the shore below. The forts finished, the Vicomte de Beaupre took command, while Cartier went with two boats to explore the rapids above Hochelaga. When at length he returned, the autumn was far advanced; and with the gloom of a Canadian November came distrust, foreboding, and homesickness. Roberval had not appeared; the Indians kept jealously aloof; the motley colony was sullen as the dull, raw air around it. There was disgust and ire at Charlesbourg-Royal, for so the place was called.

Meanwhile, unexpected delays had detained the impatient Roberval; nor was it until the sixteenth of April, 1542, that, with three ships and two hundred colonists, he set sail from Rochelle. When, on the eighth of June, he entered the harbor of St. John, he found seventeen fishing-vessels lying there at anchor. Soon after, he descried three other sail rounding the entrance of the haven, and, with anger and amazement, recognized the ships of Jacques Cartier. That voyager had broken up his colony and abandoned New France. What motives had prompted a desertion little consonant with the resolute spirit of the man it is impossible to say,—whether sickness within, or Indian enemies without, disgust with an enterprise whose unripened fruits had proved so hard and bitter, or discontent at finding himself reduced to a post of subordination in a country which he had discovered and where he had commanded. The Viceroy ordered him to return; but Cartier escaped with his vessels under cover of night, and made sail for France, carrying with him as trophies a few quartz diamonds from Cap Rouge, and grains of sham gold from the neighboring slate ledges. Thus closed the third Canadian voyage of this notable explorer. His discoveries had gained for him a patent of nobility, and he owned the seigniorial mansion of Limoilou, a rude structure of stone still standing. Here, and in the neighboring town of St. Malo, where also he had a house, he seems to have lived for many years.

Roberval once more set sail, steering northward to the Straits of Belle Isle and the dreaded Isles of Demons. And here an incident befell which the all-believing Thevet records in manifest good faith, and which, stripped of the adornments of superstition and a love of the marvellous, has without doubt a nucleus of truth. I give the tale as I find it.

The Viceroy's company was of a mixed complexion. There were nobles, officers, soldiers, sailors, adventurers, with women too, and children. Of the women, some were of birth and station, and among them a damsel called Marguerite, a niece of Roberval himself. In the ship was a young gentleman who had embarked for love of her. His love was too well requited; and the stern Viceroy, scandalized and enraged at a passion which scorned concealment and set shame at defiance, cast anchor by the haunted island, landed his indiscreet relative, gave her four arquebuses for defence, and, with an old Norman nurse named Bastienne, who had pandered to the lovers, left her to her fate. Her gallant threw himself into the surf, and by desperate effort gained the shore, with two more guns and a supply of ammunition.

The ship weighed anchor, receded, vanished, and they were left alone. Yet not so, for the demon lords of the island beset them day and night, raging around their hut with a confused and hungry clamoring, striving to force the frail barrier. The lovers had repented of their sin, though not abandoned it, and Heaven was on their side. The saints vouchsafed their aid, and the offended Virgin, relenting, held before them her protecting shield. In the form of beasts or other shapes abominably and unutterably hideous, the brood of hell, howling in baffled fury, tore at the branches of the sylvan dwelling; but a celestial hand was ever interposed, and there was a viewless barrier which they might not pass. Marguerite became pregnant. Here was a double prize, two souls in one, mother and child. The fiends grew frantic, but all in vain. She stood undaunted amid these horrors; but her lover, dismayed and heartbroken, sickened and died. Her child soon followed; then the old Norman nurse found her unhallowed rest in that accursed soil, and Marguerite was left alone. Neither her reason nor her courage failed. When the demons assailed her, she shot at them with her gun, but they answered with hellish merriment, and thenceforth she placed her trust in Heaven alone. There were foes around her of the upper, no less than of the nether world. Of these, the bears were the most redoubtable; yet, being vulnerable to mortal weapons, she killed three of them, all, says the story, "as white as an egg."

It was two years and five months from her landing on the island, when, far out at sea, the crew of a small fishing-craft saw a column of smoke curling upward from the haunted shore. Was it a device of the fiends to lure them to their ruin? They thought so, and kept aloof. But misgiving seized them. They warily drew near, and descried a female figure in wild attire waving signals from the strand. Thus at length was Marguerite rescued and restored to her native France, where, a few years later, the cosmographer Thevet met her at Natron in Perigord, and heard the tale of wonder from her own lips.

Having left his offending niece to the devils and bears of the Isles of Demons, Roberval held his course up the St. Lawrence, and dropped anchor before the heights of Cap Rouge. His company landed; there were bivouacs along the strand, a hubbub of pick and spade, axe, saw, and hammer; and soon in the wilderness uprose a goodly structure, half barrack, half castle, with two towers, two spacious halls, a kitchen, chambers, storerooms, workshops, cellars, garrets, a well, an oven, and two watermills. Roberval named it France-Roy, and it stood on that bold acclivity where Cartier had before intrenched himself, the St. Lawrence in front, and on the right the River of Cap Rouge. Here all the colony housed under the same roof, like one of the experimental communities of recent days,—officers, soldiers, nobles, artisans, laborers, and convicts, with the women and children in whom lay the future hope of New France.

Experience and forecast had both been wanting. There were storehouses, but no stores; mills, but no grist; an ample oven, and a dearth of bread. It was only when two of the ships had sailed for France that they took account of their provision and discovered its lamentable shortcoming. Winter and famine followed. They bought fish from the Indians, and dug roots and boiled them in whale-oil. Disease broke out, and, before spring, killed one third of the colony. The rest would have quarrelled, mutinied, and otherwise aggravated their inevitable woes, but disorder was dangerous under the iron rule of the inexorable Roberval. Michel Gaillon was detected in a petty theft, and hanged. Jean de Nantes, for a more venial offence, was kept in irons. The quarrels of men and the scolding of women were alike requited at the whipping-post, "by which means," quaintly says the narrative, "they lived in peace."

Thevet, while calling himself the intimate friend of the Viceroy, gives a darker coloring to his story. He says that, forced to unceasing labor, and chafed by arbitrary rules, some of the soldiers fell under Roberval's displeasure, and six of them, formerly his favorites, were hanged in one day. Others were banished to an island, and there kept in fetters; while, for various light offences, several, both men and women, were shot. Even the Indians were moved to pity, and wept at the sight of their woes.

And here, midway, our guide deserts us; the ancient narrative is broken, and the latter part is lost, leaving us to divine as we may the future of the ill-starred colony. That it did not long survive is certain. The King, in great need of Roberval, sent Cartier to bring him home, and this voyage seems to have taken place in the summer of 1543. It is said that, in after years, the Viceroy essayed to repossess himself of his Transatlantic domain, and lost his life in the attempt. Thevet, on the other hand, with ample means of learning the truth, affirms that Roberval was slain at night, near the Church of the Innocents, in the heart of Paris.

With him closes the prelude of the French-American drama. Tempestuous years and a reign of blood and fire were in store for France. The religious wars begot the hapless colony of Florida, but for more than half a century they left New France a desert. Order rose at length out of the sanguinary chaos; the zeal of discovery and the spirit of commercial enterprise once more awoke, while, closely following, more potent than they, moved the black-robed forces of the Roman Catholic reaction.

CHAPTER II.
1542-1604.
LA ROCHE.—CHAMPLAIN.—DE MONTS.

Years rolled on. France, long tossed among the surges of civil commotion, plunged at last into a gulf of fratricidal war. Blazing hamlets, sacked cities, fields steaming with slaughter, profaned altars, and ravished maidens, marked the track of the tornado. There was little room for schemes of foreign enterprise. Yet, far aloof from siege and battle, the fishermen of the western ports still plied their craft on the Banks of Newfoundland. Humanity, morality, decency, might be forgotten, but codfish must still be had for the use of the faithful in Lent and on fast days. Still the wandering Esquimaux saw the Norman and Breton sails hovering around some lonely headland, or anchored in fleets in the harbor of St. John; and still, through salt spray and driving mist, the fishermen dragged up the riches of the sea.

In January and February, 1545, about two vessels a day sailed from French ports for Newfoundland. In 1565, Pedro Menendez complains that the French "rule despotically" in those parts. In 1578, there were a hundred and fifty French fishing-vessels there, besides two hundred of other nations, Spanish, Portuguese, and English. Added to these were twenty or thirty Biscayan whalers. In 1607, there was an old French fisherman at Canseau who had voyaged to these seas for forty-two successive years.

But if the wilderness of ocean had its treasures, so too had the wilderness of woods. It needed but a few knives, beads, and trinkets, and the Indians would throng to the shore burdened with the spoils of their winter hunting. Fishermen threw up their old vocation for the more lucrative trade in bear-skins and beaver-skins. They built rude huts along the shores of Anticosti, where, at that day, the bison, it is said, could be seen wallowing in the sands. They outraged the Indians; they quarrelled with each other; and this infancy of the Canadian fur-trade showed rich promise of the disorders which marked its riper growth. Others, meanwhile, were ranging the gulf in search of walrus tusks; and, the year after the battle of Ivry, St. Malo sent out a fleet of small craft in quest of this new prize.

In all the western seaports, merchants and adventurers turned their eyes towards America; not, like the Spaniards, seeking treasures of silver and gold, but the more modest gains of codfish and train-oil, beaver-skins and marine ivory. St. Malo was conspicuous above them all. The rugged Bretons loved the perils of the sea, and saw with a jealous eye every attempt to shackle their activity on this its favorite field. When in 1588 Jacques Noel and Estienue Chaton—the former a nephew of Cartier and the latter pretending to be so—gained a monopoly of the American fur-trade for twelve year's, such a clamor arose within the walls of St. Malo that the obnoxious grant was promptly revoked.

But soon a power was in the field against which all St. Malo might clamor in vain. A Catholic nobleman of Brittany, the Marquis de la Roche, bargained with the King to colonize New France. On his part, he was to receive a monopoly of the trade, and a profusion of worthless titles and empty privileges. He was declared Lieutenant-General of Canada, Hochelaga, Newfoundland, Labrador, and the countries adjacent, with sovereign power within his vast and ill-defined domain. He could levy troops, declare war and peace, make laws, punish or pardon at will, build cities, forts, and castles, and grant out lands in fiefs, seigniories, counties, viscounties, and baronies. Thus was effete and cumbrous feudalism to make a lodgment in the New World. It was a scheme of high-sounding promise, but in performance less than contemptible. La Roche ransacked the prisons, and, gathering thence a gang of thieves and desperadoes, embarked them in a small vessel, and set sail to plant Christianity and civilization in the West. Suns rose and set, and the wretched bark, deep freighted with brutality and vice, held on her course. She was so small that the convicts, leaning over her side, could wash their hands in the water. At length, on the gray horizon they descried a long, gray line of ridgy sand. It was Sable Island, off the coast of Nova Scotia. A wreck lay stranded on the beach, and the surf broke ominously over the long, submerged arms of sand, stretched far out into the sea on the right hand and on the left.

Here La Roche landed the convicts, forty in number, while, with his more trusty followers, he sailed to explore the neighboring coasts, and choose a site for the capital of his new dominion, to which, in due time, he proposed to remove the prisoners. But suddenly a tempest from the west assailed him. The frail vessel was forced to run before the gale, which, howling on her track, drove her off the coast, and chased her back towards France.

Meanwhile the convicts watched in suspense for the returning sail. Days passed, weeks passed, and still they strained their eyes in vain across the waste of ocean. La Roche had left them to their fate. Rueful and desperate, they wandered among the sand-hills, through the stunted whortleberry bushes, the rank sand-grass, and the tangled cranberry vines which filled the hollows. Not a tree was to be seen; but they built huts of the fragments of the wreck. For food they caught fish in the surrounding sea, and hunted the cattle which ran wild about the island, sprung, perhaps, from those left here eighty years before by the Baron de Lery. They killed seals, trapped black foxes, and clothed themselves in their skins. Their native instincts clung to them in their exile. As if not content with inevitable miseries, they quarrelled and murdered one another. Season after season dragged on. Five years elapsed, and, of the forty, only twelve were left alive. Sand, sea, and sky,—there was little else around them; though, to break the dead monotony, the walrus would sometimes rear his half-human face and glistening sides on the reefs and sand-bars. At length, on the far verge of the watery desert, they descried a sail. She stood on towards the island; a boat's crew landed on the beach, and the exiles were once more among their countrymen.

When La Roche returned to France, the fate of his followers sat heavy on his mind. But the day of his prosperity was gone. A host of enemies rose against him and his privileges, and it is said that the Due de Mercaeur seized him and threw him into prison. In time, however, he gained a hearing of the King; and the Norman pilot, Chefdhotel, was despatched to bring the outcasts home.

He reached Sable Island in September, 1603, and brought back to France eleven survivors, whose names are still preserved. When they arrived, Henry the Fourth summoned them into his presence. They stood before him, says an old writer, like river-gods of yore; for from head to foot they were clothed in shaggy skins, and beards of prodigious length hung from their swarthy faces. They had accumulated, on their island, a quantity of valuable furs. Of these Chefdhotel had robbed them; but the pilot was forced to disgorge his prey, and, with the aid of a bounty from the King, they were enabled to embark on their own account in the Canadian trade. To their leader, fortune was less kind. Broken by disaster and imprisonment, La Roche died miserably.

In the mean time, on the ruin of his enterprise, a new one had been begun. Pontgrave, a merchant of St. Malo, leagued himself with Chauvin, a captain of the navy, who had influence at court. A patent was granted to them, with the condition that they should colonize the country. But their only thought was to enrich themselves.

At Tadoussac, at the mouth of the Saguenay, under the shadow of savage and inaccessible rocks, feathered with pines, firs, and birch-trees, they built a cluster of wooden huts and store-houses. Here they left sixteen men to gather the expected harvest of furs. Before the winter was over, several of them were dead, and the rest scattered through the woods, living on the charity of the Indians.

But a new era had dawned on France. Exhausted with thirty years of conflict, she had sunk at last to a repose, uneasy and disturbed, yet the harbinger of recovery. The rugged soldier whom, for the weal of France and of mankind, Providence had cast to the troubled surface of affairs, was throned in the Louvre, composing the strife of factions and the quarrels of his mistresses. The bear-hunting prince of the Pyrenees wore the crown of France; and to this day, as one gazes on the time-worn front of the Tuileries, above all other memories rises the small, strong finger, the brow wrinkled with cares of love and war, the bristling moustache, the grizzled beard, the bold, vigorous, and withal somewhat odd features of the mountaineer of Warn. To few has human liberty owed so deep a gratitude or so deep a grudge. He cared little for creeds or dogmas. Impressible, quick in sympathy, his grim lip lighted often with a smile, and his war-worn cheek was no stranger to a tear. He forgave his enemies and forgot his friends. Many loved him; none but fools trusted him. Mingled of mortal good and ill, frailty and force, of all the kings who for two centuries and more sat on the throne of France Henry the Fourth alone was a man.

Art, industry, and commerce, so long crushed and overborne, were stirring into renewed life, and a crowd of adventurous men, nurtured in war and incapable of repose, must seek employment for their restless energies in fields of peaceful enterprise.

Two small, quaint vessels, not larger than the fishing-craft of Gloucester and Marblehead,—one was of twelve, the other of fifteen tons,—held their way across the Atlantic, passed the tempestuous headlands of Newfoundland and the St. Lawrence, and, with adventurous knight-errantry, glided deep into the heart of the Canadian wilderness. On board of one of them was the Breton merchant, Pontgrave, and with him a man of spirit widely different, a Catholic of good family,—Samuel de Champlain, born in 1567 at the small seaport of Bronage on the Bay of Biscay. His father was a captain in the royal navy, where he himself seems also to have served, though during the war he had fought for the King in Brittany, under the banners of D'Aumont, St. Luc, and Brissac. His purse was small, his merit great; and Henry the Fourth out of his own slender revenues had given him a pension to maintain him near his person. But rest was penance to him. The war in Brittany was over. The rebellious Duc de Mercaeur was reduced to obedience, and the royal army disbanded. Champlain, his occupation gone, conceived a design consonant with his adventurous nature. He would visit the West Indies, and bring back to the King a report of those regions of mystery whence Spanish jealousy excluded foreigners, and where every intruding Frenchman was threatened with death. Here much knowledge was to be won and much peril to be met. The joint attraction was resistless.

The Spaniards, allies of the vanquished Leaguers, were about to evacuate Blavet, their last stronghold in Brittany. Thither Champlain repaired; and here he found an uncle, who had charge of the French fleet destined to take on board the Spanish garrison. Champlain embarked with them, and, reaching Cadiz, succeeded, with the aid of his relative, who had just accepted the post of Pilot-General of the Spanish marine, in gaining command of one of the ships about to sail for the West Indies under Don Francisco Colombo.

At Dieppe there is a curious old manuscript, in clear, decisive, and somewhat formal handwriting of the sixteenth century, garnished with sixty-one colored pictures, in a style of art which a child of ten might emulate. Here one may see ports, harbors, islands, and rivers, adorned with portraitures of birds, beasts, and fishes thereto pertaining. Here are Indian feasts and dances; Indians flogged by priests for not going to mass; Indians burned alive for heresy, six in one fire; Indians working the silver mines. Here, too, are descriptions of natural objects, each with its illustrative sketch, some drawn from life and some from memory,—as, for example, a chameleon with two legs; others from hearsay, among which is the portrait of the griffin said to haunt certain districts of Mexico,—a monster with the wings of a bat, the head of an eagle, and the tail of an alligator.

This is Champlain's journal, written and illustrated by his own hand, in that defiance of perspective and absolute independence of the canons of art which mark the earliest efforts of the pencil.

A true hero, after the chivalrous mediaeval type, his character was dashed largely with the spirit of romance. Though earnest, sagacious, and penetrating, he leaned to the marvellous; and the faith which was the life of his hard career was somewhat prone to overstep the bounds of reason and invade the domain of fancy. Hence the erratic character of some of his exploits, and hence his simple faith in the Mexican griffin.

His West-Indian adventure occupied him more than two years. He visited the principal ports of the islands, made plans and sketches of them all, after his fashion, and then, landing at Vera Cruz, journeyed inland to the city of Mexico. On his return he made his way to Panama. Here, more than two centuries and a half ago, his bold and active mind conceived the plan of a ship-canal across the isthmus, "by which," lie says, "the voyage to the South Sea would be shortened by more than fifteen hundred leagues."

On reaching France he repaired to court, and it may have been at this time that a royal patent raised him to the rank of the untitled nobility. He soon wearied of the antechambers of the Louvre. It was here, however, that his destiny awaited him, and the work of his life was unfolded. Aymar de Chastes, Commander of the Order of St. John and Governor of Dieppe, a gray-haired veteran of the civil wars, wished to mark his closing days with some notable achievement for France and the Church. To no man was the King more deeply indebted. In his darkest hour, when the hosts of the League were gathering round him, when friends were falling off, and the Parisians, exulting in his certain ruin, were hiring the windows of the Rue St. Antoine to see him led to the Bastille, De Chastes, without condition or reserve, gave up to him the town and castle of Dieppe. Thus he was enabled to fight beneath its walls the battle of Arques, the first in the series of successes which secured his triumph; and he had been heard to say that to this friend in his adversity he owed his own salvation and that of France.

De Chastes was one of those men who, amid the strife of factions and rage of rival fanaticisms, make reason and patriotism their watchwords, and stand on the firm ground of a strong and resolute moderation. He had resisted the madness of Leaguer and Huguenot alike; yet, though a foe of the League, the old soldier was a devout Catholic, and it seemed in his eyes a noble consummation of his life to plant the cross and the fleur-de-lis in the wilderness of New France. Chauvin had just died, after wasting the lives of a score or more of men in a second and a third attempt to establish the fur-trade at Tadoussac. De Chastes came to court to beg a patent of henry the Fourth; "and," says his friend Champlain, "though his head was crowned with gray hairs as with years, he resolved to proceed to New France in person, and dedicate the rest of his days to the service of God and his King."

The patent, costing nothing, was readily granted; and De Chastes, to meet the expenses of the enterprise, and forestall the jealousies which his monopoly would awaken among the keen merchants of the western ports, formed a company with the more prominent of them. Pontgrave, who had some knowledge of the country, was chosen to make a preliminary exploration.

This was the time when Champlain, fresh from the West Indies, appeared at court. De Chastes knew him well. Young, ardent, yet ripe in experience, a skilful seaman and a practised soldier, he above all others was a man for the enterprise. He had many conferences with the veteran, under whom he had served in the royal fleet off the coast of Brittany. De Chastes urged him to accept a post in his new company; and Champlain, nothing loath, consented, provided always that permission should be had from the King, "to whom," he says, "I was bound no less by birth than by the pension with which his Majesty honored me." To the King, therefore, De Chastes repaired. The needful consent was gained, and, armed with a letter to Pontgrave, Champlain set out for

Honfleur. Here he found his destined companion, and embarking with him, as we have seen, they spread their sails for the west.

Like specks on the broad bosom of the waters, the two pygmy vessels held their course up the lonely St. Lawrence. They passed abandoned Tadoussac, the channel of Orleans, and the gleaming cataract of Montmorenci; the tenantless rock of Quebec, the wide Lake of St. Peter and its crowded archipelago, till now the mountain reared before them its rounded shoulder above the forest-plain of Montreal. All was solitude. Hochelaga had vanished; and of the savage population that Cartier had found here, sixty-eight years before, no trace remained. In its place were a few wandering Algonquins, of different tongue and lineage. In a skiff, with a few Indians, Champlain essayed to pass the rapids of St. Louis. Oars, paddles, and poles alike proved vain against the foaming surges, and he was forced to return. On the deck of his vessel, the Indians drew rude plans of the river above, with its chain of rapids, its lakes and cataracts; and the baffled explorer turned his prow homeward, the objects of his mission accomplished, but his own adventurous curiosity unsated. When the voyagers reached Havre de Grace, a grievous blow awaited them. The Commander de Chastes was dead.

His mantle fell upon Pierre du Guast, Sieur de Monts, gentleman in ordinary of the King's chamber, and Governor of Polls. Undaunted by the fate of La Roche, this nobleman petitioned the king for leave to colonize La Cadie, or Acadie, a region defined as extending from the fortieth to the forty-Sixth degree of north latitude, or from Philadelphia to beyond Montreal. The King's minister, Sully, as he himself tells us, opposed the plan, on the ground that the colonization of this northern wilderness would never repay the outlay; but De Monts gained his point. He was made Lieutenant-General in Acadia, with viceregal powers; and withered Feudalism, with her antique forms and tinselled follies, was again to seek a new home among the rocks and pine-trees of Nova Scotia. The foundation of the enterprise was a monopoly of the fur-trade, and in its favor all past grants were unceremoniously annulled. St. Malo, Rouen, Dieppe, and Rochelle greeted the announcement with unavailing outcries. Patents granted and revoked, monopolies decreed and extinguished, had involved the unhappy traders in ceaseless embarrassment. De

Monts, however, preserved De Chastes's old company, and enlarged it, thus making the chief malcontents sharers in his exclusive rights, and converting them from enemies into partners.

A clause in his commission empowered him to impress idlers and vagabonds as material for his colony,—an ominous provision of which he largely availed himself. His company was strangely incongruous. The best and the meanest of France were crowded together in his two ships. Here were thieves and ruffians dragged on board by force; and here were many volunteers of condition and character, with Baron de Poutrincourt and the indefatigable Champlain. Here, too, were Catholic priests and Huguenot ministers; for, though De Monts was a Calvinist, the Church, as usual, displayed her banner in the van of the enterprise, and he was forced to promise that he would cause the Indians to be instructed in the dogmas of Rome.

CHAPTER III.
1604, 1605.
ACADIA OCCUPIED.

De Monts, with one of his vessels, sailed from Havre de Grace on the seventh of April, 1604. Pontgrave, with stores for the colony, was to follow in a few days.

Scarcely were they at sea, when ministers and priests fell first to discussion, then to quarrelling, then to blows. "I have seen our cure and the minister," says Champlain, "fall to with their fists on questions of faith. I cannot say which had the more pluck, or which hit the harder; but I know that the minister sometimes complained to the Sieur de Monts that he had been beaten. This was their way of settling points of controversy. I leave you to judge if it was a pleasant thing to see."

Sagard, the Franciscan friar, relates with horror, that, after their destination was reached, a priest and a minister happening to die at the same time, the crew buried them both in one grave, to see if they would lie peaceably together.

De Monts, who had been to the St. Lawrence with Chauvin, and learned to dread its rigorous winters, steered for a more southern, and, as he flattered himself, a milder region. The first land seen was Cap la Heve, on the southern coast of Nova Scotia. Four days later, they entered a small bay, where, to their surprise, they saw a vessel lying at anchor. here was a piece of good luck. The stranger was a fur-trader, pursuing her traffic in defiance, or more probably in ignorance, of De Monts's monopoly. The latter, as empowered by his patent, made prize of ship and cargo, consoling the commander, one Rossignol, by giving his name to the scene of his misfortune. It is now called Liverpool Harbor.

In an adjacent harbor, called by them Port Mouton, because a sheep here leaped overboard, they waited nearly a month for Pontgrave's store-ship. At length, to their great relief, she appeared, laden with the spoils of four Basque fur-traders, captured at Cansean. The supplies delivered, Pontgrave sailed for Tadoussac to trade with the Indians, while De Monts, followed by his prize, proceeded on his voyage.

He doubled Cape Sable, and entered St. Mary's Bay, where he lay two weeks, sending boats' crews to explore the adjacent coasts. A party one day went on shore to stroll through the forest, and among them was Nicolas Aubry, a priest from Paris, who, tiring of the scholastic haunts of the Rue de la Sorbonne and the Rue d'Enfer, had persisted, despite the remonstrance of his friends, in joining the expedition. Thirsty with a long walk, under the sun of June, through the tangled and rock-encumbered woods, he stopped to drink at a brook, laying his sword beside him on the grass. On rejoining his companions, he found that he had forgotten it; and turning back in search of it, more skilled in the devious windings of the Quartier Latin than in the intricacies of the Acadian forest, he soon lost his way. His comrades, alarmed, waited for a time, and then ranged the woods, shouting his name to the echoing solitudes. Trumpets were sounded, and cannon fired from the ships, but the priest did not appear. All now looked askance on a certain Huguenot, with whom Aubry had often quarrelled on questions of faith, and who was now accused of having killed him. In vain he denied the charge. Aubry was given up for dead, and the ship sailed from St. Mary's Bay; while the wretched priest roamed to and fro, famished and despairing, or, couched on the rocky soil, in the troubled sleep of exhaustion, dreamed, perhaps, as the wind swept moaning through the pines, that he heard once more the organ roll through the columned arches of Sainte Genevieve.

The voyagers proceeded to explore the Bay of Fundy, which De Monts called La Baye Francoise. Their first notable discovery was that of Annapolis Harbor. A small inlet invited them. They entered, when suddenly the narrow strait dilated into a broad and tranquil basin, compassed by sunny hills, wrapped in woodland verdure, and alive with waterfalls. Poutrincourt was delighted with the scene. The fancy seized him of removing thither from France with his family and, to this end, he asked a grant of the place from De Monts, who by his patent had nearly half the continent in his gift. The grant was made, and Poutrincourt called his new domain Port Royal.

Thence they sailed round the head of the Bay of Fundy, coasted its northern shore, visited and named the river St. John, and anchored at last in Passamaquoddy Bay.

The untiring Champlain, exploring, surveying, sounding, had made charts of all the principal roads and harbors; and now, pursuing his research, he entered a river which he calls La Riviere des Etechemins, from the name of the tribe of whom the present Passamaquoddy Indians are descendants. Near its mouth he found an islet, fenced round with rocks and shoals, and called it St. Croix, a name now borne by the river itself. With singular infelicity this spot was chosen as the site of the new colony. It commanded the river, and was well fitted for defence: these were its only merits; yet cannon were landed on it, a battery was planted on a detached rock at one end, and a fort begun on a rising ground at the other.

At St. Mary's Bay the voyagers thought they had found traces of iron and silver; and Champdore, the pilot, was now sent back to pursue the search. As he and his men lay at anchor, fishing, not far from land, one of them heard a strange sound, like a weak human voice; and, looking towards the shore, they saw a small black object in motion, apparently a hat waved on the end of a stick. Rowing in haste to the spot, they found the priest Aubry. For sixteen days he had wandered in the woods, sustaining life on berries and wild fruits; and when, haggard and emaciated, a shadow of his former self, Champdore carried him back to St. Croix, he was greeted as a man risen from the grave.

In 1783 the river St. Croix, by treaty, was made the boundary between Maine and New Brunswick. But which was the true St. Croix? In 1798, the point was settled. De Monts's island was found; and, painfully searching among the sand, the sedge, and the matted whortleberry bushes, the commissioners could trace the foundations of buildings long crumbled into dust; for the wilderness had resumed its sway, and silence and solitude brooded once more over this ancient resting-place of civilization.

But while the commissioner bends over a moss-grown stone, it is for us to trace back the dim vista of the centuries to the life, the zeal, the energy, of which this stone is the poor memorial. The rock-fenced islet was covered with cedars, and when the tide was out the shoals around were dark with the swash of sea-weed, where, in their leisure moments, the Frenchmen, we are told, amused themselves with detaching the limpets from the stones, as a savory addition to their fare. But there was little leisure at St. Croix. Soldiers, sailors, and artisans betook themselves to their task. Before the winter closed in, the northern end of the island was covered with buildings, surrounding a square, where a solitary tree had been left standing. On the right was a spacious house, well built, and surmounted by one of those enormous roofs characteristic of the time. This was the lodging of De Monts. Behind it, and near the water, was a long, covered gallery, for labor or amusement in foul weather. Champlain and the Sieur d'Orville, aided by the servants of the latter, built a house for themselves nearly opposite that of De Monts; and the remainder of the square was occupied by storehouses, a magazine, workshops, lodgings for gentlemen and artisans, and a barrack for the Swiss soldiers, the whole enclosed with a palisade. Adjacent there was an attempt at a garden, under the auspices of Champlain; but nothing would grow in the sandy soil. There was a cemetery, too, and a small rustic chapel on a projecting point of rock. Such was the "Habitation de l'Isle Saincte-Croix," as set forth by Champlain in quaint plans and drawings, in that musty little quarto of 1613, sold by Jean Berjon, at the sign of the Flying Horse, Rue St. Jean de Beauvais.

Their labors over, Poutrincourt set sail for France, proposing to return and take possession of his domain of Port Royal. Seventy-nine men remained at St. Croix. Here was De Monts, feudal lord of half a continent in virtue of two potent syllables, "Henri," scrawled on parchment by the rugged hand of the Bearnais. Here were gentlemen of birth and breeding, Champlain, D'Orville, Beaumont, Sourin, La Motte, Boulay, and Fougeray; here also were the pugnacious cure and his fellow priests, with the Hugnenot ministers, objects of their unceasing ire. The rest were laborers, artisans, and soldiers, all in the pay of the company, and some of them forced into its service.

Poutrincourt's receding sails vanished between the water and the sky. The exiles were left to their solitude. From the Spanish settlements northward to the pole, there was no domestic hearth, no lodgement of civilized men, save one weak band of Frenchmen, clinging, as it were for life, to the fringe of the vast and savage continent. The gray and sullen autumn sank upon the waste, and the bleak wind howled down the St. Croix, and swept the forest bare. Then the whirling snow powdered the vast sweep of desolate woodland, and shrouded in white the gloomy green of pine-clad mountains. Ice in sheets, or broken masses, swept by their island with the ebbing and flowing tide, often debarring all access to the main, and cutting off their supplies of wood and water. A belt of cedars, indeed, hedged the island; but De Monts had ordered them to be spared, that the north wind might spend something of its force with whistling through their shaggy boughs. Cider and wine froze in the casks, and were served out by the pound. As they crowded round their half-fed fires, shivering in the icy currents that pierced their rude tenements, many sank into a desperate apathy.

Soon the scurvy broke out, and raged with a fearful malignity. Of the seventy-nine, thirty-five died before spring, and many more were brought to the verge of death. In vain they sought that marvellous tree which had relieved the followers of Cartier. Their little cemetery was peopled with nearly half their number, and the rest, bloated and disfigured with the relentless malady, thought more of escaping from their woes than of building up a Transatlantic empire. Yet among them there was one, at least, who, amid languor and defection, held to his purpose with indomitable tenacity; and where Champlain was present, there was no room for despair.

Spring came at last, and, with the breaking up of the ice, the melting of the snow, and the clamors of the returning wild-fowl, the spirits and the health of the woe-begone company began to revive. But to misery succeeded anxiety and suspense. Where was the succor from France? Were they abandoned to their fate like the wretched exiles of La Roche? In a happy hour, they saw an approaching sail. Pontgrave, with forty men, cast anchor before their island on the sixteenth of June; and they hailed him as the condemned hails the messenger of his pardon.

Weary of St. Croix, De Monts resolved to seek out a more auspicious site, on which to rear the capital of his wilderness dominion. During the preceding September, Champlain had ranged the westward coast in a pinnace, visited and named the island of Mount Desert, and entered the mouth of the river Penobscot, called by him the Pemetigoet, or Pentegoet, and previously known to fur-traders and fishermen as the Norembega, a name which it shared with all the adjacent region. 27 Now, embarking a second time, in a bark of fifteen tons, with De Monts, several gentlemen, twenty sailors, and an Indian with his squaw, he set forth on the eighteenth of June on a second voyage of discovery. They coasted the strangely indented shores of Maine, with its reefs and surf-washed islands, rocky headlands, and deep embosomed bays, passed Mount Desert and the Penobscot, explored the mouths of the Kennebec, crossed Casco Bay, and descried the distant peaks of the White Mountains. The ninth of July brought them to Saco Bay. They were now within the limits of a group of tribes who were called by the French the Armouchiquois, and who included those whom the English afterwards called the Massachusetts. They differed in habits as well as in language from the Etechemins and Miemacs of Acadia, for they were tillers of the soil, and around their wigwams were fields of maize, beans, pumpkins, squashes, tobacco, and the so-called Jerusalem artichoke. Near Pront's Neck, more than eighty of them ran down to the shore to meet the strangers, dancing and yelping to show their joy. They had a fort of palisades on a rising ground by the Saco, for they were at deadly war with their neighbors towards the east.

On the twelfth, the French resumed their voyage, and, like some adventurous party of pleasure, held their course by the beaches of York and Wells, Portsmouth Harbor, the Isles of Shoals, Rye Beach, and Hampton Beach, till, on the fifteenth, they descried the dim outline of Cape Ann. Champlain called it Cap aux Isles, from the three adjacent islands, and in a subsequent voyage he gave the name of Beauport to the neighboring harbor of Gloucester. Thence steering southward and westward, they entered Massachusetts Bay, gave the name of Riviere du Guast to a river flowing into it, probably the Charles; passed the islands of Boston Harbor, which Champlain describes as covered with trees, and were met on the way by great numbers of canoes filled with astonished Indians. On Sunday, the seventeenth, they passed Point Allerton and Nantasket Beach, coasted the shores of Cohasset, Scituate, and Marshfield, and anchored for the night near Brant Point. On the morning of the eighteenth, a head wind forced them to take shelter in Port St. Louis, for so they called the harbor of Plymouth, where the Pilgrims made their memorable landing fifteen years later. Indian wigwams and garden patches lined the shore. A troop of the inhabitants came down to the beach and danced; while others, who had been fishing, approached in their canoes, came on board the vessel, and showed Champlain their fish-hooks, consisting of a barbed bone lashed at an acute angle to a slip of wood.

From Plymouth the party circled round the bay, doubled Cape Cod, called by Champlain Cap Blanc, from its glistening white sands, and steered southward to Nausett Harbor, which, by reason of its shoals and sand-bars, they named Port Mallebarre. Here their prosperity deserted them. A party of sailors went behind the sand-banks to find fresh water at a spring, when an Indian snatched a kettle from one of them, and its owner, pursuing, fell, pierced with arrows by the robber's comrades. The French in the vessel opened fire. Champlain's arquebuse burst, and was near killing him, while the Indians, swift as deer, quickly gained the woods. Several of the tribe chanced to be on board the vessel, but flung themselves with such alacrity into the water that only one was caught. They bound him hand and foot, but soon after humanely set him at liberty.

Champlain, who we are told "delighted marvellously in these enterprises," had busied himself throughout the voyage with taking observations, making charts, and studying the wonders of land and sea. The "horse-foot crab" seems to have awakened his special curiosity, and he describes it with amusing exactness. Of the human tenants of the New England coast he has also left the first precise and trustworthy account. They were clearly more numerous than when the Puritans landed at Plymouth, since in the interval a pestilence made great havoc among them. But Champlain's most conspicuous merit lies in the light that he threw into the dark places of American geography, and the order that he brought out of the chaos of American cartography; for it was a result of this and the rest of his voyages that precision and clearness began at last to supplant the vagueness, confusion, and contradiction of the earlier map-makers.

At Nausett Harbor provisions began to fail, and steering for St. Croix the voyagers reached that ill-starred island on the third of August. De Monts had found no spot to his liking. He now bethought him of that inland harbor of Port Royal which he had granted to Poutrincourt, and thither he resolved to remove. Stores, utensils, even portions of the buildings, were placed on board the vessels, carried across the Bay of Fundy, and landed at the chosen spot. It was on the north side of the basin opposite Goat Island, and a little below the mouth of the river Annapolis, called by the French the Equille, and, afterwards, the Dauphin. The axe-men began their task; the dense forest was cleared away, and the buildings of the infant colony soon rose in its place.

But while De Monts and his company were struggling against despair at St. Croix, the enemies of his monopoly were busy at Paris; and, by a ship from France, he was warned that prompt measures were needed to thwart their machinations. Therefore he set sail, leaving Pontgrave to command at Port Royal: while Champlain, Champdore, and others, undaunted by the past, volunteered for a second winter in the wilderness.

CHAPTER IV.
1605-1607.
LESCARBOT AND CHAMPLAIN.

Evil reports of a churlish wilderness, a pitiless climate, disease, misery, and death, had heralded the arrival of De Monts. The outlay had been great, the returns small; and when he reached Paris, he found his friends cold, his enemies active and keen. Poutrincourt, however, was still full of zeal; and, though his private affairs urgently called for his presence in France, he resolved, at no small sacrifice, to go in person to Acadia. He had, moreover, a friend who proved an invaluable ally. This was Marc Lescarbot, "avocat en Parlement," who had been roughly handled by fortune, and was in the mood for such a venture, being desirous, as he tells us, "to fly from a corrupt world," in which he had just lost a lawsuit. Unlike De Monts, Poutrincourt, and others of his associates, he was not within the pale of the noblesse, belonging to the class of "gens de robe," which stood at the head of the bourgeoisie, and which, in its higher grades, formed within itself a virtual nobility. Lescarbot was no common man,—not that his abundant gift of verse-making was likely to avail much in the woods of New France, nor yet his classic lore, dashed with a little harmless pedantry, born not of the man, but of the times; but his zeal, his good sense, the vigor of his understanding, and the breadth of his views, were as conspicuous as his quick wit and his lively fancy. One of the best, as well as earliest, records of the early settlement of North America is due to his pen; and it has been said, with a certain degree of truth, that he was no less able to build up a colony than to write its history. He professed himself a Catholic, but his Catholicity sat lightly on him; and he might have passed for one of those amphibious religionists who in the civil wars were called "Les Politiques."

De Monts and Poutrincourt bestirred themselves to find a priest, since the foes of the enterprise had been loud in lamentation that the spiritual welfare of the Indians had been slighted. But it was Holy Week. All the priests were, or professed to be, busy with exercises and confessions, and not one could be found to undertake the mission of Acadia. They were more successful in engaging mechanics and laborers for the voyage. These were paid a portion of their wages in advance, and were sent in a body to Rochelle, consigned to two merchants of that port, members of the company. De Monts and Poutrincourt went thither by post. Lescarbot soon followed, and no sooner reached Rochelle than he penned and printed his Adieu a la France, a poem which gained for him some credit.

More serious matters awaited him, however, than this dalliance with the Muse. Rochelle was the centre and citadel of Calvinism,— a town of austere and grim aspect, divided, like Cisatlantic communities of later growth, betwixt trade and religion, and, in the interest of both, exacting a deportment of discreet and well-ordered sobriety. "One must walk a strait path here," says Lescarbot, "unless he would hear from the mayor or the ministers." But the mechanics sent from Paris, flush of money, and lodged together in the quarter of St. Nicolas, made day and night hideous with riot, and their employers found not a few of them in the hands of the police. Their ship, bearing the inauspicious name of the "Jonas," lay anchored in the stream, her cargo on board, when a sudden gale blew her adrift. She struck on a pier, then grounded on the flats, bilged, careened, and settled in the mud. Her captain, who was ashore, with Poutrincourt, Lescarbot, and others, hastened aboard, and the pumps were set in motion; while all Rochelle, we are told, came to gaze from the ramparts, with faces of condolence, but at heart well pleased with the disaster. The ship and her cargo were saved, but she must be emptied, repaired, and reladen. Thus a month was lost; at length, on the thirteenth of May, 1606, the disorderly crew were all brought on board, and the "Jonas" put to sea. Poutrincourt and Lescarbot had charge of the expedition, De Monts remaining in France.

Lescarbot describes his emotions at finding himself on an element so deficient in solidity, with only a two-inch plank between him and death. Off the Azores, they spoke a supposed pirate. For the rest, they beguiled the voyage by harpooning porpoises, dancing on deck in calm weather, and fishing for cod on the Grand Bank. They were two months on their way; and when, fevered with eagerness to reach land, they listened hourly for the welcome cry, they were involved in impenetrable fogs. Suddenly the mists parted, the sun shone forth, and streamed fair and bright over the fresh hills and forests of the New World, in near view before them. But the black rocks lay between, lashed by the snow-white breakers. "Thus," writes Lescarbot, "doth a man sometimes seek the land as one doth his beloved, who sometimes repulseth her sweetheart very rudely. Finally, upon Saturday, the fifteenth of July, about two o'clock in the afternoon, the sky began to salute us as it were with cannon-shots, shedding tears, as being sorry to have kept us so long in pain;... but, whilst we followed on our course, there came from the land odors incomparable for sweetness, brought with a warm wind so abundantly that all the Orient parts could not produce greater abundance. We did stretch out our hands as it were to take them, so palpable were they, which I have admired a thousand times since."

It was noon on the twenty-seventh when the "Jonas" passed the rocky gateway of Port Royal Basin, and Lescarbot gazed with delight and wonder on the calm expanse of sunny waters, with its amphitheatre of woody hills, wherein he saw the future asylum of distressed merit and impoverished industry. Slowly, before a favoring breeze, they held their course towards the head of the harbor, which narrowed as they advanced; but all was solitude,— no moving sail, no sign of human presence. At length, on their left, nestling in deep forests, they saw the wooden walls and roofs of the infant colony. Then appeared a birch canoe, cautiously coming towards them, guided by an old Indian. Then a Frenchman, arquebuse in hand, came down to the shore; and then, from the wooden bastion, sprang the smoke of a saluting shot. The ship replied; the trumpets lent their voices to the din, and the forests and the hills gave back unwonted echoes. The voyagers landed, and found the colony of Port Royal dwindled to two solitary Frenchmen.

These soon told their story. The preceding winter had been one of much suffering, though by no means the counterpart of the woful experience of St. Croix. But when the spring had passed, the summer far advanced, and still no tidings of De Monts had come, Pontgrave grew deeply anxious. To maintain themselves without supplies and succor was impossible. He caused two small vessels to be built, and set out in search of some of the French vessels on the fishing stations. This was but twelve days before the arrival of the ship "Jonas." Two men had bravely offered themselves to stay behind and guard the buildings, guns, and munitions; and an old Indian chief, named Memberton, a fast friend of the French, and still a redoubted warrior, we are told, though reputed to number more than a hundred years, proved a stanch ally. When the ship approached, the two guardians were at dinner in their room at the fort. Memberton, always on the watch, saw the advancing sail, and, shouting from the gate, roused them from their repast. In doubt who the new-comers might be, one ran to the shore with his gun, while the other repaired to the platform where four cannon were mounted, in the valorous resolve to show fight should the strangers prove to be enemies. Happily this redundancy of mettle proved needless. He saw the white flag fluttering at the masthead, and joyfully fired his pieces as a salute.

The voyagers landed, and eagerly surveyed their new home. Some wandered through the buildings; some visited the cluster of Indian wigwams hard by; some roamed in the forest and over the meadows that bordered the neighboring river. The deserted fort now swarmed with life; and, the better to celebrate their prosperous arrival, Poutrincourt placed a hogs-head of wine in the courtyard at the discretion of his followers, whose hilarity, in consequence, became exuberant. Nor was it diminished when Pontgrave's vessels were seen entering the harbor. A boat sent by Pountrincourt, more than a week before, to explore the coasts, had met them near Cape Sable, and they joyfully returned to Port Royal.

Pontgrave, however, soon sailed for France in the "Jonas," hoping on his way to seize certain contraband fur-traders, reported to be at Canseau and Cape Breton. Poutrincourt and Champlain, bent on finding a better site for their settlement in a more southern latitude, set out on a voyage of discovery, in an ill-built vessel of eighteen tons, while Lescarbot remained in charge of Port Royal. They had little for their pains but danger, hardship, and mishap. The autumn gales cut short their exploration; and, after visiting Gloucester Harbor, doubling Monoinoy Point, and advancing as far as the neighborhood of Hyannis, on the southeast coast of Massachusetts, they turned back, somewhat disgusted with their errand. Along the eastern verge of Cape Cod they found the shore thickly studded with the wigwams of a race who were less hunters than tillers of the soil. At Chatham Harbor—called by them Port

Fortune—five of the company, who, contrary to orders, had remained on shore all night, were assailed, as they slept around their fire, by a shower of arrows from four hundred Indians. Two were killed outright, while the survivors fled for their boat, bristling like porcupines with the feathered missiles,—a scene oddly portrayed by the untutored pencil of Champlain. He and Poutrincourt, with eight men, hearing the war-whoops and the cries for aid, sprang up from sleep, snatched their weapons, pulled ashore in their shirts, and charged the yelling multitude, who fled before their spectral assailants, and vanished in the woods. "Thus," observes Lescarbot, "did thirty-five thousand Midianites fly before Gideon and his three hundred." The French buried their dead comrades; but, as they chanted their funeral hymn, the Indians, at a safe distance on a neighboring hill, were dancing in glee and triumph, and mocking them with unseemly gestures; and no sooner had the party re-embarked, than they dug up the dead bodies, burnt them, and arrayed themselves in their shirts. Little pleased with the country or its inhabitants, the voyagers turned their prow towards Port Royal, though not until, by a treacherous device, they had lured some of their late assailants within their reach, killed them, and cut off their heads as trophies. Near Mount Desert, on a stormy night, their rudder broke, and they had a hair-breadth escape from destruction. The chief object of their voyage, that of discovering a site for their colony under a more southern sky, had failed. Pontgravé's son had his hand blown off by the bursting of his gun; several of their number had been killed; others were sick or wounded; and thus, on the fourteenth of November, with somewhat downcast visages, they guided their helpless vessel with a pair of oars to the landing at Port Royal.

"I will not," says Lescarbot, "compare their perils to those of Ulysses, nor yet of Aeneas, lest thereby I should sully our holy enterprise with things impure."

He and his followers had been expecting them with great anxiety. His alert and buoyant spirit had conceived a plan for enlivening the courage of the company, a little dashed of late by misgivings and forebodings. Accordingly, as Poutrincourt, Champlain, and their weather-beaten crew approached the wooden gateway of Port Royal, Neptune issued forth, followed by his tritons, who greeted the voyagers in good French verse, written in all haste for the occasion by Lescarbot. And, as they entered, they beheld, blazoned over the arch, the arms of Prance, circled with laurels, and flanked by the scuteheons of De Monts and Poutrincourt.

The ingenious author of these devices had busied himself, during the absence of his associates, in more serious labors for the welfare of the colony. He explored the low borders of the river Equille, or Annapolis. Here, in the solitude, he saw great meadows, where the moose, with their young, were grazing, and where at times the rank grass was beaten to a pulp by the trampling of their hoofs. He burned the grass, and sowed crops of wheat, rye, and barley in its stead. His appearance gave so little promise of personal vigor, that some of the party assured him that he would never see France again, and warned him to husband his strength; but he knew himself better, and set at naught these comforting monitions. He was the most diligent of workers. He made gardens near the fort, where, in his zeal, he plied the hoe with his own hands late into the moonlight evenings. The priests, of whom at the outset there had been no lack, had all succumbed to the scurvy at St. Croix; and Lescarbot, so far as a layman might, essayed to supply their place, reading on Sundays from the Scriptures, and adding expositions of his own after a fashion not remarkable for rigorous Catholicity. Of an evening, when not engrossed with his garden, he was reading or writing in his room, perhaps preparing the material of that History of New France in which, despite the versatility of his busy brain, his good sense and capacity are clearly made manifest.

Now, however, when the whole company were reassembled, Lescarbot found associates more congenial than the rude soldiers, mechanics, and laborers who gathered at night around the blazing logs in their rude hall. Port Royal was a quadrangle of wooden buildings, enclosing a spacious court. At the southeast corner was the arched gateway, whence a path, a few paces in length, led to the water. It was flanked by a sort of bastion of palisades, while at the southwest corner was another bastion, on which four cannon were mounted. On the east side of the quadrangle was a range of magazines and storehouses; on the west were quarters for the men; on the north, a dining-hall and lodgings for the principal persons of the company; while on the south, or water side, were the kitchen, the forge, and the oven. Except the Garden-patches and the cemetery, the adjacent ground was thickly studded with the Stumps of the newly felled trees.

Most bountiful provision had been made for the temporal wants of the colonists, and Lescarbot is profuse in praise of the liberality of Du Monte and two merchants of Rochelle, who had freighted the ship "Jonas." Of wine, in particular, the supply was so generous, that every man in Port Royal was served with three pints daily.

The principal persons of the colony sat, fifteen in number, at Poutrincourt's table, which, by an ingenious device of Champlain, was always well furnished. He formed the fifteen into a new order, christened "L'Ordre de Bon-Temps." Each was Grand Master in turn, holding office for one day. It was his function to cater for the company; and, as it became a point of honor to fill the post with credit, the prospective Grand Master was usually busy, for several days before coming to his dignity, in hunting, fishing, or bartering provisions with the Indians. Thus did Poutrincourt's table groan beneath all the luxuries of the winter forest,—flesh of moose, caribou, and deer, beaver, otter, and hare, bears and wild-cats; with ducks, geese, grouse, and plover; sturgeon, too, and trout, and fish innumerable, speared through the ice of the Equille, or drawn from the depths of the neighboring bay. "And," says Lescarbot, in closing his bill of fare, "whatever our gourmands at home may think, we found as good cheer at Port Royal as they at their Rue aux Ours in Paris, and that, too, at a cheaper rate." For the preparation of this manifold provision, the Grand Master was also answerable; since, during his day of office, he was autocrat of the kitchen.

Nor did this bounteous repast lack a solemn and befitting ceremonial. When the hour had struck, after the manner of our fathers they dined at noon, the Grand Master entered the hall, a napkin on his shoulder, his staff of office in his hand, and the collar of the Order—valued by Lescarbot at four crowns—about his neck. The brotherhood followed, each bearing a dish. The invited guests were Indian chiefs, of whom old Memberton was daily present, seated at table with the French, who took pleasure in this red-skin companionship. Those of humbler degree, warriors, squaws, and children, sat on the floor, or crouched together in the corners of the hall, eagerly waiting their portion of biscuit or of bread, a novel and much coveted luxury. Being always treated with kindness, they became fond of the French, who often followed them on their moose-hunts, and shared their winter bivouac.

At the evening meal there was less of form and circumstance; and when the winter night closed in, when the flame crackled and the sparks streamed up the wide-throated chimney, and the founders of New France with their tawny allies were gathered around the blaze, then did the Grand Master resign the collar and the staff to the successor of his honors, and, with jovial courtesy, pledge him in a cup of wine. Thus these ingenious Frenchmen beguiled the winter of their exile.

It was an unusually mild winter. Until January, they wore no warmer garment than their doublets. They made hunting and fishing parties, in which the Indians, whose lodges were always to be seen under the friendly shelter of the buildings, failed not to bear part. "I remember," says Lescarbot, "that on the fourteenth of January, of a Sunday afternoon, we amused ourselves with singing and music on the river Equille; and that in the same month we went to see the wheat-fields two leagues from the fort, and dined merrily in the sunshine."

Good spirits and good cheer saved them in great measure from the scurvy; and though towards the end of winter severe cold set in, yet only four men died. The snow thawed at last, and as patches of the black and oozy soil began to appear, they saw the grain of their last autumn's sowing already piercing the mould. The forced inaction of the winter was over. The carpenters built a water-mill on the stream now called Allen's River; others enclosed fields and laid out gardens; others, again, with scoop-nets and baskets, caught the herrings and alewives as they ran up the innumerable rivulets. The leaders of the colony set a contagious example of activity. Poutrincourt forgot the prejudices of his noble birth, and went himself into the woods to gather turpentine from the pines, which he converted into tar by a process of his own invention; while Lescarbot, eager to test the qualities of the soil, was again, hoe in hand, at work all day in his garden.

All seemed full of promise; but alas for the bright hope that kindled the manly heart of Champlain and the earnest spirit of the vivacions advocate! A sudden blight fell on them, and their rising prosperity withered to the ground. On a morning, late in spring, as the French were at breakfast, the ever watchful Membertou came in with news of an approaching sail. They hastened to the shore; but the vision of the centenarian sagamore put them all to shame. They could see nothing. At length their doubts were resolved. A small vessel stood on towards them, and anchored before the fort. She was commanded by one Chevalier, a young man from St. Malo, and was freighted with disastrous tidings. Dc Monts's monopoly was rescinded. The life of the enterprise was stopped, and the establishment at Port Royal could no longer be supported; for its expense was great, the body of the colony being laborers in the pay of the company. Nor was the annulling of the patent the full extent of the disaster; for, during the last summer, the Dutch had found their way to the St. Lawrence, and carried away a rich harvest of furs, while other interloping traders had plied a busy traffic along the coasts, and, in the excess of their avidity, dug up the bodies of buried Indians to rob them of their funeral robes.

It was to the merchants and fishermen of the Norman, Breton, and Biscayan ports, exasperated at their exclusion from a lucrative trade, and at the confiscations which had sometimes followed their attempts to engage in it, that this sudden blow was due. Money had been used freely at court, and the monopoly, unjustly granted, had been more unjustly withdrawn. De Monts and his company, who had spent a hundred thousand livres, were allowed six thousand in requital, to be collected, if possible, from the fur-traders in the form of a tax.

Chevalier, captain of the ill-omened bark, was entertained with a hospitality little deserved, since, having been intrusted with sundry hams, fruits, spices, sweetmeats, jellies, and other dainties, sent by the generous De Monts to his friends of New France, he with his crew had devoured them on the voyage, alleging that, in their belief, the inmates of Port Royal would all be dead before their arrival.

Choice there was none, and Port Royal must be abandoned. Built on a false basis, sustained only by the fleeting favor of a government, the generous enterprise had come to naught. Yet Poutrincourt, who in virtue of his grant from De Monts owned the place, bravely resolved that, come what might, he would see the adventure to an end, even should it involve emigration with his family to the wilderness. Meanwhile, he began the dreary task of abandonment, sending boat-loads of men and stores to Canseau, where lay the ship "Jonas," eking out her diminished profits by fishing for cod.

Membertou was full of grief at the departure of his friends. He had built a palisaded village not far from Port Royal, and here were mustered some four hundred of his warriors for a foray into the country of the Armouchiquois, dwellers along the coasts of Massachusetts, New Hampshire, and Western Maine. One of his tribesmen had been killed by a chief from the Saco, and he was bent on revenge. He proved himself a sturdy beggar, pursuing Pontrincourt with daily petitions,—now for a bushel of beans, now for a basket of bread, and now for a barrel of wine to regale his greasy crew. Memberton's long life had not been one of repose. In deeds of blood and treachery he had no rival in the Acadian forest; and, as his old age was beset with enemies, his alliance with the French had a foundation of policy no less than of affection. In right of his rank of Sagamore, he claimed perfect equality both with Poutrincourt and with the King, laying his shrivelled forefingers together in token of friendship between peers. Calumny did not spare him; and a rival chief intimated to the French, that, under cover of a war with the Armouchiquois, the crafty veteran meant to seize and plunder Port Royal. Precautions, therefore, were taken; but they were seemingly needless; for, their feasts and dances over, the warriors launched their birchen flotilla and set out. After an absence of six weeks they reappeared with howls of victory, and their exploits were commemorated in French verse by the muse of the indefatigable Lescarbot.

With a heavy heart the advocate bade farewell to the dwellings, the cornfields, the gardens, and all the dawning prosperity of Port Royal, and sailed for Canseau in a small vessel on the thirtieth of July. Pontrincourt and Champlain remained behind, for the former was resolved to learn before his departure the results of his agricultural labors. Reaching a harbor on the southern coast of Nova Scotia, six leagues west of Cansean, Lescarbot found a fishing-vessel commanded and owned by an old Basque, named Savalet, who for forty-two successive years had carried to France his annual cargo of codfish. He was in great glee at the success of his present venture, reckoning his profits at ten thousand francs. The Indians, however, annoyed him beyond measure, boarding him from their canoes as his fishing-boats came alongside, and helping themselves at will to his halibut and cod. At Cansean—a harbor near the strait now bearing the name—the ship Jonas still lay, her hold well stored with fish; and here, on the twenty-seventh of August, Lescarbot was rejoined by Poutrincourt and Champlain, who had come from Port Royal in an open boat. For a few days, they amused themselves with gathering raspberries on the islands; then they spread their sails for France, and early in October, 1607, anchored in the harbor of St. Malo.

First of Europeans, they had essayed to found an agricultural colony in the New World. The leaders of the enterprise had acted less as merchants than as citizens; and the fur-trading monopoly, odious in itself, had been used as the instrument of a large and generous design. There was a radical defect, however, in their scheme of settlement. Excepting a few of the leaders, those engaged in it had not chosen a home in the wilderness of New France, but were mere hirelings, without wives or families, and careless of the welfare of the colony. The life which should have pervaded all the members was confined to the heads alone. In one respect, however, the enterprise of De Monts was truer in principle than the Roman Catholic colonization of Canada, on the one hand, or the Puritan colonization of Massachusetts, on the other, for it did not attempt to enforce religious exclusion.

Towards the fickle and bloodthirsty race who claimed the lordship of the forests, these colonists, excepting only in the treacherous slaughter at Port Fortune, bore themselves in a spirit of kindness contrasting brightly with the rapacious cruelty of the Spaniards and the harshness of the English settlers. When the last boat-load left Port Royal, the shore resounded with lamentation; and nothing could console the afflicted savages but reiterated promises of a speedy return.

CHAPTER V.
1610, 1611.
THE JESUITS AND THEIR PATRONESS.

Poutrincourt, we have seen, owned Port Royal in virtue of a grant from De Monts. The ardent and adventurous baron was in evil case, involved in litigation and low in purse; but nothing could damp his zeal. Acadia must become a new France, and he, Poutrincourt, must be its father. He gained from the King a confirmation of his grant, and, to supply the lack of his own weakened resources, associated with himself one Robin, a man of family and wealth. This did not save him from a host of delays and vexations; and it was not until the spring of 1610 that he found himself in a condition to embark on his new and doubtful venture.

Meanwhile an influence, of sinister omen as he thought, had begun to act upon his schemes. The Jesuits were strong at court. One of their number, the famous Father Coton, was confessor to Henry the Fourth, and, on matters of this world as of the next, was ever whispering at the facile ear of the renegade King. New France offered a fresh field of action to the indefatigable Society of Jesus, and Coton urged upon the royal convert, that, for the saving of souls, some of its members should be attached to the proposed enterprise. The King, profoundly indifferent in matters of religion, saw no evil in a proposal which at least promised to place the Atlantic betwixt him and some of those busy friends whom at heart he deeply mistrusted. Other influences, too, seconded the confessor. Devout ladies of the court, and the Queen herself, supplying the lack of virtue with an overflowing piety, burned, we are assured, with a holy zeal for snatching the tribes of the West from the bondage of Satan. Therefore it was insisted that the projected colony should combine the spiritual with the temporal character,—or, in other words, that Poutrincourt should take Jesuits with him. Pierre Biard, Professor of Theology at Lyons, was named for the mission, and repaired in haste to Bordeaux, the port of embarkation, where he found no vessel, and no sign of preparation; and here, in wrath and discomfiture, he remained for a whole year.

That Poutrincourt was a good Catholic appears from a letter to the Pope, written for him in Latin by Lescarbot, asking a blessing on his enterprise, and assuring his Holiness that one of his grand objects was the saving of souls. But, like other good citizens, he belonged to the national party in the Church, those liberal Catholics, who, side by side with the Huguenots, had made head against the League, with its Spanish allies, and placed Henry the Fourth upon the throne. The Jesuits, an order Spanish in origin and policy, determined champions of ultramontane principles, the sword and shield of the Papacy in its broadest pretensions to spiritual and temporal sway, were to him, as to others of his party, objects of deep dislike and distrust. He feared them in his colony, evaded what he dared not refuse, left Biarci waiting in solitude at Bordeax, and sought to postpone the evil day by assuring Father Coton that, though Port Royal was at present in no state to receive the missionaries, preparation should be made to entertain them the next year after a befitting fashion.

Poutrincourt owned the barony of St. Just in Champagne, inherited a few years before from his mother. Hence, early in February, 1610, he set out in a boat loaded to the gunwales with provisions, furniture, goods, and munitions for Port Royal, descended the rivers Aube and Seine, and reached Dieppe safely with his charge. Here his ship was awaiting him; and on the twenty-sixth of February he set sail, giving the slip to the indignant Jesuit at Bordeaux.

The tedium of a long passage was unpleasantly broken by a mutiny among the crew. It was suppressed, however, and Poutrincourt entered at length the familiar basin of Port Royal. The buildings were still standing, whole and sound save a partial falling in of the roofs. Even furniture was found untouched in the deserted chambers. The centenarian Membertou was still alive, his leathern, wrinkled visage beaming with welcome.

Pontrincourt set himself without delay to the task of Christianizing New France, in an access of zeal which his desire of proving that Jesuit aid was superfluous may be supposed largely to have reinforced. He had a priest with him, one La Fleche, whom he urged to the pious work. No time was lost. Membertou first was catechised, confessed his sins, and renounced the Devil, whom we are told he had faithfully served during a hundred and ten years.

His squaws, his children, his grandchildren, and his entire clan were next won over. It was in June, the day of St. John the Baptist, when the naked proselytes, twenty-one in number, were gathered on the shore at Port Royal. Here was the priest in the vestments of his office; here were gentlemen in gay attire, soldiers, laborers, lackeys, all the infant colony. The converts kneeled; the sacred rite was finished, Te Deum was sung, and the roar of cannon proclaimed this triumph over the powers of darkness. Membertou was named Henri, after the King; his principal squaw, Marie, after the Queen. One of his sons received the name of the Pope, another that of the Dauphin; his daughter was called Marguerite, after the divorced Marguerite de Valois, and, in like manner, the rest of the squalid company exchanged their barbaric appellatives for the names of princes, nobles, and ladies of rank.

The fame of this chef-d'aeuvre of Christian piety, as Lescarbot gravely calls it, spread far and wide through the forest, whose denizens,—partly out of a notion that the rite would bring good luck, partly to please the French, and partly to share in the good cheer with which the apostolic efforts of Father La Fleche had been sagaciously seconded—came flocking to enroll themselves under the banners of the Faith. Their zeal ran high. They would take no refusal. Membertou was for war on all who would not turn Christian. A living skeleton was seen crawling from hut to hut in search of the priest and his saving waters; while another neophyte, at the point of death, asked anxiously whether, in the realms of bliss to which he was bound, pies were to be had comparable to those with which the French regaled him.

A formal register of baptisms was drawn up to be carried to France in the returning ship, of which Pontrincourt's son, Biencourt, a spirited youth of eighteen, was to take charge. He sailed in July, his father keeping him company as far as Port la Have, whence, bidding the young man farewell, he attempted to return in an open boat to Port Royal. A north wind blew him out to sea; and for six days he was out of sight of land, subsisting on rain-water wrung from the boat's sail, and on a few wild-fowl which he had shot on an island. Five weeks passed before he could rejoin his colonists, who, despairing of his safety, were about to choose a new chief.

Meanwhile, young Biencourt, speeding on his way, heard dire news from a fisherman on the Grand Bank. The knife of Ravaillac had done its work. Henry the Fourth was dead.

There is an ancient street in Paris, where a great thoroughfare contracts to a narrow pass, the Rue de la Ferronnerie. Tall buildings overshadow it, packed from pavement to tiles with human life, and from the dingy front of one of them the sculptured head of a man looks down on the throng that ceaselessly defiles beneath. On the fourteenth of May, 1610, a ponderous coach, studded with fleurs-de-lis and rich with gilding, rolled along this street. In it was a small man, well advanced in life, whose profile once seen could not be forgotten,—a hooked nose, a protruding chin, a brow full of wrinkles, grizzled hair, a short, grizzled beard, and stiff, gray moustaches, bristling like a cat's. One would have thought him some whiskered satyr, grim from the rack of tumultuous years; but his alert, upright port bespoke unshaken vigor, and his clear eye was full of buoyant life. Following on the footway strode a tall, strong, and somewhat corpulent man, with sinister, deep-set eyes and a red beard, his arm and shoulder covered with his cloak. In the throat of the thoroughfare, where the sculptured image of Henry the Fourth still guards the spot, a collision of two carts stopped the coach. Ravaillac quickened his pace. In an instant he was at the door. With his cloak dropped from his shoulders, and a long knife in his hand, he set his foot upon a guardstone, thrust his head and shoulders into the coach, and with frantic force stabbed thrice at the King's heart. A broken exclamation, a gasping convulsion,—and then the grim visage drooped on the bleeding breast. Henry breathed his last, and the hope of Europe died with him.

The omens were sinister for Old France and for New. Marie de Medicis, "cette grosse banquiere," coarse scion of a bad stock, false wife and faithless queen, paramour of an intriguing foreigner, tool of the Jesuits and of Spain, was Regent in the minority of her imbecile son. The Huguenots drooped, the national party collapsed, the vigorous hand of Sully was felt no more, and the treasure gathered for a vast and beneficent enterprise became the instrument of despotism and the prey of corruption. Under such dark auspices, young Biencourt entered the thronged chambers of the Louvre.

He gained audience of the Queen, and displayed his list of baptisms; while the ever present Jesuits failed not to seize him by the button, assuring him, not only that the late King had deeply at heart the establishment of their Society in Acadia, but that to this end he had made them a grant of two thousand livres a year. The Jesuits had found an ally and the intended mission a friend at court, whose story and whose character are too striking to pass unnoticed.

This was a lady of honor to the Queen, Antoinette de Pons, Marquise de Guercheville, once renowned for grace and beauty, and not less conspicuous for qualities rare in the unbridled court of Henry's predecessor, where her youth had been passed. When the civil war was at its height, the royal heart, leaping with insatiable restlessness from battle to battle, from mistress to mistress, had found a brief repose in the affections of his Corisande, famed in tradition and romance; but Corisande was suddenly abandoned, and the young widow, Madame de Guercheville, became the load-star of his erratic fancy. It was an evil hour for the Bearnais. Henry sheathed in rusty steel, battling for his crown and his life, and Henry robed in royalty and throned triumphant in the Louvre, alike urged their suit in vain. Unused to defeat, the King's passion rose higher for the obstacle that barred it. On one occasion he was met with an answer not unworthy of record:—

"Sire, my rank, perhaps, is not high enough to permit me to be your wife, but my heart is too high to permit me to be your mistress."

She left the court and retired to her chateau of La Roche-Guyon, on the Seine, ten leagues below Paris, where, fond of magnificence, she is said to have lived in much expense and splendor. The indefatigable King, haunted by her memory, made a hunting-party in the neighboring forests; and, as evening drew near, separating himself from his courtiers, he sent a gentleman of his train to ask of Madame de Guercheville the shelter of her roof. The reply conveyed a dutiful acknowledgment of the honor, and an offer of the best entertainment within her power. It was night when Henry with his little band of horsemen, approached the chateau, where lights were burning in every window, after a fashion of the day on occasions of welcome to an honored guest. Pages stood in the gateway, each with a blazing torch; and here, too, were gentlemen of the neighborhood, gathered to greet their sovereign. Madame de Guercheville came forth, followed by the women of her household; and when the King, unprepared for so benign a welcome, giddy with love and hope, saw her radiant in pearls and more radiant yet in a beauty enhanced by the wavy torchlight and the surrounding shadows, he scarcely dared trust his senses:—

"Que vois-je, madame; est-ce bien vous, et suis-je ce roi meprise?"

He gave her his hand, and she led him within the chateau, where, at the door of the apartment destined for him, she left him, with a graceful reverence. The King, nowise disconcerted, did not doubt that she had gone to give orders for his entertainment, when an attendant came to tell him that she had descended to the courtyard and called for her coach. Thither he hastened in alarm:

"What! am I driving you from your house?"

"Sire," replied Madame de Guercheville, "where a king is, he should be the sole master; but, for my part, I like to preserve some little authority wherever I may be."

With another deep reverence, she entered her coach and disappeared, seeking shelter under the roof of a friend, some two leagues off, and leaving the baffled King to such consolation as he might find in a magnificent repast, bereft of the presence of the hostess.

Henry could admire the virtue which he could not vanquish; and, long after, on his marriage, he acknowledged his sense of her worth by begging her to accept an honorable post near the person of the Queen.

"Madame," he said, presenting her to Marie de Medicis, "I give you a lady of honor who is a lady of honor indeed."

Some twenty years had passed since the adventure of La Roche-Guyon. Madame de Guercheville had outlived the charms which had attracted her royal suitor, but the virtue which repelled him was reinforced by a devotion no less uncompromising. A rosary in her hand and a Jesuit at her side, she realized the utmost wishes of the subtle fathers who had moulded and who guided her. She readily took fire when they told her of the benighted souls of New France, and the wrongs of Father Biard kindled her utmost indignation. She declared herself the protectress of the American missions; and the only difficulty, as a Jesuit writer tells us, was to restrain her zeal within reasonable bounds.

She had two illustrious coadjutors. The first was the jealous Queen, whose unbridled rage and vulgar clamor had made the Louvre a hell. The second was Henriette d'Entragues, Marquise de Vernenil, the crafty and capricious siren who had awakened these conjugal tempests. To this singular coalition were joined many other ladies of the court; for the pious flame, fanned by the Jesuits, spread through hall and boudoir, and fair votaries of the Loves and Graces found it a more grateful task to win heaven for the heathen than to merit it for themselves.

Young Biencourt saw it vain to resist. Biard must go with him in the returning ship, and also another Jesuit, Enemond Masse. The two fathers repaired to Dieppe, wafted on the wind of court favor, which they never doubted would bear them to their journey s end. Not so, however. Poutrincourt and his associates, in the dearth of their own resources, had bargained with two Huguenot merchants of Dieppe, Du Jardin and Du Quesne, to equip and load the vessel, in consideration of their becoming partners in the expected profits. Their indignation was extreme when they saw the intended passengers. They declared that they would not aid in building up a colony for the profit of the King of Spain, nor risk their money in a venture where Jesuits were allowed to intermeddle; and they closed with a fiat refusal to receive them on board, unless, they added with patriotic sarcasm, the Queen would direct them to transport the whole order beyond sea. Biard and Masse insisted, on which the merchants demanded reimbursement for their outlay, as they would have no further concern in the business.

Biard communicated with Father Coton, Father Coton with Madame de Guercheville. No more was needed. The zealous lady of honor, "indignant," says Biard, "to see the efforts of hell prevail," and resolved "that Satan should not remain master of the field," set on foot a subscription, and raised an ample fund within the precincts of the court. Biard, in the name of the "Province of France of the Order of Jesus," bought out the interest of the two merchants for thirty-eight hundred livres, thus constituting the Jesuits equal partners in business with their enemies. Nor was this all; for, out of the ample proceeds of the subscription, he lent to the needy associates a further sum of seven hundred and thirty-seven livres, and advanced twelve hundred and twenty-five more to complete the outfit of the ship. Well pleased, the triumphant priests now embarked, and friend and foe set sail together on the twenty-sixth of January, 1611.

CHAPTER VI.
1611, 1612.
JESUITS IN ACADIA.

The voyage was one of inordinate length,—beset, too, with icebergs, larger and taller, according to the Jesuit voyagers, than the Church of Notre Dame; but on the day of Pentecost their ship, "The Grace of God," anchored before Port Royal. Then first were seen in the wilderness of New France the close black cap, the close black robe, of the Jesuit father, and the features seamed with study and thought and discipline. Then first did this mighty Proteus, this many-colored Society of Jesus, enter upon that rude field of toil and woe, where, in after years, the devoted zeal of its apostles was to lend dignity to their order and do honor to humanity.

Few were the regions of the known world to which the potent brotherhood had not stretched the vast network of its influence. Jesuits had disputed in theology with the bonzes of Japan, and taught astronomy to the mandarins of China; had wrought prodigies of sudden conversion among the followers of Bralinra, preached the papal supremacy to Abyssinian schismatics, carried the cross among the savages of Caffraria, wrought reputed miracles in Brazil, and gathered the tribes of Paraguay beneath their paternal sway. And now, with the aid of the Virgin and her votary at court, they would build another empire among the tribes of New France. The omens were sinister and the outset was unpropitious. The Society was destined to reap few laurels from the brief apostleship of Biard and Masse.

When the voyagers landed, they found at Port Royal a band of half-famished men, eagerly expecting their succor. The voyage of four months had, however, nearly exhausted their own very moderate stock of provisions, and the mutual congratulations of the old colonists and the new were damped by a vision of starvation. A friction, too, speedily declared itself between the spiritual and the temporal powers. Pontgrave's son, then trading on the coast, had exasperated the Indians by an outrage on one of their women, and, dreading the wrath of Poutrincourt, had fled to the woods. Biard saw fit to take his part, remonstrated for him with vehemence, gained his pardon, received his confession, and absolved him. The Jesuit says that he was treated with great consideration by Poutrincourt, and that he should be forever beholden to him. The latter, however, chafed at Biard's interference.

"Father," he said, "I know my duty, and I beg you will leave me to do it. I, with my sword, have hopes of paradise, as well as you with your breviary. Show me my path to heaven. I will show you yours on earth."

He soon set sail for France, leaving his son Biencourt in charge. This hardy young sailor, of ability and character beyond his years, had, on his visit to court, received the post of Vice-Admiral in the seas of New France, and in this capacity had a certain authority over the trading-vessels of St. Malo and Rochelle, several of which were upon the coast. To compel the recognition of this authority, and also to purchase provisions, he set out along with Biard in a boat filled with armed followers. His first collision was with young Pontgrave, who with a few men had built a trading-hut on the St. John, where he proposed to winter. Meeting with resistance, Biencourt took the whole party prisoners, in spite of the remonstrances of Biard. Next, proceeding along the coast, he levied tribute on four or five traders wintering at St. Croix, and, continuing his course to the Kennebec, found the Indians of that region greatly enraged at the conduct of certain English adventurers, who three or four years before had, as they said, set dogs upon them and otherwise maltreated them. These were the colonists under Popham and Gilbert, who in 1607 and 1608 made an abortive attempt to settle near the mouth of the river. Nothing now was left of them but their deserted fort. The neighboring Indians were Abenakis, one of the tribes included by the French under the general name of Armouchiquois. Their disposition was doubtful, and it needed all the coolness of young Biencourt to avoid a fatal collision. On one occasion a curious incident took place. The French met six canoes full of warriors descending the Kennebec, and, as neither party trusted the other, the two encamped on opposite banks of the river. In the evening the Indians began to sing and dance. Biard suspected these proceedings to be an invocation of the Devil, and "in order," he says, "to thwart this accursed tyrant, I made our people sing a few church hymns, such as the Salve, the Ave Mans Stella, and others.

But being once in train, and getting to the end of their spiritual songs, they fell to singing such others as they knew, and when these gave out they took to mimicking the dancing and singing of the Armouchiquois on the other side of the water; and as Frenchmen are naturally good mimics, they did it so well that the Armouchiquois stopped to listen; at which our people stopped too; and then the Indians began again. You would have laughed to hear them, for they were like two choirs answering each other in concert, and you would hardly have known the real Armouchiquois from the sham ones."

Before the capture of young Pontgrave, Biard made him a visit at his camp, six leagues up the St. John. Pontgrave's men were sailors from St. Malo, between whom and the other Frenchmen there was much ill blood, Biard had hardly entered the river when he saw the evening sky crimsoned with the dancing fires of a superb aurora borealis, and he and his attendants marvelled what evil thing the prodigy might portend. Their Indian companions said that it was a sign of war. In fact, the night after they had joined Pontgrave a furious quarrel broke out in the camp, with abundant shouting, gesticulating and swearing; and, says the father, "I do not doubt that an accursed band of furious and sanguinary spirits were hovering about us all night, expecting every moment to see a horrible massacre of the few Christians in those parts; but the goodness of God bridled their malice. No blood was shed, and on the next day the squall ended in a fine calm."

He did not like the Indians, whom he describes as "lazy, gluttonous, irreligious, treacherous, cruel, and licentious." He makes an exception in favor of Memberton, whom he calls "the greatest, most renowned, and most redoubted savage that ever lived in the memory of man," and especially commends him for contenting himself with but one wife, hardly a superlative merit in a centenarian. Biard taught him to say the Lord's Prayer, though at the petition, "Give us this clay our daily bread," the chief remonstrated, saying, "If I ask for nothing but bread, I shall get no fish or moose meat." His protracted career was now drawing to a close, and, being brought to the settlement in a dying state, he was placed in Biard's bed and attended by the two Jesuits. He was as remarkable in person as in character, for he was bearded like a Frenchman. Though, alone among La Fleche's converts, the Faith seemed to have left some impression upon him, he insisted on being buried with his heathen forefathers, but was persuaded to forego a wish fatal to his salvation, and slept at last in consecrated ground.

Another of the scanty fruits of the mission was a little girl on the point of death, whom Biard had asked her parents to give him for baptism. "Take her and keep her, if you like," was the reply, "for she is no better than a dead dog." "We accepted the offer," says Biard, "in order to show them the difference between Christianity and their impiety; and after giving her what care we could, together with some instruction, we baptized her. We named her after Madame the Marquise de Guercheville, in gratitude for the benefits we have received from that lady, who can now rejoice that her name is already in heaven; for, a few days after baptism, the chosen soul flew to that place of glory."

Biard's greatest difficulty was with the Micmac language. Young Biencourt was his best interpreter, and on common occasions served him well; but the moment that religion was in question he was, as it were, stricken dumb,—the reason being that the language was totally without abstract terms. Biard resolutely set himself to the study of it,—a hard and thorny path, on which he made small progress, and often went astray. Seated, pencil in hand, before some Indian squatting on the floor, whom with the bribe of a mouldy biscuit he had lured into the hut, he plied him with questions which he often neither would nor could answer. What was the Indian word for Faith, Hope, Charity, Sacrament, Baptism, Eucharist, Trinity, Incarnation? The perplexed savage, willing to amuse himself, and impelled, as Biard thinks, by the Devil, gave him scurrilous and unseemly phrases as the equivalent of things holy, which, studiously incorporated into the father's Indian catechism, produced on his pupils an effect the reverse of that intended. Biard's colleague, Masse, was equally zealous, and still less fortunate. He tried a forest life among the Indians 'with signal ill success. Hard fare, smoke, filth, the scolding of squaws, and the cries of children reduced him to a forlorn condition of body and mind, wore him to a skeleton, and sent him back to Port Royal without a single convert.

The dark months wore slowly on. A band of half-famished men gathered about the huge fires of their barn-like hall, moody, sullen, and quarrelsome. Discord was here in the black robe of the Jesuit and the brown capote of the rival trader. The position of the wretched little colony may well provoke reflection. Here lay the shaggy continent, from Florida to the Pole, outstretched in savage slumber along the sea, the stern domain of Nature,—or, to adopt the ready solution of the Jesuits, a realm of the powers of night, blasted beneath the sceptre of hell. On the banks of James River was a nest of woe-begone Englishmen, a handful of Dutch fur-traders at the mouth of the Hudson, and a few shivering Frenchmen among the snow-drifts of Acadia; while deep within the wild monotony of desolation, on the icy verge of the great northern river, the hand of Champlain upheld the fleur-de-lis on the rock of Quebec. These were the advance guard, the forlorn hope of civilization, messengers of promise to a desert continent. Yet, unconscious of their high function, not content with inevitable woes, they were rent by petty jealousies and miserable feuds; while each of these detached fragments of rival nationalities, scarcely able to maintain its own wretched existence on a few square miles, begrudged to the others the smallest share in a domain which all the nations of Europe could hardly have sufficed to fill.

One evening, as the forlorn tenants of Port Royal sat together disconsolate, Biard was seized with a spirit of prophecy. He called upon Biencourt to serve out the little of wine that remained,—a proposal which met with high favor from the company present, though apparently with none from the youthful Vice-Admiral. The wine was ordered, however, and, as an unwonted cheer ran round the circle, the Jesuit announced that an inward voice told him how, within a month, they should see a ship from France. In truth, they saw one within a week. On the twentythird of January, 1612, arrived a small vessel laden with a moderate store of provisions and abundant seeds of future strife.

This was the expected succor sent by Poutrincourt. A series of ruinous voyages had exhausted his resources but he had staked all on the success of the colony, had even brought his family to Acadia, and he would not leave them and his companions to perish. His credit was gone; his hopes were dashed; yet assistance was proffered, and, in his extremity, he was forced to accept it. It came from Madame de Guercheville and her Jesuit advisers. She offered to buy the interest of a thousand crowns in the enterprise.

The ill-omened succor could not be refused; but this was not all. The zealous protectress of the missions obtained from De Monts, whose fortunes, like those of Poutrincouirt, had ebbed low, a transfer of all his claims to the lands of Acadia; while the young King, Louis the Thirteenth, was persuaded to give her, in addition, a new grant of all the territory of North America, from the St. Lawrence to Florida. Thus did Madame de Guercheville, or in other words, the Jesuits who used her name as a cover, become proprietors of the greater part of the future United States and British Provinces. The English colony of Virginia and the Dutch trading-houses of New York were included within the limits of this destined Northern Paraguay; while Port Royal, the seigniory of the unfortunate Poutrincourt, was encompassed, like a petty island, by the vast domain of the Society of Jesus. They could not deprive him of it, since his title had been confirmed by the late King, but they flattered themselves, to borrow their own language, that he would be "confined as in a prison." His grant, however, had been vaguely worded, and, while they held him restricted to an insignificant patch of ground, he claimed lordship over a wide and indefinite territory. Here was argument for endless strife. Other interests, too, were adverse. Poutrincourt, in his discouragement, had abandoned his plan of liberal colonization, and now thought of nothing but beaver-skins. He wished to make a trading-post; the Jesuits wished to make a mission.

When the vessel anchored before Port Royal, Biencourt, with disgust and anger, saw another Jesuit landed at the pier. This was Gilbert du Thet, a lay brother, versed in affairs of this world, who had come out as representative and administrator of Madame de Guercheville. Poutrincourt, also, had his agent on board; and, without the loss of a day, the two began to quarrel. A truce ensued; then a smothered feud, pervading the whole colony, and ending in a notable explosion. The Jesuits, chafing under the sway of Biencourt, had withdrawn without ceremony, and betaken themselves to the vessel, intending to sail for France. Biencourt, exasperated at such a breach of discipline, and fearing their representations at court, ordered them to return, adding that, since the Queen had commended them to his especial care, he could not, in conscience, lose sight of them. The indignant fathers excommunicated him. On this, the sagamore Louis, son of the grisly convert Membertou, begged leave to kill them; but Biencourt

- 174 -

would not countenance this summary mode of relieving his embarrassment. He again, in the King's name, ordered the clerical mutineers to return to the fort. Biard declared that he would not, threatened to excommunicate any who should lay hand on him, and called the Vice-Admiral a robber. His wrath, however, soon cooled; he yielded to necessity, and came quietly ashore, where, for the next three months, neither he nor his colleagues would say mass, or perform any office of religion. At length a change came over him; he made advances of peace, prayed that the past might be forgotten, said mass again, and closed with a petition that Brother du Thet might be allowed to go to France in a trading vessel then on the coast. His petition being granted, he wrote to Poutrincourt a letter overflowing with praises of his son; and, charged with this missive, Du Thet set sail.

CHAPTER VII.
1613.
LA SAUSSAYE.—ARGALL

Pending these squabbles, the Jesuits at home were far from idle. Bent on ridding themselves of Poutrincourt, they seized, in satisfaction of debts due them, all the cargo of his returning vessel, and involved him in a network of litigation. If we accept his own statements in a letter to his friend Lescarbot, he was outrageously misused, and indeed defrauded, by his clerical copartners, who at length had him thrown into prison. Here, exasperated, weary, sick of Acadia, and anxious for the wretched exiles who looked to him for succor, the unfortunate man fell ill. Regaining his liberty, he again addressed himself with what strength remained to the forlorn task of sending relief to his son and his comrades.

Scarcely had Brother Gilbert du Thet arrived in France, when Madame de Guercheville and her Jesuits, strong in court favor and in the charity of wealthy penitents, prepared to take possession of their empire beyond sea. Contributions were asked, and not in vain; for the sagacious fathers, mindful of every spring of influence, had deeply studied the mazes of feminine psychology, and then, as now, were favorite confessors of the fair. It was on the twelfth of March, 1613, that the "Mayflower" of the Jesuits sailed from Honfleur for the shores of New England. She was the "Jonas," formerly in the service of De Monts, a small craft bearing forty-eight sailors and colonists, including two Jesuits, Father Quentin and Brother Du Thet. She carried horses, too, and goats, and was abundantly stored with all things needful by the pious munificence of her patrons. A courtier named La Saussaye was chief of the colony, Captain Charles Fleury commanded the ship, and, as she winged her way across the Atlantic, benedictions hovered over her from lordly halls and perfumed chambers.

On the sixteenth of May, La Saussaye touched at La Heve, where he heard mass, planted a cross, and displayed the scutcheon of Madame de Guercheville. Thence, passing on to Port Royal, he found Biard, Masse, their servant-boy, an apothecary, and one man beside. Biencourt and his followers were scattered about the woods and shores, digging the tuberous roots called ground-nuts, catching alewives in the brooks, and by similar expedients sustaining their miserable existence. Taking the two Jesuits on board, the voyagers steered for the Penobscot. A fog rose upon the sea. They sailed to and fro, groping their way in blindness, straining their eyes through the mist, and trembling each instant lest they should descry the black outline of some deadly reef and the ghostly death-dance of the breakers, But Heaven heard their prayers. At night they could see the stars. The sun rose resplendent on a laughing sea, and his morning beams streamed fair and full on the wild heights of the island of Mount Desert. They entered a bay that stretched inland between iron-bound shores, and gave it the name of St. Sauveur. It is now called Frenchman's Bay. They saw a coast-line of weather-beaten crags set thick with spruce and fir, the surf-washed cliffs of Great Head and Schooner Head, the rocky front of Newport Mountain, patched with ragged woods, the arid domes of Dry Mountain and Green Mountain, the round bristly backs of the Porcupine Islands, and the waving outline of the Gouldsborough Hills.

La Saussaye cast anchor not far from Schooner Head, and here he lay till evening. The jet-black shade betwixt crags and sea, the pines along the cliff, pencilled against the fiery sunset, the dreamy slumber of distant mountains bathed in shadowy purples—such is the scene that in this our day greets the wandering artist, the roving collegian bivouacked on the shore, or the pilgrim from stifled cities renewing his laded strength in the mighty life of Nature. Perhaps they then greeted the adventurous Frenchmen. There was peace on the wilderness and peace on the sea; but none in this missionary bark, pioneer of Christianity and civilization. A rabble of angry sailors clamored on her deck, ready to mutiny over the terms of their engagement. Should the time of their stay be reckoned from their landing at La Heve, or from their anchoring at Mount Desert? Fleury, the naval commander, took their part. Sailor, courtier, and priest gave tongue together in vociferous debate. Poutrincourt was far away, a ruined man, and the intractable Vice-Admiral had ceased from troubling; yet not the less were the omens of the pious enterprise sinister and dark. The company, however, went ashore, raised a cross, and heard mass.

At a distance in the woods they saw the signal smoke of Indians, whom Biard lost no time in visiting. Some of them were from a village on the shore, three leagues westward. They urged the French to go with them to their wigwams. The astute savages had learned already how to deal with a Jesuit.

"Our great chief, Asticou, is there. He wishes for baptism. He is very sick. He will die unbaptized. He will burn in hell, and it will be all your fault."

This was enough. Biard embarked in a canoe, and they paddled him to the spot, where he found the great chief, Asticou, in his wigwam, with a heavy cold in the head. Disappointed of his charitable purpose, the priest consoled himself with observing the beauties of the neighboring shore, which seemed to him better fitted than St. Sauveur for the intended settlement. It was a gentle slope, descending to the water, covered with tall grass, and backed by rocky hills. It looked southeast upon a harbor where a fleet might ride at anchor, sheltered from the gales by a cluster of islands.

The ship was brought to the spot, and the colonists disembarked. First they planted a cross; then they began their labors, and with their labors their quarrels. La Saussaye, zealous for agriculture, wished to break ground and raise crops immediately; the rest opposed him, wishing first to be housed and fortified. Fleury demanded that the ship should be unladen, and La Saussaye would not consent. Debate ran high, when suddenly all was harmony, and the disputants were friends once more in the pacification of a common danger.

Far out at sea, beyond the islands that sheltered their harbor, they saw an approaching sail; and as she drew near, straining their anxious eyes, they could descry the red flags that streamed from her masthead and her stern; then the black muzzles of her cannon,—they counted seven on a side; then the throng of men upon her decks. The wind was brisk and fair; all her sails were set; she came on, writes a spectator, more swiftly than an arrow.

Six years before, in 1607, the ships of Captain Newport had conveyed to the banks of James River the first vital germ of English colonization on the continent. Noble and wealthy speculators with Hispaniola, Mexico, and Peru for their inspiration, had combined to gather the fancied golden harvest of Virginia, received a charter from the Crown, and taken possession of their

El Dorado. From tavern, gaming-house, and brothel was drawn the staple the colony,—ruined gentlemen, prodigal sons, disreputable retainers, debauched tradesmen. Yet it would be foul slander to affirm that the founders of Virginia were all of this stamp; for among the riotous crew were men of worth, and, above them all, a hero disguised by the homeliest of names. Again and again, in direst woe and jeopardy, the infant settlement owed its life to the heart and hand of John Smith.

Several years had elapsed since Newport's voyage; and the colony, depleted by famine, disease, and an Indian war, had been recruited by fresh emigration, when one Samuel Argall arrived at Jamestown, captain of an illicit trading-vessel. He was a man of ability and force,—one of those compounds of craft and daring in which the age was fruitful; for the rest, unscrupulous and grasping. In the spring of 1613 he achieved a characteristic exploit,—the abduction of Pocahontas, that most interesting of young squaws, or, to borrow the style of the day, of Indian princesses. Sailing up the Potomac he lured her on board his ship, and then carried off the benefactress of the colony a prisoner to Jamestown. Here a young man of family, Rolfe, became enamoured of her, married her with more than ordinary ceremony, and thus secured a firm alliance between her tribesmen and the English.

Meanwhile Argall had set forth on another enterprise. With a ship of one hundred and thirty tons, carrying fourteen guns and sixty men, he sailed in May for islands off the coast of Maine to fish, as he says for cod. He had a more important errand; for Sir Thomas Dale, Governor of Virginia, had commissioned him to expel the French from any settlement they might have made within the limits of King James's patents. Thick fogs involved him; and when the weather cleared he found himself not far from the Bay of Penobscot. Canoes came out from shore; the Indians climbed the ship's side, and, as they gained the deck, greeted the astonished English with an odd pantomime of bows and flourishes, which, in the belief of the latter, could have been learned from none but Frenchmen. By signs, too, and by often repeating the word Norman,—by which they always designated the French,—they betrayed the presence of the latter. Argall questioned them as well as his total ignorance of their language would permit, and learned, by signs, the position and numbers of the colonists. Clearly they were no match for him. Assuring the Indians that the Normans were his friends, and that he longed to see them, he retained one of the visitors as a guide, dismissed the rest with presents, and shaped his course for Mount Desert.

Now the wild heights rose in view; now the English could see the masts of a small ship anchored in the sound; and now, as they rounded the islands, four white tents were visible on the grassy slope between the water and the woods. They were a gift from the Queen to Madame de Guercheville and her missionaries. Argall's men prepared for fight, while their Indian guide, amazed, broke into a howl of lamentation.

On shore all was confusion. Bailleul, the pilot, went to reconnoitre, and ended by hiding among the islands. La Saussaye lost presence of mind, and did nothing for defence. La Motte, his lieutenant, with Captain Fleury, an ensign, a sergeant, the Jesuit Du Thet, and a few of the bravest men, hastened on board the vessel, but had no time to cast loose her cables. Argall bore down on them, with a furious din of drums and trumpets, showed his broadside, and replied to their hail with a volley of cannon and musket shot. "Fire! Fire!" screamed Fleury. But there was no gunner to obey, till Du Thet seized and applied the match. "The cannon made as much noise as the enemy's," writes Biard; but, as the inexperienced artillerist forgot to aim the piece, no other result ensued. Another storm of musketry, and Brother Gilbert du Thet rolled helpless on the deck.

The French ship was mute. The English plied her for a time with shot, then lowered a boat and boarded. Under the awnings which covered her, dead and wounded men lay strewn about her deck, and among them the brave lay brother, smothering in his blood. He had his wish; for, on leaving France, he had prayed with uplifted hands that he might not return, but perish in that holy enterprise. Like the Order of which he was a humble member, he was a compound of qualities in appearance contradictory. La Motte, sword in hand, showed fight to the last, and won the esteem of his captors.

The English landed without meeting any show of resistance, and ranged at will among the tents, the piles of baggage and stores, and the buildings and defences newly begun. Argall asked for the commander, but La Saussaye had fled to the woods. The crafty Englishman seized his chests, caused the locks to be picked, searched till he found the royal letters and commissions, withdrew them, replaced everything else as he had found it, and again closed the lids. In the morning, La Saussaye, between the English and starvation, preferred the former, and issued from his hiding place. Argall received him with studious courtesy. That country, he said, belonged to his master, King James. Doubtless they had authority from their own sovereign for thus encroaching upon it; and, for his part, he was prepared to yield all respect to the commissions of the King of France, that the peace between the two nations might not be disturbed. Therefore he prayed that the commissions might be shown to him. La Saussaye opened his chests. The royal signature was nowhere to be found. At this, Argall's courtesy was changed to wrath. He denounced the Frenchmen as robbers and pirates who deserved the gallows, removed their property on board his ship, and spent the afternoon in dividing it among his followers, The disconsolate French remained on the scene of their woes, where the greedy sailors as they came ashore would snatch from them, now a cloak, now a hat, and now a doublet, till the unfortunate colonists were left half naked. In other respects the English treated their captives well,—except two of them, whom they flogged; and Argall, whom Biard, after recounting his knavery, calls "a gentleman of noble courage," having gained his point, returned to his former courtesy.

But how to dispose of the prisoners? Fifteen of them, including La Saussaye and the Jesuit Masse, were turned adrift in an open boat, at the mercy of the wilderness and the sea. Nearly all were lands-men; but while their unpractised hands were struggling with the oars, they were joined among the islands by the fugitive pilot and his boat's crew. Worn and half starved, the united bands made their perilous way eastward, stopping from time to time to hear mass, make a procession, or catch codfish. Thus sustained in the spirit and in the flesh, cheered too by the Indians, who proved fast friends in need, they crossed the Bay of Fundy, doubled Cape Sable, and followed the southern coast of Nova Scotia, till they happily fell in with two French trading-vessels, which bore them in safety to St. Malo.

CHAPTER VIII.
1613-1615.
RUIN OF FRENCH ACADIA.

"Praised be God, behold two thirds of our company safe in France, telling their strange adventures to their relatives and friends. And now you will wish to know what befell the rest of us." Thus writes Father Biard, who with his companions in misfortune, fourteen in all, prisoners on board Argall's ship and the prize, were borne captive to Virginia. Old Point Comfort was reached at length, the site of Fortress Monroe; Hampton Roads, renowned in our day for the sea-fight of the Titans; Sewell's Point; the Rip Raps; Newport News,—all household words in the ears of this generation. Now, far on their right, buried in the damp shade of immemorial verdure, lay, untrodden and voiceless, the fields where stretched the leaguering lines of Washington where the lilies of France floated beside the banners of the new-born republic, and where in later years embattled treason confronted the manhood of an outraged nation. And now before them they could descry the mast of small craft at anchor, a cluster of rude dwellings fresh from the axe, scattered tenements, and fields green with tobacco.

Throughout the voyage the prisoners had been soothed with flattering tales of the benignity of the Governor of Virginia, Sir Thomas Dale; of his love of the French, and his respect for the memory of Henry the Fourth, to whom, they were told, he was much beholden for countenance and favor. On their landing at Jamestown, this consoling picture was reversed. The Governor fumed and blustered, talked of halter and gallows, and declared that he would hang them all. In vain Argall remonstrated, urging that he had pledged his word for their lives. Dale, outraged by their invasion of British territory, was deaf to all appeals; till Argall, driven to extremity, displayed the stolen commissions, and proclaimed his stratagem, of which the French themselves had to that moment been ignorant. As they were accredited by their government, their lives at least were safe. Yet the wrath of Sir Thomas Dale still burned high. He summoned his council, and they resolved promptly to wipe off all stain of French intrusion from shores which King James claimed as his own.

Their action was utterly unauthorized. The two kingdoms were at peace. James the First, by the patents of 1606, had granted all North America, from the thirty-fourth to the forty-fifth degree of latitude, to the two companies of London and Plymouth,—Virginia being assigned to the former, while to the latter were given Maine and Acadia, with adjacent regions. Over these, though as yet the claimants had not taken possession of them, the authorities of Virginia had no color of jurisdiction. England claimed all North America, in virtue of the discovery of Cabot; and Sir Thomas Dale became the self-constituted champion of British rights, not the less zealous that his championship promised a harvest of booty.

Argall's ship, the captured ship of La Saussaye, and another smaller vessel, were at once equipped and despatched on their errand of havoc. Argall commanded; and Biard, with Quentin and several others of the prisoners, were embarked with him. They shaped their course first for Mount Desert. Here they landed, levelled La Saussaye's unfinished defences, cut down the French cross, and planted one of their own in its place. Next they sought out the island of St. Croix, seized a quantity of salt, and razed to the ground all that remained of the dilapidated buildings of De Monts. They crossed the Bay of Fundy to Port Royal, guided, says Biard, by an Indian chief,—an improbable assertion, since the natives of these coasts hated the English as much as they loved the French, and now well knew the designs of the former. The unfortunate settlement was tenantless. Biencourt, with some of his men, was on a visit to neighboring bands of Indians, while the rest were reaping in the fields on the river, two leagues above the fort. Succor from Poutrincourt had arrived during the summer. The magazines were by no means empty, and there were cattle, horses, and hogs in adjacent fields and enclosures. Exulting at their good fortune, Argall's men butchered or carried off the animals, ransacked the buildings, plundered them even to the locks and bolts of the doors, and then laid the whole in ashes; "and may it please the Lord," adds the pious Biard, "that the sins therein committed may likewise have been consumed in that burning."

Having demolished Port Royal, the marauders went in boats up the river to the fields where the reapers were at work. These fled, and took refuge behind the ridge of a hill, whence they gazed helplessly on the destruction of their harvest. Biard approached them, and, according to the declaration of Poutrincourt made and attested before the Admiralty of Guienne, tried to persuade them to desert his son, Biencourt, and take service with Argall. The reply of one of the men gave little encouragement for further parley:—

"Begone, or I will split your head with this hatchet."

There is flat contradiction here between the narrative of the Jesuit and the accounts of Poutrincourt and contemporary English writers, who agree in affirming that Biard, "out of indigestible malice that he had conceived against Biencourt," encouraged the attack on the settlements of St. Croix and Port Royal, and guided the English thither. The priest himself admits that both French and English regarded him as a traitor, and that his life was in danger. While Argall's ship was at anchor, a Frenchman shouted to the English from a distance that they would do well to kill him. The master of the ship, a Puritan, in his abomination of priests, and above all of Jesuits, was at the same time urging his commander to set Biard ashore and leave him to the mercy of his countrymen. In this pass he was saved, to adopt his own account, by what he calls his simplicity; for he tells us, that, while—instigated, like the rest of his enemies, by the Devil—the robber and the robbed were joining hands to ruin him, he was on his knees before Argall, begging him to take pity on the French, and leave them a boat, together with provisions to sustain their miserable lives through the winter. This spectacle of charity, he further says, so moved the noble heart of the commander, that he closed his ears to all the promptings of foreign and domestic malice.

The English had scarcely re-embarked, when Biencourt arrived with his followers, and beheld the scene of destruction. Hopelessly outnumbered, he tried to lure Argall and some of his officers into an ambuscade, but they would not be entrapped. Biencourt now asked for an interview. The word of honor was mutually given, and the two chiefs met in a meadow not far from the demolished dwellings. An anonymous English writer says that Biencourt offered to transfer his allegiance to King James, on condition of being permitted to remain at Port Royal and carry on the fur-trade under a guaranty of English protection, but that Argall would not listen to his overtures. The interview proved a stormy one. Biard says that the Frenchmen vomited against him every species of malignant abuse. "In the mean time," he adds, "you will considerately observe to what madness the evil spirit exciteth those who sell themselves to him."

According to Pontrincourt, Argall admitted that the priest had urged him to attack Port Royal. Certain it is that Biencourt demanded his surrender, frankly declaring that he meant to hang him. "Whilest they were discoursing together," says the old English writer above mentioned, "one of the savages, rushing suddenly forth from the Woods, and licentiated to come neere, did after his manner, with such broken French as he had, earnestly mediate a peace, wondring why they that seemed to be of one Country should vse others with such hostilitie, and that with such a forme of habit and gesture as made them both to laugh."

His work done, and, as he thought, the French settlements of Acadia effectually blotted out, Argall set sail for Virginia on the thirteenth of November. Scarcely was he at sea when a storm scattered the vessels. Of the smallest of the three nothing was ever heard. Argall, severely buffeted, reached his port in safety, having first, it is said, compelled the Dutch at Manhattan to acknowledge for a time the sovereignty of King James. The captured ship of La Saussaye, with Biard and his colleague Quentin on board, was forced to yield to the fury of the western gales and bear away for the Azores. To Biard the change of destination was not unwelcome. He stood in fear of the truculent Governor of Virginia, and his tempest-rocked slumbers were haunted with unpleasant visions of a rope's end. It seems that some of the French at Port Royal, disappointed in their hope of hanging him, had commended him to Sir Thomas Dale as a proper subject for the gallows drawing up a paper, signed by six of them, and containing allegations of a nature well fitted to kindle the wrath of that vehement official. The vessel was commanded by Turnel, Argall's lieutenant, apparently an officer of merit, a scholar and linguist. He had treated his prisoner with great kindness, because, says the latter, "he esteemed and loved him for his naive simplicity and ingenuous candor." But of late, thinking his kindness misplaced, he had changed it for an extreme coldness, preferring, in the words of Biard himself, "to think that the Jesuit had lied, rather than so many who accused him."

Water ran low, provisions began to fail, and they eked out their meagre supply by butchering the horses taken at Port Royal. At length they came within sight of Fayal, when a new terror seized the minds of the two Jesuits. Might not the Englishmen fear that their prisoners would denounce them to the fervent Catholics of that island as pirates and sacrilegious kidnappers of priests? From such hazard the escape was obvious. What more simple than to drop the priests into the sea? In truth, the English had no little dread of the results of conference between the Jesuits and the Portuguese authorities of Fayal; but the conscience or humanity of Turnel revolted at the expedient which awakened such apprehension in the troubled mind of Biard. He contented himself with requiring that the two priests should remain hidden while the ship lay off the port: Biard does not say that he enforced the demand either by threats or by the imposition of oaths. He and his companion, however, rigidly complied with it, lying close in the hold or under the boats, while suspicious officials searched the ship, a proof, he triumphantly declares, of the audacious malice which has asserted it as a tenet of Rome that no faith need be kept with heretics.

Once more at sea, Turnel shaped his course for home, having, with some difficulty, gained a supply of water and provisions at Fayal. All was now harmony between him and his prisoners. When he reached Pembroke, in Wales, the appearance of the vessel—a French craft in English hands—again drew upon him the suspicion of piracy. The Jesuits, dangerous witnesses among the Catholics of Fayal, could at the worst do little harm with the Vice-Admiral at Pembroke. To him, therefore, he led the prisoners, in the sable garb of their order, now much the worse for wear, and commended them as persons without reproach, "wherein," adds the modest father, "he spoke the truth." The result of their evidence was, we are told, that Turnel was henceforth treated, not as a pirate, but, according to his deserts, as an honorable gentleman. This interview led to a meeting with certain dignitaries of the Anglican Church, who, much interested in an encounter with Jesuits in their robes, were filled, says Biard, with wonder and admiration at what they were told of their conduct. He explains that these churchmen differ widely in form and doctrine from the English Calvinists, who, he says, are called Puritans; and he adds that they are superior in every respect to these, whom they detest as an execrable pest.

Biard was sent to Dover and thence to Calais, returning, perhaps, to the tranquil honors of his chair of theology at Lyons. La Saussaye, La Motte, Fleury, and other prisoners were at various times sent from Virginia to England, and ultimately to France. Madame de Guercheville, her pious designs crushed in the bud, seems to have gained no further satisfaction than the restoration of the vessel. The French ambassador complained of the outrage, but answer was postponed; and, in the troubled state of France, the matter appears to have been dropped.

Argall, whose violent and crafty character was offset by a gallant bearing and various traits of martial virtue, became Deputy-Governor of Virginia, and, under a military code, ruled the colony with a rod of iron. He enforced the observance of Sunday with an edifying rigor. Those who absented themselves from church were, for the first offence, imprisoned for the night, and reduced to slavery for a week; for the second offence, enslaved a month and for the third, a year. Nor was he less strenuous in his devotion to mammon. He enriched himself by extortion and wholesale peculation; and his audacious dexterity, aided by the countenance of the Earl of Warwick, who is said to have had a trading connection with him, thwarted all the efforts of the company to bring him to account. In 1623, he was knighted by the hand of King James.

Early in the spring following the English attack, Pontrincourt came to Port Royal. He found the place in ashes, and his unfortunate son, with the men under his command, wandering houseless in the forests. They had passed a winter of extreme misery, sustaining their wretched existence with roots, the buds of trees, and lichens peeled from the rocks.

Despairing of his enterprise, Poutrincourt returned to France. In the next year, 1615, during the civil disturbances which followed the marriage of the King, command was given him of the royal forces destined for the attack on Mery; and here, happier in his death than in his life, he fell, sword in hand.

In spite of their reverses, the French kept hold on Acadia. Biencourt, partially at least, rebuilt Port Royal; while winter after winter the smoke of fur traders' huts curled into the still, sharp air of these frosty wilds, till at length, with happier auspices, plans of settlement were resumed.

Rude hands strangled the "Northern Paraguay" in its birth. Its beginnings had been feeble, but behind were the forces of a mighty organization, at once devoted and ambitious, enthusiastic and calculating. Seven years later the "Mayflower" landed her emigrants at Plymouth. What would have been the issues had the zeal of the pious lady of honor preoccupied New England with a Jesuit colony?

In an obscure stroke of lawless violence began the strife of France and England, Protestantism and Rome, which for a century and a half shook the struggling communities of North America, and closed at last in the memorable triumph on the Plains of Abraham.

CHAPTER—IX.
1608, 1609.
CHAMPLAIN AT QUEBEC.

A LONELY ship sailed up the St. Lawrence. The white whales floundering in the Bay of Tadoussac, and the wild duck diving as the foaming prow drew near,—there was no life but these in all that watery solitude, twenty miles from shore to shore. The ship was from Honfleur, and was commanded by Samuel de Champlain. He was the AEneas of a destined people, and in her womb lay the embryo life of Canada.

De Monts, after his exclusive privilege of trade was revoked and his Acadian enterprise ruined, had, as we have seen, abandoned it to Poutrincourt. Perhaps would it have been well for him had he abandoned with it all Transatlantic enterprises; but the passion for discovery and the noble ambition of founding colonies had taken possession of his mind. These, rather than a mere hope of gain, seem to have been his controlling motives; yet the profits of the fur-trade were vital to the new designs he was meditating, to meet the heavy outlay they demanded, and he solicited and obtained a fresh monopoly of the traffic for one year.

Champlain was, at the time, in Paris; but his unquiet thoughts turned westward. He was enamoured of the New World, whose rugged charms had seized his fancy and his heart; and as explorers of Arctic seas have pined in their repose for polar ice and snow, so did his restless thoughts revert to the fog-wrapped coasts, the piny odors of forests, the noise of waters, the sharp and piercing sunlight, so dear to his remembrance. He longed to unveil the mystery of that boundless wilderness, and plant the Catholic faith and the power of France amid its ancient barbarism.

Five years before, he had explored the St. Lawrence as far as the rapids above Montreal. On its banks, as he thought, was the true site for a settlement,—a fortified post, whence, as from a secure basis, the waters of the vast interior might be traced back towards their sources, and a western route discovered to China and Japan. For the fur-trade, too, the innumerable streams that descended to the great river might all be closed against foreign intrusion by a single fort at some commanding point, and made tributary to a rich and permanent commerce; while—and this was nearer to his heart, for he had often been heard to say that the saving of a soul was worth more than the conquest of an empire—countless savage tribes, in the bondage of Satan, might by the same avenues be reached and redeemed.

De Monts embraced his views; and, fitting out two ships, gave command of one to the elder Pontgrave, of the other to Champlain. The former was to trade with the Indians and bring back the cargo of furs which, it was hoped, would meet the expense of the voyage. To Champlain fell the harder task of settlement and exploration.

Pontgrave, laden with goods for the Indian trade of Tadoussac sailed from Honfleur on the fifth of April, 1608. Champlain, with men, arms, and stores for the colony, followed, eight days later. On the fifteenth of May he was on the Grand Bank; on the thirtieth he passed Gaspe, and on the third of June neared Tadoussac. No living thing was to be seen. He anchored, lowered a boat, and rowed into the port, round the rocky point at the southeast, then, from the fury of its winds and currents, called La Pointe de Tous les Diables. There was life enough within, and more than he cared to find. In the still anchorage under the cliffs lay Pontgrave's vessel, and at her side another ship, which proved to be a Basque furtrader.

Poutgrave, arriving a few days before, had found himself anticipated by the Basques, who were busied in a brisk trade with bands of Indians cabined along the borders of the cove. He displayed the royal letters, and commanded a cessation of the prohibited traffic; but the Basques proved refractory, declared that they would trade in spite of the King, fired on Pontgrave with cannon and musketry, wounded him and two of his men, and killed a third. They then boarded his vessel, and carried away all his cannon, small arms, and ammunition, saying that they would restore them when they had finished their trade and were ready to return home.

Champlain found his comrade on shore, in a disabled condition. The Basques, though still strong enough to make fight, were alarmed for the consequences of their conduct, and anxious to come to terms. A peace, therefore, was signed on board their vessel; all differences were referred to the judgment of the French courts, harmony was restored, and the choleric strangers betook themselves to catching whales.

This port of Tadoussac was long the centre of the Canadian fur trade. A desolation of barren mountains closes round it, betwixt whose ribs of rugged granite, bristling with savins, birches, and firs, the Saguenay rolls its gloomy waters from the northern wilderness. Centuries of civilization have not tamed the wildness of the place; and still, in grim repose, the mountains hold their guard around the waveless lake that glistens in their shadow, and doubles, in its sullen mirror, crag, precipice, and forest.

Near the brink of the cove or harbor where the vessels lay, and a little below the mouth of a brook which formed one of the outlets of this small lake, stood the remains of the wooden barrack built by Chauvin eight years before. Above the brook were the lodges of an Indian camp,—stacks of poles covered with birch-bark. They belonged to an Algonquin horde, called Montagnais, denizens of surrounding wilds, and gatherers of their only harvest,—skins of the moose, caribou, and bear; fur of the beaver, marten, otter, fox, wild-cat, and lynx. Nor was this all, for there were intermediate traders betwixt the French and the shivering bands who roamed the weary stretch of stunted forest between the head-waters of the Saguenay and Hudson's Bay. Indefatigable canoe-men, in their birchen vessels, light as eggshells, they threaded the devious tracks of countless rippling streams, shady by-ways of the forest, where the wild duck scarcely finds depth to swim; then descended to their mart along those scenes of picturesque yet dreary grandeur which steam has made familiar to modern tourists. With slowly moving paddles they glided beneath the cliff whose shaggy brows frown across the zenith, and whose base the deep waves wash with a hoarse and hollow cadence; and they passed the sepulchral Bay of the Trinity, dark as the tide of Acheron,—a sanctuary of solitude and silence: depths which, as the fable runs, no sounding line can fathom, and heights at whose dizzy verge the wheeling eagle seems a speck.

Peace being established with the Basques, and the wounded Pontgrave busied, as far as might be, in transferring to the hold of his ship the rich lading of the Indian canoes, Champlain spread his sails, and again held his course up the St. Lawrence. Far to the south, in sun and shadow, slumbered the woody mountains whence fell the countless springs of the St. John, behind tenantless shores, now white with glimmering villages,—La Chenaic, Granville, Kamouraska, St. Roche, St. Jean, Vincelot, Berthier. But on the north the jealous wilderness still asserts its sway, crowding to the river's verge its walls, domes, and towers of granite; and, to this hour, its solitude is scarcely broken.

Above the point of the Island of Orleans, a constriction of the vast channel narrows it to less than a mile, with the green heights of Point Levi on one side, and on the other the cliffs of Quebec. Here, a small stream, the St. Charles, enters the St. Lawrence, and in the angle betwixt them rises the promontory on two sides a natural fortress. Between the cliffs and the river lay a strand covered with walnuts and other trees. From this strand, by a rough passage gullied downward from the place where Prescott Gate now guards the way, one might climb the height to the broken plateau above, now burdened with its ponderous load of churches, convents, dwellings, ramparts, and batteries. Thence, by a gradual ascent, the rock sloped upward to its highest summit, Cape Diamond, looking down on the St. Lawrence from a height of three hundred and fifty feet. Here the citadel now stands; then the fierce sun fell on the bald, baking rock, with its crisped mosses and parched lichens. Two centuries and a half have quickened the solitude with swarming life, covered the deep bosom of the river with barge and steamer and gliding sail, and reared cities and villages on the site of forests; but nothing can destroy the surpassing grandeur of the scene.

On the strand between the water and the cliffs Champlain's axemen fell to their work. They were pioneers of an advancing host,—advancing, it is true, with feeble and uncertain progress,— priests, soldiers, peasants, feudal scutcheons, royal insignia: not the Middle Age, but engendered of it by the stronger life of modern centralization, sharply stamped with a parental likeness, heir to parental weakness and parental force.

In a few weeks a pile of wooden buildings rose on the brink of the St. Lawrence, on or near the site of the marketplace of the Lower Town of Quebec. The pencil of Champlain, always regardless of proportion and perspective, has preserved its likeness. A strong wooden wall, surmounted by a gallery loop-holed for musketry, enclosed three buildings, containing quarters for himself and his men, together with a courtyard, from one side of which rose a tall dove-cot, like a belfry. A moat surrounded the whole, and two or three small cannon were planted on salient platforms towards the river. There was a large storehouse near at hand, and a part of the adjacent ground was laid out as a garden.

In this garden Champlain was one morning directing his laborers, when Tetu, his pilot, approached him with an anxious countenance, and muttered a request to speak with him in private. Champlain assenting, they withdrew to the neighboring woods, when the pilot disburdened himself of his secret. One Antoine Natel, a locksmith, smitten by conscience or fear, had revealed to him a conspiracy to murder his commander and deliver Quebec into the hands of the Basques and Spaniards then at Tadoussac. Another locksmith, named Duval, was author of the plot, and, with the aid of three accomplices, had befooled or frightened nearly all the company into taking part in it. Each was assured that he should make his fortune, and all were mutually pledged to poniard the first betrayer of the secret. The critical point of their enterprise was the killing of Champlain. Some were for strangling him, some for raising a false alarm in the night and shooting him as he came out from his quarters.

Having heard the pilot's story, Champlain, remaining in the woods, desired his informant to find Antoine Natel, and bring him to the spot. Natel soon appeared, trembling with excitement and fear, and a close examination left no doubt of the truth of his statement. A small vessel, built by Pontgrave at Tadoussac, had lately arrived, and orders were now given that it should anchor close at hand. On board was a young man in whom confidence could be placed. Champlain sent him two bottles of wine, with a direction to tell the four ringleaders that they had been given him by his Basque friends at Tadoussac, and to invite them to share the good cheer. They came aboard in the evening, and were seized and secured. "Voyla done mes galants bien estonnez," writes Champlain.

It was ten o'clock, and most of the men on shore were asleep. They were wakened suddenly, and told of the discovery of the plot and the arrest of the ringleaders. Pardon was then promised them, and they were dismissed again to their beds, greatly relieved; for they had lived in trepidation, each fearing the other. Duval's body, swinging from a gibbet, gave wholesome warning to those he had seduced; and his head was displayed on a pike, from the highest roof of the buildings, food for birds and a lesson to sedition. His three accomplices were carried by Pontgrave to France, where they made their atonement in the galleys.

It was on the eighteenth of September that Pontgrave set sail, leaving Champlain with twenty-eight men to hold Quebec through the winter. Three weeks later, and shores and hills glowed with gay prognostics of approaching desolation,—the yellow and scarlet of the maples, the deep purple of the ash, the garnet hue of young oaks, the crimson of the tupelo at the water's edge, and the golden plumage of birch saplings in the fissures of the cliff. It was a short-lived beauty. The forest dropped its festal robes. Shrivelled and faded, they rustled to the earth. The crystal air and laughing sun of October passed away, and November sank upon the shivering waste, chill and sombre as the tomb.

A roving band of Montagnais had built their huts near the buildings, and were busying themselves with their autumn eel-fishery, on which they greatly relied to sustain their miserable lives through the winter. Their slimy harvest being gathered, and duly smoked and dried, they gave it for safe-keeping to Champlain, and set out to hunt beavers. It was deep in the winter before they came back, reclaimed their eels, built their birch cabins again, and disposed themselves for a life of ease, until famine or their enemies should put an end to their enjoyments. These were by no means without alloy. While, gorged with food, they lay dozing on piles of branches in their smoky huts, where, through the crevices of the thin birch bark, streamed in a cold capable at times of congealing mercury, their slumbers were beset with nightmare visions of Iroquois forays, scalpings, butcherings, and burnings. As dreams were their oracles, the camp was wild with fright. They sent out no scouts and placed no guard; but, with each repetition of these nocturnal terrors, they came flocking in a body to beg admission within the fort. The women and children were allowed to enter the yard and remain during the night, while anxious fathers and jealous husbands shivered in the darkness without.

On one occasion, a group of wretched beings was seen on the farther bank of the St. Lawrence, like wild animals driven by famine to the borders of the settler's clearing. The river was full of drifting ice, and there was no crossing without risk of life. The Indians, in their desperation, made the attempt; and midway their canoes were ground to atoms among the tossing masses. Agile as wild-cats, they all leaped upon a huge raft of ice, the squaws carrying their children on their shoulders, a feat at which Champlain marveled when he saw their starved and emaciated condition. Here they began a wail of despair; when happily the pressure of other masses thrust the sheet of ice against the northern shore. They landed and soon made their appearance at the fort, worn to skeletons and horrible to look upon. The French gave them food, which they devoured with a frenzied avidity, and, unappeased, fell upon a dead dog left on the snow by Champlain for two months past as a bait for foxes. They broke this carrion into fragments, and thawed and devoured it, to the disgust of the spectators, who tried vainly to prevent them.

This was but a severe access of the periodical famine which, during winter, was a normal condition of the Algonquin tribes of Acadia and the Lower St. Lawrence, who, unlike the cognate tribes of New England, never tilled the soil, or made any reasonable provision against the time of need.

One would gladly know how the founders of Quebec spent the long hours of their first winter; but on this point the only man among them, perhaps, who could write, has not thought it necessary to enlarge. He himself beguiled his leisure with trapping foxes, or hanging a dead dog from a tree and watching the hungry martens in their efforts to reach it. Towards the close of winter, all found abundant employment in nursing themselves or their neighbors, for the inevitable scurvy broke out with virulence. At the middle of May, only eight men of the twenty-eight were alive, and of these half were suffering from disease.

This wintry purgatory wore away; the icy stalactites that hung from the cliffs fell crashing to the earth; the clamor of the wild geese was heard; the bluebirds appeared in the naked woods; the water-willows were covered with their soft caterpillar-like blossoms; the twigs of the swamp maple were flushed with ruddy bloom; the ash hung out its black tufts; the shad-bush seemed a wreath of snow; the white stars of the bloodroot gleamed among dank, fallen leaves; and in the young grass of the wet meadows the marsh-marigolds shone like spots of gold.

Great was the joy of Champlain when, on the fifth of June, he saw a sailboat rounding the Point of Orleans, betokening that the spring had brought with it the longed for succors. A son-in-law of Pontgrave, named Marais, was on board, and he reported that Pontgrave was then at Tadoussac, where he had lately arrived. Thither Champlain hastened, to take counsel with his comrade. His constitution or his courage had defied the scurvy. They met, and it was determined betwixt them, that, while Pontgrave remained in charge of Quebec, Champlain should enter at once on his long meditated explorations, by which, like La Salle seventy years later, he had good hope of finding a way to China.

But there was a lion in the path. The Indian tribes, to whom peace was unknown, infested with their scalping parties the streams and pathways of the forest, and increased tenfold its inseparable risks. The after career of Champlain gives abundant proof that he was more than indifferent to all such chances; yet now an expedient for evading them offered itself, so consonant with his instincts that he was glad to accept it.

During the last autumn, a young chief from the banks of the then unknown Ottawa had been at Quebec; and, amazed at what he saw, he had begged Champlain to join him in the spring against his enemies. These enemies were a formidable race of savages,— the Iroquois, or Five Confederate Nations, who dwelt in fortified villages within limits now embraced by the State of New York, and who were a terror to all the surrounding forests. They were deadly foes of their kindred the Hurons, who dwelt on the lake which bears their name, and were allies of Algonquin bands on the Ottawa. All alike were tillers of the soil, living at ease when compared with the famished Algonquins of the Lower St. Lawrence.

By joining these Hurons and Algonquins against their Iroquois enemies, Champlain might make himself the indispensable ally and leader of the tribes of Canada, and at the same time fight his way to discovery in regions which otherwise were barred against him. From first to last it was the policy of France in America to mingle in Indian politics, hold the balance of power between adverse tribes, and envelop in the network of her power and diplomacy the remotest hordes of the wilderness. Of this policy the Father of New France may perhaps be held to have set a rash and premature example. Yet while he was apparently following the dictates of his own adventurous spirit, it became evident, a few years later, that under his thirst for discovery and spirit of knight-errantry lay a consistent and deliberate purpose. That it had already assumed a definite shape is not likely; but his after course makes it plain that, in embroiling himself and his colony with the most formidable savages on the continent, he was by no means acting so recklessly as at first sight would appear.

CHAPTER X.
1609.
LAKE CHAMPLAIN.

It was past the middle of June, and the expected warriors from the upper country had not come,—a delay which seems to have given Champlain little concern, for, without waiting longer, he set out with no better allies than a band of Montagnais. But, as he moved up the St. Lawrence, he saw, thickly clustered in the bordering forest, the lodges of an Indian camp, and, landing, found his Huron and Algonquin allies. Few of them had ever seen a white man, and they surrounded the steel-clad strangers in speechless wonder. Champlain asked for their chief, and the staring throng moved with him towards a lodge where sat, not one chief, but two; for each band had its own. There were feasting, smoking, and speeches; and, the needful ceremony over, all descended together to Quebec; for the strangers were bent on seeing those wonders of architecture, the fame of which had pierced the recesses of their forests.

On their arrival, they feasted their eyes and glutted their appetites; yelped consternation at the sharp explosions of the arquebuse and the roar of the cannon; pitched their camps, and bedecked themselves for their war-dance. In the still night, their fire glared against the black and jagged cliff, and the fierce red light fell on tawny limbs convulsed with frenzied gestures and ferocious stampings on contorted visages, hideous with paint; on brandished weapons, stone war-clubs, stone hatchets, and stone-pointed lances; while the drum kept up its hollow boom, and the air was split with mingled yells.

The war-feast followed, and then all embarked together. Champlain was in a small shallop, carrying, besides himself, eleven men of Pontgrave's party, including his son-in-law Marais and the pilot La Routte. They were armed with the arquebuse,—a matchlock or firelock somewhat like the modern carbine, and from its shortness not ill suited for use in the forest. On the twenty-eighth of June they spread their sails and held their course against the current, while around them the river was alive with canoes, and hundreds of naked arms plied the paddle with a steady, measured sweep. They crossed the Lake of St. Peter, threaded the devious channels among its many islands, and reached at last the mouth of the Riviere des Iroquois, since called the Richelien, or the St. John. Here, probably on the site of the town of Sorel, the leisurely warriors encamped for two days, hunted, fished, and took their ease, regaling their allies with venison and wildfowl. They quarrelled, too; three fourths of their number seceded, took to their canoes in dudgeon, and paddled towards their homes, while the rest pursued their course up the broad and placid stream.

Walls of verdure stretched on left and right. Now, aloft in the lonely air rose the cliffs of Belceil, and now, before them, framed in circling forests, the Basin of Chambly spread its tranquil mirror, glittering in the sun. The shallop outsailed the canoes. Champlain, leaving his allies behind, crossed the basin and tried to pursue his course; but, as he listened in the stillness, the unwelcome noise of rapids reached his ear, and, by glimpses through the dark foliage of the Islets of St. John he could see the gleam of snowy foam and the flash of hurrying waters. Leaving the boat by the shore in charge of four men, he went with Marais, La Routte, and five others, to explore the wild before him. They pushed their way through the damps and shadows of the wood, through thickets and tangled vines, over mossy rocks and mouldering logs. Still the hoarse surging of the rapids followed them; and when, parting the screen of foliage, they looked out upon the river, they saw it thick set with rocks where, plunging over ledges, gurgling under drift-logs, darting along clefts, and boiling in chasms, the angry waters filled the solitude with monotonous ravings.

Champlain retraced his steps. He had learned the value of an Indian's word. His allies had promised him that his boat could pass unobstructed throughout the whole journey. "It afflicted me," he says, "and troubled me exceedingly to be obliged to return without having seen so great a lake, full of fair islands and bordered with the fine countries which they had described to me."

When he reached the boat, he found the whole savage crew gathered at the spot. He mildly rebuked their bad faith, but added, that, though they had deceived him, he, as far as might be, would fulfil his pledge. To this end, he directed Marais, with the boat and the greater part of the men, to return to Quebec, while he, with two who offered to follow him, should proceed in the Indian canoes.

The warriors lifted their canoes from the water, and bore them on their shoulders half a league through the forest to the smoother stream above. Here the chiefs made a muster of their forces, counting twenty-four canoes and sixty warriors. All embarked again, and advanced once more, by marsh, meadow, forest, and scattered islands,—then full of game, for it was an uninhabited land, the war-path and battleground of hostile tribes. The warriors observed a certain system in their advance. Some were in front as a vanguard; others formed the main body; while an equal number were in the forests on the flanks and rear, hunting for the subsistence of the whole; for, though they had a provision of parched maize pounded into meal, they kept it for use when, from the vicinity of the enemy, hunting should become impossible.

Late in the day they landed and drew up their canoes, ranging them closely, side by side. Some stripped sheets of bark, to cover their camp sheds; others gathered wood, the forest being full of dead, dry trees; others felled the living trees, for a barricade. They seem to have had steel axes, obtained by barter from the French; for in less than two hours they had made a strong defensive work, in the form of a half-circle, open on the river side, where their canoes lay on the strand, and large enough to enclose all their huts and sheds. 28 Some of their number had gone forward as scouts, and, returning, reported no signs of an enemy. This was the extent of their precaution, for they placed no guard, but all, in full security, stretched themselves to sleep,—a vicious custom from which the lazy warrior of the forest rarely departs.

They had not forgotten, however, to consult their oracle. The medicine-man pitched his magic lodge in the woods, formed of a small stack of poles, planted in a circle and brought together at the tops like stacked muskets. Over these he placed the filthy deer-skins which served him for a robe, and, creeping in at a narrow opening, hid himself from view. Crouched in a ball upon the earth, he invoked the spirits in mumbling inarticulate tones; while his naked auditory, squatted on the ground like apes, listened in wonder and awe. Suddenly, the lodge moved, rocking with violence to and fro,—by the power of the spirits, as the Indians thought, while Champlain could plainly see the tawny fist of the medicine-man shaking the poles. They begged him to keep a watchful eye on the peak of the lodge, whence fire and smoke would presently issue; but with the best efforts of his vision, he discovered none. Meanwhile the medicine-man was seized with such convulsions, that, when his divination was over, his naked body streamed with perspiration. In loud, clear tones, and in an unknown tongue, he invoked the spirit, who was understood to be present in the form of a stone, and whose feeble and squeaking accents were heard at intervals, like the wail of a young puppy.

In this manner they consulted the spirit—as Champlain thinks, the Devil—at all their camps. His replies, for the most part, seem to have given them great content; yet they took other measures, of which the military advantages were less questionable. The principal chief gathered bundles of sticks, and, without wasting his breath, stuck them in the earth in a certain order, calling each by the name of some warrior, a few taller than the rest representing the subordinate chiefs. Thus was indicated the position which each was to hold in the expected battle. All gathered round and attentively studied the sticks, ranged like a child's wooden soldiers, or the pieces on a chessboard; then, with no further instruction, they formed their ranks, broke them, and reformed them again and again with excellent alacrity and skill.

Again the canoes advanced, the river widening as they went. Great islands appeared, leagues in extent,—Isle a la Motte, Long Island, Grande Isle; channels where ships might float and broad reaches of water stretched between them, and Champlain entered the lake which preserves his name to posterity. Cumberland Head was passed, and from the opening of the great channel between Grande Isle and the main he could look forth on the wilderness sea. Edged with woods, the tranquil flood spread southward beyond the sight. Far on the left rose the forest ridges of the Green Mountains, and on the right the Adirondacks,—haunts in these later years of amateur sportsmen from counting-rooms or college halls. Then the Iroquois made them their hunting-ground; and beyond, in the valleys of the Mohawk, the Onondaga, and the Genesce, stretched the long line of their five cantons and palisaded towns.

At night they encamped again. The scene is a familiar one to many a tourist; and perhaps, standing at sunset on the peaceful strand, Champlain saw what a roving student of this generation has seen on those same shores, at that same hour,—the glow of the vanished sun behind the western mountains, darkly piled in mist and shadow along the sky; near at hand, the dead pine, mighty in decay, stretching its ragged arms athwart the burning heaven, the crow perched on its top like an image carved in jet; and aloft, the nighthawk, circling in his flight, and, with a strange whirring sound, diving through the air each moment for the insects he makes his prey.

The progress of the party was becoming dangerous. They changed their mode of advance and moved only in the night. All day they lay close in the depth of the forest, sleeping, lounging, smoking tobacco of their own raising, and beguiling the hours, no doubt, with the shallow banter and obscene jesting with which knots of Indians are wont to amuse their leisure. At twilight they embarked again, paddling their cautious way till the eastern sky began to redden. Their goal was the rocky promontory where Fort Ticonderoga was long afterward built. Thence, they would pass the outlet of Lake George, and launch their canoes again on that Como of the wilderness, whose waters, limpid as a fountain-head, stretched far southward between their flanking mountains. Landing at the future site of Fort William Henry, they would carry their canoes through the forest to the river Hudson, and, descending it, attack perhaps some outlying town of the Mohawks. In the next century this chain of lakes and rivers became the grand highway of savage and civilized war, linked to memories of momentous conflicts.

The allies were spared so long a progress. On the morning of the twenty-ninth of July, after paddling all night, they hid as usual in the forest on the western shore, apparently between Crown Point and Ticonderoga. The warriors stretched themselves to their slumbers, and Champlain, after walking till nine or ten o'clock through the surrounding woods, returned to take his repose on a pile of spruce-boughs. Sleeping, he dreamed a dream, wherein he beheld the Iroquois drowning in the lake; and, trying to rescue them, he was told by his Algonquin friends that they were good for nothing, and had better be left to their fate. For some time past he had been beset every morning by his superstitious allies, eager to learn about his dreams; and, to this moment, his unbroken slumbers had failed to furnish the desired prognostics. The announcement of this auspicious vision filled the crowd with joy, and at nightfall they embarked, flushed with anticipated victories.

It was ten o'clock in the evening, when, near a projecting point of land, which was probably Ticonderoga, they descried dark objects in motion on the lake before them. These were a flotilla of Iroquois canoes, heavier and slower than theirs, for they were made of oak bark. Each party saw the other, and the mingled war-cries pealed over the darkened water. The Iroquois, who were near the shore, having no stomach for an aquatic battle, landed, and, making night hideous with their clamors, began to barricade themselves. Champlain could see them in the woods, laboring like beavers, hacking down trees with iron axes taken from the Canadian tribes in war, and with stone hatchets of their own making. The allies remained on the lake, a bowshot from the hostile barricade, their canoes made fast together by poles lashed across. All night they danced with as much vigor as the frailty of their vessels would permit, their throats making amends for the enforced restraint of their limbs. It was agreed on both sides that the fight should be deferred till daybreak; but meanwhile a commerce of abuse, sarcasm, menace, and boasting gave unceasing exercise to the lungs and fancy of the combatants, "much," says Champlain, "like the besiegers and besieged in a beleaguered town."

As day approached, he and his two followers put on the light armor of the time. Champlain wore the doublet and long hose then in vogue. Over the doublet he buckled on a breastplate, and probably a back-piece, while his thighs were protected by cuisses of steel, and his head by a plumed casque. Across his shoulder hung the strap of his bandoleer, or ammunition-box; at his side was his sword, and in his hand his arquebuse. Such was the equipment of this ancient Indian-fighter, whose exploits date eleven years before the landing of the Puritans at Plymouth, and sixty-six years before King Philip's War.

Each of the three Frenchmen was in a separate canoe, and, as it grew light, they kept themselves hidden, either by lying at the bottom, or covering themselves with an Indian robe. The canoes approached the shore, and all landed without opposition at some distance from the Iroquois, whom they presently could see filing out of their barricade,-tall, strong men, some two hundred in number, the boldest and fiercest warriors of North America. They advanced through the forest with a steadiness which excited the admiration of Champlain. Among them could be seen three chiefs, made conspicuous by their tall plumes. Some bore shields of wood and hide, and some were covered with a kind of armor made of tough twigs interlaced with a vegetable fibre supposed by Champlain to be cotton. 29

The allies, growing anxious, called with loud cries for their champion, and opened their ranks that he might pass to the front. He did so, and, advancing before his red companions in arms, stood revealed to the gaze of the Iroquois, who, beholding the warlike apparition in their path, stared in mute amazement. "I looked at them," says Champlain, "and they looked at me. When I saw them getting ready to shoot their arrows at us, I levelled my arquebuse, which I had loaded with four balls, and aimed straight at one of the three chiefs. The shot brought down two, and wounded another. On this, our Indians set up such a yelling that one could not have heard a thunder-clap, and all the while the arrows flew thick on both sides. The Iroquois were greatly astonished and frightened to see two of their men killed so quickly, in spite of their arrow-proof armor. As I was reloading, one of my companions fired a shot from the woods, which so increased their astonishment that, seeing their chiefs dead, they abandoned the field and fled into the depth of the forest." The allies dashed after them. Some of the Iroquois were killed, and more were taken. Camp, canoes, provisions, all were abandoned, and many weapons flung down in the panic flight. The victory was complete.

At night, the victors led out one of the prisoners, told him that he was to die by fire, and ordered him to sing his death-song if he dared. Then they began the torture, and presently scalped their victim alive, 30 when Champlain, sickening at the sight, begged leave to shoot him. They refused, and he turned away in anger and disgust; on which they called him back and told him to do as he pleased. He turned again, and a shot from his arquebuse put the wretch out of misery.

The scene filled him with horror; but a few months later, on the Place de la Greve at Paris, he might have witnessed tortures equally revolting and equally vindictive, inflicted on the regicide Ravaillac by the sentence of grave and learned judges.

The allies made a prompt retreat from the scene of their triumph. Three or four days brought them to the mouth of the Richelien. Here they separated; the Hurons and Algonquins made for the Ottawa, their homeward route, each with a share of prisoners for future torments. At parting, they invited Champlain to visit their towns and aid them again in their wars, an invitation which this paladin of the woods failed not to accept.

The companions now remaining to him were the Montagnais. In their camp on the Richelien, one of them dreamed that a war party of Iroquois was close upon them; on which, in a torrent of rain, they left their huts, paddled in dismay to the islands above the Lake of St. Peter, and hid themselves all night in the rushes. In the morning they took heart, emerged from their hiding-places, descended to Quebec, and went thence to Tadoussac, whither Champlain accompanied them. Here the squaws, stark naked, swam out to the canoes to receive the heads of the dead Iroquois, and, hanging them from their necks, danced in triumph along the shore, One of the heads and a pair of arms were then bestowed on Champlain,—touching memorials of gratitude, which, however, he was by no means to keep for himself, but to present to the King.

Thus did New France rush into collision with the redoubted warriors of the Five Nations. Here was the beginning, and in some measure doubtless the cause, of a long suite of murderous conflicts, bearing havoc and flame to generations yet unborn. Champlain had invaded the tiger's den; and now, in smothered fury, the patient savage would lie biding his day of blood.

CHAPTER XI.
1610-1612.
WAR.—TRADE.—DISCOVERY.

Champlain and Pontgrave returned to France, while Pierre Chauvin of Dieppe held Quebec in their absence. The King was at Fontainebleau,—it was a few months before his assassination,—and here Champlain recounted his adventures, to the great satisfaction of the lively monarch. He gave him also, not the head of the dead Iroquois, but a belt wrought in embroidery of dyed quills of the Canada porcupine, together with two small birds of scarlet plumage, and the skull of a gar-fish.

De Monts was at court, striving for a renewal of his monopoly. His efforts failed; on which, with great spirit but little discretion, he resolved to push his enterprise without it. Early in the spring of 1610, the ship was ready, and Champlain and Pontgrave were on board, when a violent illness seized the former, reducing him to the most miserable of all conflicts, the battle of the eager spirit against the treacherous and failing flesh. Having partially recovered, he put to sea, giddy and weak, in wretched plight for the hard career of toil and battle which the New World offered him. The voyage was prosperous, no other mishap occurring than that of an ardent youth of St. Malo, who drank the health of Pontgrave with such persistent enthusiasm that he fell overboard and was drowned.

There were ships at Tadoussac, fast loading with furs; and boats, too, higher up the river, anticipating the trade, and draining De Monts's resources in advance. Champlain, who was left free to fight and explore wherever he should see fit, had provided, to use his own phrase, "two strings to his bow." On the one hand, the Montagnais had promised to guide him northward to Hudson's Bay; on the other, the Hurons were to show him the Great Lakes, with the mines of copper on their shores; and to each the same reward was promised,—to join them against the common foe, the Iroquois. The rendezvous was at the mouth of the river Richelien. Thither the Hurons were to descend in force, together with Algonquins of the Ottawa; and thither Champlain now repaired, while around his boat swarmed a multitude of Montagnais canoes, filled with warriors whose lank hair streamed loose in the wind.

There is an island in the St. Lawrence near the mouth of the Richelien. On the nineteenth of June it was swarming with busy and clamorous savages, Champlain's Montagnais allies, cutting down the trees and clearing the ground for a dance and a feast; for they were hourly expecting the Algonquin warriors, and were eager to welcome them with befitting honors. But suddenly, far out on the river, they saw an advancing canoe. Now on this side, now on that, the flashing paddles urged it forward as if death were on its track; and as it drew near, the Indians on board cried out that the Algonquins were in the forest, a league distant, engaged with a hundred warriors of the Iroquois, who, outnumbered, were fighting savagely within a barricade of trees. The air was split with shrill outcries. The Montagnais snatched their weapons,—shields, bows, arrows, war-clubs, sword-blades made fast to poles,—and ran headlong to their canoes, impeding each other in their haste, screeching to Champlain to follow, and invoking with no less vehemence the aid of certain fur-traders, just arrived in four boats from below. These, as it was not their cue to fight, lent them a deaf ear; on which, in disgust and scorn, they paddled off, calling to the recusants that they were women, fit for nothing but to make war on beaver-skins.

Champlain and four of his men were in the canoes. They shot across the intervening water, and, as their prows grated on the pebbles, each warrior flung down his paddle, snatched his weapons, and ran into the woods. The five Frenchmen followed, striving vainly to keep pace with the naked, light-limbed rabble, bounding like shadows through the forest. They quickly disappeared. Even their shrill cries grew faint, till Champlain and his men, discomforted and vexed, found themselves deserted in the midst of a swamp. The day was sultry, the forest air heavy, close, and filled with hosts of mosquitoes, "so thick," says the chief sufferer, "that we could scarcely draw breath, and it was wonderful how cruelly they persecuted us." Through black mud, spongy moss, water knee-deep, over fallen trees, among slimy logs and entangling roots, tripped by vines, lashed by recoiling boughs, panting under their steel head-pieces and heavy corselets, the Frenchmen struggled on, bewildered and indignant. At length they descried two Indians running in the distance, and shouted to them in desperation, that, if they wanted their aid, they must guide them to the enemy.

At length they could hear the yells of the combatants; there was light in the forest before them, and they issued into a partial clearing made by the Iroquois axemen near the river. Champlain saw their barricade. Trees were piled into a circular breastwork, trunks, boughs, and matted foliage forming a strong defence, within which the Iroquois stood savagely at bay. Around them flocked the allies, half hidden in the edges of the forest, like hounds around a wild boar, eager, clamorous, yet afraid to rush in. They had attacked, and had met a bloody rebuff. All their hope was now in the French; and when they saw them, a yell arose from hundreds of throats that outdid the wilderness voices whence its tones were borrowed,—the whoop of the homed owl, the scream of the cougar, the howl of starved wolves on a winter night. A fierce response pealed from the desperate band within; and, amid a storm of arrows from both sides, the Frenchmen threw themselves into the fray, firing at random through the fence of trunks, boughs, and drooping leaves, with which the Iroquois had encircled themselves. Champlain felt a stone-headed arrow splitting his ear and tearing through the muscles of his neck, he drew it out, and, the moment after, did a similar office for one of his men. But the Iroquois had not recovered from their first terror at the arquebuse; and when the mysterious and terrible assailants, clad in steel and armed with thunder-bolts, ran up to the barricade, thrust their pieces through the openings, and shot death among the crowd within, they could not control their fright, but with every report threw themselves flat on the ground. Animated with unwonted valor, the allies, covered by their large shields, began to drag out the felled trees of the barricade, while others, under Champlain's direction, gathered at the edge of the forest, preparing to close the affair with a final rush. New actors soon appeared on the scene. These were a boat's crew of the fur-traders under a young man of St. Malo, one Des Prairies, who, when he heard the firing, could not resist the impulse to join the fight. On seeing them, Champlain checked the assault, in order, as he says, that the new-comers might have their share in the sport. The traders opened fire, with great zest and no less execution; while the Iroquois, now wild with terror, leaped and writhed to dodge the shot which tore through their frail armor of twigs. Champlain gave the signal; the crowd ran to the barricade, dragged down the boughs or clambered over them, and bore themselves, in his own words, "so well and manfully," that, though scratched and torn by the sharp points, they quickly forced an entrance. The French ceased their fire, and, followed by a smaller body of Indians, scaled the barricade on the farther side. Now, amid howlings, shouts, and screeches, the work was finished. Some of the Iroquois were cut down as they stood, hewing with their war-clubs, and foaming like slaughtered tigers; some climbed the barrier and were killed by the furious crowd without; some were drowned in the river; while fifteen, the only survivors, were made prisoners. "By the grace of God," writes Champlain, "behold the battle won!" Drunk with ferocious ecstasy, the conquerors scalped the dead and gathered fagots for the living; while some of the fur-traders, too late to bear part in the fight, robbed the carcasses of their blood-bedrenched robes of beaver-skin amid the derision of the surrounding Indians.

That night, the torture fires blazed along the shore. Champlain saved one prisoner from their clutches, but nothing could save the rest. One body was quartered and eaten. 31 "As for the rest of the prisoners," says Champlain, "they were kept to be put to death by the women and girls, who in this respect are no less inhuman than the men, and, indeed, much more so; for by their subtlety they invent more cruel tortures, and take pleasure in it."

On the next day, a large band of Hurons appeared at the rendezvous, greatly vexed that they had come too late. The shores were thickly studded with Indian huts, and the woods were full of them. Here were warriors of three designations, including many subordinate tribes, and representing three grades of savage society,—the Hurons, the Algonquins of the Ottawa, and the Montagnais; afterwards styled by a Franciscan friar, than whom few men better knew them, the nobles, the burghers, and the peasantry and paupers of the forest. Many of them, from the remote interior, had never before seen a white man; and, wrapped like statues in their robes, they stood gazing on the French with a fixed stare of wild and wondering eyes.

Judged by the standard of Indian war, a heavy blow had been struck on the common enemy. Here were hundreds of assembled warriors; yet none thought of following up their success. Elated with unexpected fortune, they danced and sang; then loaded their canoes, hung their scalps on poles, broke up their camps, and set out triumphant for their homes. Champlain had fought their battles, and now might claim, on their part, guidance and escort to the distant interior. Why he did not do so is scarcely apparent. There were cares, it seems, connected with the very life of his puny colony, which demanded his return to France. Nor were his anxieties lessened by the arrival of a ship from his native town of Brouage, with tidings of the King's assassination. Here was a death-blow to all that had remained of De Monts's credit at court; while that unfortunate nobleman, like his old associate, Pontrincourt, was moving with swift strides toward financial ruin. With the revocation of his monopoly, fur-traders had swarmed to the St. Lawrence. Tadoussac was full of them, and for that year the trade was spoiled. Far from aiding to support a burdensome enterprise of colonization, it was in itself an occasion of heavy loss.

Champlain bade farewell to his garden at Quebec, where maize, wheat, rye, and barley, with vegetables of all kinds, and a small vineyard of native grapes,—for he was a zealous horticulturist,—held forth a promise which he was not to see fulfilled. He left one Du Parc in command, with sixteen men, and, sailing on the eighth of August, arrived at Honfleur with no worse accident than that of running over a sleeping whale near the Grand Bank.

With the opening spring he was afloat again. Perils awaited him worse than those of Iroquois tomahawks; for, approaching Newfoundland, the ship was entangled for days among drifting fields and bergs of ice. Escaping at length, she arrived at Tadoussac on the thirteenth of May, 1611. She had anticipated the spring. Forests and mountains, far and near, all were white with snow. A principal object with Champlain was to establish such relations with the great Indian communities of the interior as to secure to De Monts and his associates the advantage of trade with them; and to this end he now repaired to Montreal, a position in the gateway, as it were, of their yearly descents of trade or war. On arriving, he began to survey the ground for the site of a permanent post.

A few days convinced him, that, under the present system, all his efforts would be vain. Wild reports of the wonders of New France had gone abroad, and a crowd of hungry adventurers had hastened to the land of promise, eager to grow rich, they scarcely knew how, and soon to return disgusted. A fleet of boats and small vessels followed in Champlain's wake. Within a few days, thirteen of them arrived at Montreal, and more soon appeared. He was to break the ground; others would reap the harvest. Travel, discovery, and battle, all must inure to the profit, not of the colony, but of a crew of greedy traders.

Champlain, however, chose the site and cleared the ground for his intended post. It was immediately above a small stream, now running under arches of masonry, and entering the St. Lawrence at Point Callieres, within the modern city. He called it Place Royale; and here, on the margin of the river, he built a wall of bricks made on the spot, in order to measure the destructive effects of the "ice-shove" in the spring.

Now, down the surges of St. Louis, where the mighty floods of the St. Lawrence, contracted to a narrow throat, roll in fury among their sunken rocks,—here, through foam and spray and the roar of the angry torrent, a fleet of birch canoes came dancing like dry leaves on the froth of some riotous brook. They bore a band of Hurons first at the rendezvous. As they drew near the landing, all the fur-traders' boats blazed out a clattering fusillade, which was designed to bid them welcome, but in fact terrified many of them to such a degree that they scarcely dared to come ashore. Nor were they reassured by the bearing of the disorderly crowd, who, in jealous competition for their beaver-skins, left them not a moment's peace, and outraged all their notions of decorum. More soon appeared, till hundreds of warriors were encamped along the shore, all restless, suspicious, and alarmed. Late one night they awakened Champlain. On going with them to their camp, he found chiefs and warriors in solemn conclave around the glimmering firelight. Though they were fearful of the rest, their trust in him was boundless. "Come to our country, buy our beaver, build a fort, teach us the true faith, do what you will, but do not bring this crowd with you." The idea had seized them that these lawless bands of rival traders, all well armed, meant to plunder and kill them. Champlain assured them of safety, and the whole night was consumed in friendly colloquy. Soon afterward, however, the camp broke up, and the uneasy warriors removed to the borders of the Lake of St. Louis, placing the rapids betwixt themselves and the objects of their alarm. Here Champlain visited them, and hence these intrepid canoe-men, kneeling in their birchen egg-shells, carried him homeward down the rapids, somewhat, as he admits, to the discomposure of his nerves. 32

The great gathering dispersed: the traders descended to Tadoussac, and Champlain to Quebec; while the Indians went, some to their homes, some to fight the Iroquois. A few months later, Champlain was in close conference with De Monts at Pons, a place near Rochelle, of which the latter was governor. The last two years had made it apparent, that, to keep the colony alive and maintain a basis for those discoveries on which his heart was bent, was impossible without a change of system. De Monts, engrossed with the cares of his government, placed all in the hands of his associate; and Champlain, fully empowered to act as he should judge expedient, set out for Paris. On the way, Fortune, at one stroke, wellnigh crushed him and New France together; for his horse fell on him, and he narrowly escaped with life. When he was partially recovered, he resumed his journey, pondering on means of rescue for the fading colony. A powerful protector must be had,— a great name to shield the enterprise from assaults and intrigues of jealous rival interests. On reaching Paris he addressed himself to a prince of the blood, Charles de Bourbon, Comte de Soissons; described New France, its resources, and its boundless extent; urged the need of unfolding a mystery pregnant perhaps with results of the deepest moment; laid before him maps and memoirs, and begged him to become the guardian of this new world. The royal consent being obtained, the Comte de Soissons became Lieutenant-General for the King in New France, with vice-regal powers. These, in turn, he conferred upon Champlain, making him his lieutenant, with full control over the trade in furs at and above Quebec, and with power to associate with himself such persons as he saw fit, to aid in the exploration and settlement of the country.

Scarcely was the commission drawn when the Comte de Soissons, attacked with fever, died,—to the joy of the Breton and Norman traders, whose jubilation, however, found a speedy end. Henri de Bourbon, Prince de Conde, first prince of the blood, assumed the vacant protectorship. He was grandson of the gay and gallant Conde of the civil wars, was father of the great Conde, the youthful victor of Rocroy, and was husband of Charlotte de Moutmorency, whose blond beauties had fired the inflammable heart of Henry the Fourth. To the unspeakable wrath of that keen lover, the prudent Conde fled with his bride, first to Brussels, and then to Italy; nor did he return to France till the regicide's knife had put his jealous fears to rest. After his return, he began to intrigue against the court. He was a man of common abilities, greedy of money and power, and scarcely seeking even the decency of a pretext to cover his mean ambition. His chief honor—an honor somewhat equivocal—is, as Voltaire observes, to have been father of the great Conde. Busy with his intrigues, he cared little for colonies and discoveries; and his rank and power were his sole qualifications for his new post.

In Champlain alone was the life of New France. By instinct and temperament he was more impelled to the adventurous toils of exploration than to the duller task of building colonies. The profits of trade had value in his eyes only as means to these ends, and settlements were important chiefly as a base of discovery. Two great objects eclipsed all others,—to find a route to the Indies, and to bring the heathen tribes into the embraces of the Church, since, while he cared little for their bodies, his solicitude for their souls knew no bounds.

It was no part of his plan to establish an odious monopoly. He sought rather to enlist the rival traders in his cause; and he now, in concurrence with Du Monts, invited them to become sharers in the traffic, under certain regulations, and on condition of aiding in the establishment and support of the colony. The merchants of St. Malo and Rouen accepted the terms, and became members of the new company; but the intractable heretics of Rochelle, refractory in commerce as in religion, kept aloof, and preferred the chances of an illicit trade. The prospects of New France were far from flattering; for little could be hoped from this unwilling league of selfish traders, each jealous of the rest. They gave the Prince of Conde large gratuities to secure his countenance and support. The hungry viceroy took them, and with these emoluments his interest in the colony ended.

CHAPTER XII.
1612, 1613.
THE IMPOSTOR VIGNAU.

The arrangements just indicated were a work of time. In the summer of 1612, Champlain was forced to forego his yearly voyage to New France; nor, even in the following spring, were his labors finished and the rival interests brought to harmony. Meanwhile, incidents occurred destined to have no small influence on his movements. Three years before, after his second fight with the Iroquois, a young man of his company had boldly volunteered to join the Indians on their homeward journey, and winter among them. Champlain gladly assented, and in the following summer the adventurer returned. Another young man, one Nicolas de Vignan, next offered himself; and he also, embarking in the Algonquin canoes, passed up the Ottawa, and was seen no more for a twelvemonth. In 1612 he reappeared in Paris, bringing a tale of wonders; for, says Champlain, "he was the most impudent liar that has been seen for many a day." He averred that at the sources of the Ottawa he had found a great lake; that he had crossed it, and discovered a river flowing northward; that he had descended this river, and reached the shores of the sea; that here he had seen the wreck of an English ship, whose crew, escaping to land, had been killed by the Indians; and that this sea was distant from Montreal only seventeen days by canoe. The clearness, consistency, and apparent simplicity of his story deceived Champlain, who had heard of a voyage of the English to the northern seas, coupled with rumors of wreck and disaster, and was thus confirmed in his belief of Vignau's honesty. The Marechal de Brissac, the President Jeannin, and other persons of eminence about the court, greatly interested by these dexterous fabrications, urged Champlain to follow up without delay a discovery which promised results so important; while he, with the Pacific, Japan, China, the Spice Islands, and India stretching in flattering vista before his fancy, entered with eagerness on the chase of this illusion. Early in the spring of 1613 the unwearied voyager crossed the Atlantic, and sailed up the St. Lawrence. On Monday, the twenty-seventh of May, he left the island of St. Helen, opposite Montreal, with four Frenchmen, one of whom was Nicolas de Vignau, and one Indian, in two small canoes. They passed the swift current at St. Ann's, crossed the Lake of Two Mountains, and advanced up the Ottawa till the rapids of Carillon and the Long Saut checked their course. So dense and tangled was the forest, that they were forced to remain in the bed of the river, trailing their canoes along the bank with cords, or pushing them by main force up the current. Champlain's foot slipped; he fell in the rapids, two boulders, against which he braced himself, saving him from being swept down, while the cord of the canoe, twisted round his hand, nearly severed it. At length they reached smoother water, and presently met fifteen canoes of friendly Indians. Champlain gave them the most awkward of his Frenchmen and took one of their number in return,—an exchange greatly to his profit.

All day they plied their paddles, and when night came they made their camp-fire in the forest. He who now, when two centuries and a half are passed, would see the evening bivouac of Champlain, has but to encamp, with Indian guides, on the upper waters of this same Ottawa, or on the borders of some lonely river of New Brunswick or of Maine.

Day dawned. The east glowed with tranquil fire, that pierced with eyes of flame the fir-trees whose jagged tops stood drawn in black against the burning heaven. Beneath, the glossy river slept in shadow, or spread far and wide in sheets of burnished bronze; and the white moon, paling in the face of day, hung like a disk of silver in the western sky. Now a fervid light touched the dead top of the hemlock, and creeping downward bathed the mossy beard of the patriarchal cedar, unstirred in the breathless air; now a fiercer spark beamed from the east; and now, half risen on the sight, a dome of crimson fire, the sun blazed with floods of radiance across the awakened wilderness.

The canoes were launched again, and the voyagers held their course. Soon the still surface was flecked with spots of foam; islets of froth floated by, tokens of some great convulsion. Then, on their left, the falling curtain of the Rideau shone like silver betwixt its bordering woods, and in front, white as a snowdrift, the cataracts of the Chaudiere barred their way. They saw the unbridled river careering down its sheeted rocks, foaming in unfathomed chasms, wearying the solitude with the hoarse outcry of its agony and rage.

On the brink of the rocky basin where the plunging torrent boiled like a caldron, and puffs of spray sprang out from its concussion like smoke from the throat of a cannon, Champlain's two Indians took their stand, and, with a loud invocation, threw tobacco into the foam,—an offering to the local spirit, the Manitou of the cataract.

They shouldered their canoes over the rocks, and through the woods; then launched them again, and, with toil and struggle, made their amphibious way, pushing dragging, lifting, paddling, shoving with poles; till, when the evening sun poured its level rays across the quiet Lake of the Chaudiere, they landed, and made their camp on the verge of a woody island.

Day by day brought a renewal of their toils. Hour by hour, they moved prosperously up the long windings of the solitary stream; then, in quick succession, rapid followed rapid, till the bed of the Ottawa seemed a slope of foam. Now, like a wall bristling at the top with woody islets, the Falls of the Chats faced them with the sheer plunge of their sixteen cataracts; now they glided beneath overhanging cliffs, where, seeing but unseen, the crouched wildcat eyed them from the thicket; now through the maze of water-girded rocks, which the white cedar and the spruce clasped with serpent-like roots, or among islands where old hemlocks darkened the water with deep green shadow. Here, too, the rock-maple reared its verdant masses, the beech its glistening leaves and clean, smooth stem, and behind, stiff and sombre, rose the balsam-fir. Here in the tortuous channels the muskrat swam and plunged, and the splashing wild duck dived beneath the alders or among the red and matted roots of thirsty water willows. Aloft, the white-pine towered above a sea of verdure; old fir-trees, hoary and grim, shaggy with pendent mosses, leaned above the stream, and beneath, dead and submerged, some fallen oak thrust from the current its bare, bleached limbs, like the skeleton of a drowned giant. In the weedy cove stood the moose, neck-deep in water to escape the flies, wading shoreward, with glistening sides, as the canoes drew near, shaking his broad antlers and writhing his hideous nostril, as with clumsy trot he vanished in the woods.

In these ancient wilds, to whose ever verdant antiquity the pyramids are young and Nineveh a mushroom of yesterday; where the sage wanderer of the Odyssey, could he have urged his pilgrimage so far, would have surveyed the same grand and stern monotony, the same dark sweep of melancholy woods;—here, while New England was a solitude, and the settlers of Virginia scarcely dared venture inland beyond the sound of a cannon-shot, Champlain was planting on shores and islands the emblems of his faith. Of the pioneers of the North American forests, his name stands foremost on the list. It was he who struck the deepest and boldest strokes into the heart of their pristine barbarism. At Chantilly, at Fontainebleau, Paris, in the cabinets of princes and of royalty itself, mingling with the proud vanities of the court; then lost from sight in the depths of Canada, the companion of savages, sharer of their toils, privations, and battles, more hardy, patient, and bold than they;—such, for successive years, were the alternations of this man's life.

To follow on his trail once more. His Indians said that the rapids of the river above were impassable. Nicolas de Vignan affirmed the contrary; but, from the first, Vignau had been found always in the wrong. His aim seems to have been to involve his leader in difficulties, and disgust him with a journey which must soon result in exposing the imposture which had occasioned it. Champlain took counsel of the Indians. The party left the river, and entered the forest.

"We had a hard march," says Champlain. "I carried for my share of the luggage three arquebuses, three paddles, my overcoat, and a few bagatelles. My men carried a little more than I did, and suffered more from the mosquitoes than from their loads. After we had passed four small ponds and advanced two leagues and a half, we were so tired that we could go no farther, having eaten nothing but a little roasted fish for nearly twenty-four hours. So we stopped in a pleasant place enough by the edge of a pond, and lighted a fire to drive off the mosquitoes, which plagued us beyond all description; and at the same time we set our nets to catch a few fish."

On the next day they fared still worse, for their way was through a pine forest where a tornado had passed, tearing up the trees and piling them one upon another in a vast "windfall," where boughs, roots, and trunks were mixed in confusion. Sometimes they climbed over and sometimes crawled through these formidable barricades, till, after an exhausting march, they reached the banks of Muskrat Lake, by the edge of which was an Indian settlement.

This neighborhood was the seat of the principal Indian population of the river, and, as the canoes advanced, unwonted signs of human life could be seen on the borders of the lake. Here was a rough clearing. The trees had been burned; there was a rude and desolate gap in the sombre green of the pine forest. Dead trunks, blasted and black with fire, stood grimly upright amid the charred stumps and prostrate bodies of comrades half consumed. In the intervening spaces, the soil had been feebly scratched with hoes of wood or bone, and a crop of maize was growing, now some four inches high. The dwellings of these slovenly farmers, framed of poles covered with sheets of bark, were scattered here and there, singly or in groups, while their tenants were running to the shore in amazement. The chief, Nibachis, offered the calumet, then harangued the crowd: "These white men must have fallen from the clouds. How else could they have reached us through the woods and rapids which even we find it hard to pass? The French chief can do anything. All that we have heard of him must he true." And they hastened to regale the hungry visitors with a repast of fish.

Champlain asked for guidance to the settlements above. It was readily granted. Escorted by his friendly hosts, he advanced beyond the foot of Muskrat Lake, and, landing, saw the unaccustomed sight of pathways through the forest. They led to the clearings and cabins of a chief named Tessonat, who, amazed at the apparition of the white strangers, exclaimed that he must be in a dream. Next, the voyagers crossed to the neighboring island, then deeply wooded with pine, elm, and oak. Here were more desolate clearings, more rude cornfields and bark-built cabins. Here, too, was a cemetery, which excited the wonder of Champlain, for the dead were better cared for than the living. Each grave was covered with a double row of pieces of wood, inclined like a roof till they crossed at the ridge, a long which was laid a thick tablet of wood, meant apparently either to bind the whole together or protect it from rain. At one end stood an upright tablet, or flattened post, rudely carved with an intended representation of the features of the deceased. If a chief, the head was adorned with a plume. If a warrior, there were figures near it of a shield, a lance, a war-club, and a bow and arrows; if a boy, of a small bow and one arrow; and if a woman or a girl, of a kettle, an earthen pot, a wooden spoon, and a paddle. The whole was decorated with red and yellow paint; and beneath slept the departed, wrapped in a robe of skins, his earthly treasures about him, ready for use in the land of souls.

Tessouat was to give a tabagie, or solemn feast, in honor of Champlain, and the chiefs and elders of the island were invited. Runners were sent to summon the guests from neighboring hamlets; and, on the morrow, Tessonat's squaws swept his cabin for the festivity. Then Champlain and his Frenchmen were seated on skins in the place of honor, and the naked guests appeared in quick succession, each with his wooden dish and spoon, and each ejaculating his guttural salute as he stooped at the low door. The spacious cabin was full. The congregated wisdom and prowess of the nation sat expectant on the bare earth. Each long, bare arm thrust forth its dish in turn as the host served out the banquet, in which, as courtesy enjoined, he himself was to have no share. First, a mess of pounded maize, in which were boiled, without salt, morsels of fish and dark scraps of meat; then, fish and flesh broiled on the embers, with a kettle of cold water from the river. Champlain, in wise distrust of Ottawa cookery, confined himself to the simpler and less doubtful viands. A few minutes, and all alike had vanished. The kettles were empty. Then pipes were filled and touched with fire brought in by the squaws, while the young men who had stood thronged about the entrance now modestly withdrew, and the door was closed for counsel.

First, the pipes were passed to Champlain. Then, for full half an hour, the assembly smoked in silence. At length, when the fitting time was come, he addressed them in a speech in which he declared, that, moved by affection for them, he visited their country to see its richness and its beauty, and to aid them in their wars; and he now begged them to furnish him with four canoes and eight men, to convey him to the country of the Nipissings, a tribe dwelling northward on the lake which bears their name.

His audience looked grave, for they were but cold and jealous friends of the Nipissings. For a time they discoursed in murmuring tones among themselves, all smoking meanwhile with redoubled vigor. Then Tessouat, chief of these forest republics, rose and spoke in behalf of all:—"We always knew you for our best friend among the Frenchmen. We love you like our own children. But why did you break your word with us last year when we all went down to meet you at Montreal, to give you presents and go with you to war? You were not there, but other Frenchmen were there who abused us. We will never go again. As for the four canoes, you shall have them if you insist upon it; but it grieves us to think of the hardships you must endure. The Nipissings have weak hearts. They are good for nothing in war, but they kill us with charms, and they poison us. Therefore we are on bad terms with them. They will kill you, too."

Such was the pith of Tessouat's discourse, and at each clause the conclave responded in unison with an approving grunt.

Champlain urged his petition; sought to relieve their tender scruples in his behalf; assured them that he was charm-proof, and that he feared no hardships. At length he gained his point. The canoes and the men were promised, and, seeing himself as he thought on the highway to his phantom Northern Sea, he left his entertainers to their pipes, and with a light heart issued from the close and smoky den to breathe the fresh air of the afternoon. He visited the Indian fields, with their young crops of pumpkins, beans, and French peas,—the last a novelty obtained from the traders. Here, Thomas, the interpreter, soon joined him with a countenance of ill news. In the absence of Champlain, the assembly had reconsidered their assent. The canoes were denied.

With a troubled mind he hastened again to the hall of council, and addressed the naked senate in terms better suited to his exigencies than to their dignity:

"I thought you were men; I thought you would hold fast to your word: but I find you children, without truth. You call yourselves my friends, yet you break faith with me. Still I would not incommode you; and if you cannot give me four canoes, two will Serve."

The burden of the reply was, rapids, rocks, cataracts, and the wickedness of the Nipissings. "We will not give you the canoes, because we are afraid of losing you," they said.

"This young man," rejoined Champlain, pointing to Vignau, who sat by his side, "has been to their country, and did not find the road or the people so bad as you have said."

"Nicolas," demanded Tessouat, "did you say that you had been to the Nipissings?"

The impostor sat mute for a time, and then replied, "Yes, I have been there."

Hereupon an outcry broke from the assembly, and they turned their eyes on him askance, "as if," says Champlain, "they would have torn and eaten him."

"You are a liar," returned the unceremonious host; "you know very well that you slept here among my children every night, and got up again every morning; and if you ever went to the Nipissings, it must have been when you were asleep. How can you be so impudent as to lie to your chief, and so wicked as to risk his life among so many dangers? He ought to kill you with tortures worse than those with which we kill our enemies."

Champlain urged him to reply, but he sat motionless and dumb. Then he led him from the cabin, and conjured him to declare if in truth he had seen this sea of the north. Vignan, with oaths, affirmed that all he had said was true. Returning to the council, Champlain repeated the impostor's story—how he had seen the sea, the wreck of an English ship, the heads of eighty Englishmen, and an English boy, prisoner among the Indians.

At this, an outcry rose louder than before, and the Indians turned in ire upon Vignan.

"You are a liar." "Which way did you go?" "By what rivers?" "By what lakes?" "Who went with you?"

Vignan had made a map of his travels, which Champlain now produced, desiring him to explain it to his questioners; but his assurance failed him, and he could not utter a word.

Champlain was greatly agitated. His heart was in the enterprise, his reputation was in a measure at stake; and now, when he thought his triumph so near, he shrank from believing himself the sport of an impudent impostor. The council broke up,—the

Indians displeased and moody, and he, on his part, full of anxieties and doubts.

"I called Vignau to me in presence of his companions," he says. "I told him that the time for deceiving me was ended; that he must tell me whether or not he had really seen the things he had told of; that I had forgotten the past, but that, if he continued to mislead me, I would have him hanged without mercy."

Vignau pondered for a moment; then fell on his knees, owned his treachery, and begged forgiveness. Champlain broke into a rage, and, unable, as he says, to endure the sight of him, ordered him from his presence, and sent the interpreter after him to make further examination. Vanity, the love of notoriety, and the hope of reward, seem to have been his inducements; for he had in fact spent a quiet winter in Tessonat's cabin, his nearest approach to the northern sea; and he had flattered himself that he might escape the necessity of guiding his commander to this pretended discovery. The Indians were somewhat exultant.

"Why did you not listen to chiefs and warriors, instead of believing the lies of this fellow?" And they counselled Champlain to have him killed at once, adding, "Give him to us, and we promise you that he shall never lie again."

No motive remaining for farther advance, the party set out on their return, attended by a fleet of forty canoes bound to Montreal for trade. They passed the perilous rapids of the Calumet, and were one night encamped on an island, when an Indian, slumbering in an uneasy posture, was visited with a nightmare. He leaped up with a yell, screamed, that somebody was killing him, and ran for refuge into the river. Instantly all his companions sprang to their feet, and, hearing in fancy the Iroquois war-whoop, took to the water, splashing, diving, and wading up to their necks, in the blindness of their fright. Champlain and his Frenchmen, roused at the noise, snatched their weapons and looked in vain for an enemy. The panic-stricken warriors, reassured at length, waded crestfallen ashore, and the whole ended in a laugh.

At the Chaudiere, a contribution of tobacco was collected on a wooden platter, and, after a solemn harangue, was thrown to the guardian Manitou. On the seventeenth of June they approached Montreal, where the assembled traders greeted them with discharges of small arms and cannon. Here, among the rest, was Champlain's lieutenant, Du Parc, with his men, who had amused their leisure with hunting, and were revelling in a sylvan abundance, while their baffled chief, with worry of mind, fatigue of body, and a Lenten diet of half-cooked fish, was grievously fallen away in flesh and strength. He kept his word with DeVignau, left the scoundrel unpunished, bade farewell to the Indians, and, promising to rejoin then the next year, embarked in one of the trading-ships for France.

CHAPTER XIII.
1615.
DISCOVERY OF LAKE HURON.

In New France, spiritual and temporal interests were inseparably blended, and, as will hereafter appear, the conversion of the Indians was used as a means of commercial and political growth. But, with the single-hearted founder of the colony, considerations of material advantage, though clearly recognized, were no less clearly subordinate. He would fain rescue from perdition a people living, as he says, "like brute beasts, without faith, without law, without religion, without God." While the want of funds and the indifference of his merchant associates, who as yet did not fully see that their trade would find in the missions its surest ally, were threatening to wreck his benevolent schemes, he found a kindred spirit in his friend Houd, secretary to the King, and comptroller-general of the salt-works of Bronage. Near this town was a convent of Recollet friars, some of whom were well known to Houel. To them he addressed himself; and several of the brotherhood, "inflamed," we are told, "with charity," were eager to undertake the mission. But the Recollets, mendicants by profession, were as weak in resources as Champlain himself. He repaired to Paris, then filled with bishops, cardinals, and nobles, assembled for the States-General. Responding to his appeal, they subscribed fifteen hundred livres for the purchase of vestments, candles, and ornaments for altars. The King gave letters patent in favor of the mission, and the Pope gave it his formal authorization. By this instrument the papacy in the person of Paul the Fifth virtually repudiated the action of the papacy in the person of Alexander the Sixth, who had proclaimed all America the exclusive property of Spain.

The Recollets form a branch of the great Franciscan Order, founded early in the thirteenth century by Saint Francis of Assisi. Saint, hero, or madman, according to the point of view from which he is regarded, he belonged to an era of the Church when the tumult of invading heresies awakened in her defence a band of impassioned champions, widely different from the placid saints of an earlier age. He was very young when dreams and voices began to reveal to him his vocation, and kindle his high-wrought nature to sevenfold heat. Self-respect, natural affection, decency, became in his eyes but stumbling-blocks and snares. He robbed his father to build a church; and, like so many of the Roman Catholic saints, confounded filth with humility, exchanged clothes with beggars, and walked the streets of Assisi in rags amid the hootings of his townsmen. He vowed perpetual poverty and perpetual beggary, and, in token of his renunciation of the world, stripped himself naked before the Bishop of Assisi, and then begged of him in charity a peasant's mantle. Crowds gathered to his fervid and dramatic eloquence. His handful of disciples multiplied, till Europe became thickly dotted with their convents. At the end of the eighteenth century, the three Orders of Saint Francis numbered a hundred and fifteen thousand friars and twenty-eight thousand nuns. Four popes, forty-five cardinals, and forty-six canonized martyrs were enrolled on their record, besides about two thousand more who had shed their blood for the faith. Their missions embraced nearly all the known world; and, in 1621, there were in Spanish America alone five hundred Franciscan convents.

In process of time the Franciscans had relaxed their ancient rigor; but much of their pristine spirit still subsisted in the Recollets, a reformed branch of the Order, sometimes known as Franciscans of the Strict Observance.

Four of their number were named for the mission of New France,—Denis Jamay, Jean Dolbean, Joseph le Caron, and the lay brother Pacifique du Plessis. "They packed their church ornaments," says Champlain, "and we, our luggage." All alike confessed their sins, and, embarking at Honfleur, reached Quebec at the end of May, 1615. Great was the perplexity of the Indians as the apostolic mendicants landed beneath the rock. Their garb was a form of that common to the brotherhood of Saint Francis, consisting of a rude garment of coarse gray cloth, girt at the waist with the knotted cord of the Order, and furnished with a peaked hood, to be drawn over the head. Their naked feet were shod with wooden sandals, more than an inch thick.

Their first care was to choose a site for their convent, near the fortified dwellings and storehouses built by Champlain. This done, they made an altar, and celebrated the first mass ever said in Canada. Dolbean was the officiating priest; all New France kneeled on the bare earth around him, and cannon from the ship and the ramparts hailed the mystic rite. Then, in imitation of the Apostles, they took counsel together, and assigned to each his province in the vast field of their mission,—to Le Caron the Hurons, and to Dolbean the Montagnais; while Jamay and Du Plessis were to remain for the present near Quebec.

Dolbean, full of zeal, set out for his post, and in the next winter tried to follow the roving hordes of Tadoussac to their frozen hunting-grounds. He was not robust, and his eyes were weak. Lodged in a hut of birch bark, full of abominations, dogs, fleas, stench, and all uncleanness, he succumbed at length to the smoke, which had wellnigh blinded him, forcing him to remain for several days with his eyes closed. After debating within himself whether God required of him the sacrifice of his sight, he solved his doubts with a negative, and returned to Quebec, only to depart again with opening spring on a tour so extensive that it brought him in contact with outlying bands of the Esquimaux. Meanwhile Le Caron had long been absent on a more noteworthy mission.

While his brethren were building their convent and garnishing their altar at Quebec, the ardent friar had hastened to the site of Montreal, then thronged with a savage concourse come down for the yearly trade. he mingled with them, studied their manners, tried to learn their languages, and, when Champlain and Pontgrave arrived, declared his purpose of wintering in their villages. Dissuasion availed nothing. "What," he demanded, "are privations to him whose life is devoted to perpetual poverty, and who has no ambition but to serve God?"

The assembled Indians were more eager for temporal than for spiritual succor, and beset Champlain with clamors for aid against the Iroquois. He and Pontgrave were of one mind. The aid demanded must be given, and that from no motive of the hour, but in pursuance of a deliberate policy. It was evident that the innumerable tribes of New France, otherwise divided, were united in a common fear and hate of these formidable bands, who, in the strength of their fivefold league, spread havoc and desolation through all the surrounding wilds. It was the aim of Champlain, as of his successors, to persuade the threatened and endangered hordes to live at peace with each other, and to form against the common foe a virtual league, of which the French colony would be the heart and the head, and which would continually widen with the widening area of discovery. With French soldiers to fight their battles, French priests to baptize them, and French traders to supply their increasing wants, their dependence would be complete. They would become assured tributaries to the growth of New France. It was a triple alliance of soldier, priest, and trader. The soldier might be a roving knight, and the priest a martyr and a saint; but both alike were subserving the interests of that commerce which formed the only solid basis of the colony. The scheme of English colonization made no account of the Indian tribes. In the scheme of French colonization they were all in all.

In one point the plan was fatally defective, since it involved the deadly enmity of a race whose character and whose power were as yet but ill understood,—the fiercest, boldest, most politic, and most ambitious savages to whom the American forest has ever given birth.

The chiefs and warriors met in council,—Algonquins of the Ottawa, and Hurons from the borders of the great Fresh-Water Sea. Champlain promised to join them with all the men at his command, while they, on their part, were to muster without delay twenty-five hundred warriors for an inroad into the country of the Iroquois. He descended at once to Quebec for needful preparation; but when, after a short delay, he returned to Montreal, he found, to his chagrin, a solitude. The wild concourse had vanished; nothing remained but the skeleton poles of their huts, the smoke of their fires, and the refuse of their encampments. Impatient at his delay, they had set out for their villages, and with them had gone Father Joseph le Caron.

Twelve Frenchmen, well armed, had attended him. Summer was at its height, and as his canoe stole along the bosom of the glassy river, and he gazed about him on the tawny multitude whose fragile craft covered the water like swarms of gliding insects, he thought, perhaps, of his whitewashed cell in the convent of Brouage, of his book, his table, his rosary, and all the narrow routine of that familiar life from which he had awakened to contrasts so startling. That his progress up the Ottawa was far from being an excursion of pleasure is attested by his letters, fragments of which have come down to us.

"It would be hard to tell you," he writes to a friend, "how tired I was with paddling all day, with all my strength, among the Indians; wading the rivers a hundred times and more, through the mud and over the sharp rocks that cut my feet; carrying the canoe and luggage through the woods to avoid the rapids and frightful cataracts; and half starved all the while, for we had nothing to eat but a little sagantite, a sort of porridge of water and pounded maize, of which they gave us a very small allowance every morning and night. But I must needs tell you what abundant consolation I found under all my troubles; for when one sees so many infidels needing nothing but a drop of water to make them children of God, one feels an inexpressible ardor to labor for their conversion, and sacrifice to it one's repose and life."

Another Recollet, Gabriel Sagard, followed the same route in similar company a few years later, and has left an account of his experience, of which Le Caron's was the counterpart. Sagard reckons from eighty to a hundred waterfalls and rapids in the course of the journey, and the task of avoiding them by pushing through the woods was the harder for him because he saw fit to go barefoot, "in imitation of our seraphic father, Saint Francis." "We often came upon rocks, mudholes, and fallen trees, which we had to scramble over, and sometimes we must force our way with head and hands through dense woods and thickets, without road or path. When the time came, my Indians looked for a good place to pass the night. Some went for dry wood; others for poles to make a shed; others kindled a fire, and hung the kettle to a stick stuck aslant in the ground; and others looked for two flat stones to bruise the Indian corn, of which they make sagamite."

This sagamite was an extremely thin porridge; and, though scraps of fish were now and then boiled in it, the friar pined away daily on this weak and scanty fare, which was, moreover, made repulsive to him by the exceeding filthiness of the cookery. Nevertheless, he was forced to disguise his feelings. "One must always keep a smiling, modest, contented face, and now and then sing a hymn, both for his own consolation and to please and edify the savages, who take a singular pleasure in hearing us sing the praises of our God." Among all his trials, none afflicted him so much as the flies and mosquitoes. "If I had not kept my face wrapped in a cloth, I am almost sure they would have blinded me, so pestiferous and poisonous are the bites of these little demons. They make one look like a leper, hideous to the sight. I confess that this is the worst martyrdom I suffered in this country; hunger, thirst, weariness, and fever are nothing to it. These little beasts not only persecute you all day, but at night they get into your eyes and mouth, crawl under your clothes, or stick their long stings through them, and make such a noise that it distracts your attention, and prevents you from saying your prayers." He reckons three or four kinds of them, and adds, that in the Montagnais country there is still another kind, so small that they can hardly be seen, but which "bite like devils' imps." The sportsman who has bivouacked in the woods of Maine will at once recognize the minute tormentors there known as "no-see-'ems."

While through tribulations like these Le Caron made his way towards the scene of his apostleship, Champlain was following on his track. With two canoes, ten Indians, Etienne Brule his interpreter, and another Frenchman, he pushed up the Ottawa till he reached the Algonquin villages which had formed the term of his former journeying. He passed the two lakes of the Allumettes; and now, for twenty miles, the river stretched before him, straight as the bee can fly, deep, narrow, and black, between its mountain shores. He passed the rapids of the Joachims and the Caribou, the Rocher Capitamne, and the Deux Rivieres, and reached at length the trihutary waters of the Mattawan. He turned to the left, ascended this little stream forty miles or more, and, crossing a portage track, well trodden, reached the margin of Lake Nipissing. The canoes were launched again, and glided by leafy shores and verdant islands till at length appeared signs of human life and clusters of bark lodges, half hidden in the vastness of the woods. It was the village of an Algonquin band, called the Nipissings,—a race so beset with spirits, infested by demons, and abounding in magicians, that the Jesuits afterwards stigmatized them as "the Sorcerers." In this questionable company Champlain spent two days, feasted on fish, deer, and bears. Then, descending to the outlet of the lake, he steered his canoes westward down the current of French River.

Days passed, and no sign of man enlivened the rocky desolation. Hunger was pressing them hard, for the ten gluttonous Indians had devoured already nearly all their provision for the voyage, and they were forced to subsist on the blueberries and wild raspberries that grew abundantly in the meagre soil, when suddenly they encountered a troop of three hundred savages, whom, from their strange and startling mode of wearing their hair, Champlain named the Cheveux Releves. "Not one of our courtiers," he says, "takes so much pains in dressing his locks." Here, however, their care of the toilet ended; for, though tattooed on various parts of the body, painted, and armed with bows, arrows, and shields of bison-hide, they wore no clothing whatever. Savage as was their aspect, they were busied in the pacific task of gathering blueberries for their winter store. Their demeanor was friendly; and from them the voyager learned that the great lake of the Hurons was close at hand.

Now, far along the western sky was traced the watery line of that inland ocean, and, first of white men except the Friar Le Caron, Champlain beheld the "Mer Douce," the Fresh-Water Sea of the Hurons. Before him, too far for sight, lay the spirit-haunted Manitonalins, and, southward, spread the vast bosom of the Georgian Bay. For more than a hundred miles, his course was along its eastern shores, among islets countless as the sea-sands,—an archipelago of rocks worn for ages by the wash of waves. He crossed Byng Inlet, Franklin Inlet, Parry Sound, and the wider bay of Matchedash, and seems to have landed at the inlet now called Thunder Bay, at the entrance of the Bay of Matchedash, and a little west of the Harbor of Penetanguishine.

An Indian trail led inland, through woods and thickets, across broad meadows, over brooks, and along the skirts of green acclivities. To the eye of Champlain, accustomed to the desolation he had left behind, it seemed a land of beauty and abundance. He reached at last a broad opening in the forest, with fields of maize, pumpkins ripening in the sun, patches of sunflowers, from the seeds of which the Indians made hair-oil, and, in the midst, the Huron town of Otonacha. In all essential points, it resembled that which Cartier, eighty years before, had seen at Montreal,—the same triple palisade of crossed and intersecting trunks, and the same long lodges of bark, each containing several families. Here, within an area of thirty or forty miles, was the seat of one of the most remarkable savage communities on the continent. By the Indian standard, it was a mighty nation; yet the entire Huron population did not exceed that of a third or fourth class American city.

To the south and southeast lay other tribes of kindred race and tongue, all stationary, all tillers of the soil, and all in a state of social advancement when compared with the roving bands of Eastern Canada: the Neutral Nation west of the Niagara, and the Eries and Andastes in Western New York and Pennsylvania; while from the Genesee eastward to the Hudson lay the banded tribes of the Iroquois, leading members of this potent family, deadly foes of their kindred, and at last their destroyers.

In Champlain the Hurons saw the champion who was to lead them to victory. There was bountiful feasting in his honor in the great lodge at Otonacha; and other welcome, too, was tendered, of which the Hurons were ever liberal, but which, with all courtesy, was declined by the virtuous Champlain. Next, he went to Carmaron, a league distant, and then to Tonagnainchain and Tequenonquihayc; till at length he reached Carhagouha, with its triple palisade thirty-five feet high. Here he found Le Caron. The Indians, eager to do him honor, were building for him a bark lodge in the neighboring forest, fashioned like their own, but much smaller. In it the friar made an altar, garnished with those indispensable decorations which he had brought with him through all the vicissitudes of his painful journeying; and hither, night and day, came a curious multitude to listen to his annunciation of the new doctrine. It was a joyful hour when he saw Champlain approach his hermitage; and the two men embraced like brothers long sundered.

The twelfth of August was a day evermore marked with white in the friar's calendar. Arrayed in priestly vestments, he stood before his simple altar; behind him his little band of Christians,—the twelve Frenchmen who had attended him, and the two who had followed Champlain. Here stood their devout and valiant chief, and, at his side, that pioneer of pioneers, Etienne Brule the interpreter. The Host was raised aloft; the worshippers kneeled. Then their rough voices joined in the hymn of praise, Te Deum laudamus; and then a volley of their guns proclaimed the triumph of the faith to the okies, the manitous, and all the brood of anomalous devils who had reigned with undisputed sway in these wild realms of darkness. The brave friar, a true soldier of the

Church, had led her forlorn hope into the fastnesses of hell; and now, with contented heart, he might depart in peace, for he had said the first mass in the country of the Hurons.

CHAPTER XIV.
1615, 1616.
THE GREAT WAR PARTY.

The lot of the favored guest of an Indian camp or village is idleness without repose, for he is never left alone, with the repletion of incessant and inevitable feasts. Tired of this inane routine, Champlain, with some of his Frenchmen, set forth on a tour of observation. Journeying at their ease by the Indian trails, they visited, in three days, five palisaded villages. The country delighted them, with its meadows, its deep woods, its pine and cedar thickets, full of hares and partridges, its wild grapes and plums, cherries, crab-apples, nuts, and raspberries. It was the seventeenth of August when they reached the Huron metropolis, Cahiague, in the modern township of Orillia, three leagues west of the river Severn, by which Lake Simcoe pours its waters into the bay of Matchedash. A shrill clamor of rejoicing, the fixed stare of wondering squaws, and the screaming flight of terrified children hailed the arrival of Champlain. By his estimate, the place contained two hundred lodges; but they must have been relatively small, since, had they been of the enormous capacity sometimes found in these structures, Cahiague alone would have held the whole Huron population. Here was the chief rendezvous, and the town swarmed with gathering warriors. There was cheering news; for an allied nation, called Carantonans, probably identical with the Andastes, had promised to join the Hurons in the enemy's country, with five hundred men. Feasts and the war-dance consumed the days, till at length the tardy bands had all arrived; and, shouldering their canoes and scanty baggage, the naked host set forth.

At the outlet of Lake Simcoe they all stopped to fish,—their simple substitute for a commissariat. Hence, too, the intrepid Etienne Brule, at his own request, was sent with twelve Indians to hasten forward the five hundred allied warriors,—a dangerous venture, since his course must lie through the borders of the Iroquois.

He set out on the eighth of September, and on the morning of the tenth, Champlain, shivering in his blanket, awoke to see the meadows sparkling with an early frost, soon to vanish under the bright autumnal sun. The Huron fleet pursued its course along Lake Simcoe, across the portage to Balsam or Sturgeon Lake, and down the chain of lakes which form the sources of the river Trent. As the long line of canoes moved on its way, no human life was seen, no sign of friend or foe; yet at times, to the fancy of Champlain, the borders of the stream seemed decked with groves and shrubbery by the hands of man, and the walnut trees, laced with grape-vines, seemed decorations of a pleasure-ground.

They stopped and encamped for a deer-hunt. Five hundred Indians, in line, like the skirmishers of an army advancing to battle, drove the game to the end of a woody point; and the canoe-men killed them with spears and arrows as they took to the river. Champlain and his men keenly relished the sport, but paid a heavy price for their pleasure. A Frenchman, firing at a buck, brought down an Indian, and there was need of liberal gifts to console the sufferer and his friends.

The canoes now issued from the mouth of the Trent. Like a flock of venturous wild-fowl, they put boldly out upon Lake Ontario, crossed it in safety, and landed within the borders of New York, on or near the point of land west of Hungry Bay. After hiding their light craft in the woods, the warriors took up their swift and wary march, filing in silence between the woods and the lake, for four leagues along the strand. Then they struck inland, threaded the forest, crossed the outlet of Lake Oneida, and after a march of four days, were deep within the limits of the Iroquois. On the ninth of October some of their scouts met a fishing-party of this people, and captured them,—eleven in number, men, women, and children. They were brought to the camp of the exultant Hurons. As a beginning of the jubilation, a chief cut off a finger of one of the women, but desisted from further torturing on the angry protest of Champlain, reserving that pleasure for a more convenient season.

On the next day they reached an open space in the forest. The hostile town was close at hand, surrounded by rugged fields with a slovenly and savage cultivation. The young Hurons in advance saw the Iroquois at work among the pumpkins and maize, gathering their rustling harvest. Nothing could restrain the hare-brained and ungoverned crew. They screamed their war-cry and rushed in; but the Iroquois snatched their weapons, killed and wounded five or six of the assailants, and drove back the rest discomfited. Champlain and his Frenchmen were forced to interpose; and the report of their pieces from the border of the woods stopped the pursuing enemy, who withdrew to their defences, bearing with them their dead and wounded.

It appears to have been a fortified town of the Onondagas, the central tribe of the Iroquois confederacy, standing, there is some reason to believe, within the limits of Madison County, a few miles south of Lake Oneida. Champlain describes its defensive works as much stronger than those of the Huron villages. They consisted of four concentric rows of palisades, formed of trunks of trees, thirty feet high, set aslant in the earth, and intersecting each other near the top, where they supported a kind of gallery, well defended by shot-proof timber, and furnished with wooden gutters for quenching fire. A pond or lake, which washed one side of the palisade, and was led by sluices within the town, gave an ample supply of water, while the galleries were well provided with magazines of stones.

Champlain was greatly exasperated at the desultory and futile procedure of his Huron allies. Against his advice, they now withdrew to the distance of a cannon-shot from the fort, and encamped in the forest, out of sight of the enemy. "I was moved," he says, "to speak to them roughly and harshly enough, in order to incite them to do their duty; for I foresaw that if things went according to their fancy, nothing but harm could come of it, to their loss and ruin. He proceeded, therefore, to instruct them in the art of war."

In the morning, aided doubtless by his ten or twelve Frenchmen, they set themselves with alacrity to their prescribed task. A wooden tower was made, high enough to overlook the palisade, and large enough to shelter four or five marksmen. Huge wooden shields, or movable parapets, like the mantelets of the Middle Ages, were also constructed. Four hours sufficed to finish the work, and then the assault began. Two hundred of the strongest warriors dragged the tower forward, and planted it within a pike's length of the palisade. Three arquebusiers mounted to the top, where, themselves well sheltered, they opened a raking fire along the galleries, now thronged with wild and naked defenders. But nothing could restrain the ungovernable Hurons. They abandoned their mantelets, and, deaf to every command, swarmed out like bees upon the open field, leaped, shouted, shrieked their war-cries, and shot off their arrows; while the Iroquois, yelling defiance from their ramparts, sent back a shower of stones and arrows in reply. A Huron, bolder than the rest, ran forward with firebrands to burn the palisade, and others followed with wood to feed the flame. But it was stupidly kindled on the leeward side, without the protecting shields designed to cover it; and torrents of water, poured down from the gutters above, quickly extinguished it. The confusion was redoubled. Champlain strove in vain to restore order. Each warrior was yelling at the top of his throat, and his voice was drowned in the outrageous din. Thinking, as he says, that his head would split with shouting, he gave over the attempt, and busied himself and his men with picking off the Iroquois along their ramparts.

The attack lasted three hours, when the assailants fell back to their fortified camp, with seventeen warriors wounded. Champlain, too, had received an arrow in the knee, and another in the leg, which, for the time, disabled him. He was urgent, however, to renew the attack; while the Hurons, crestfallen and disheartened, refused to move from their camp unless the five hundred allies, for some time expected, should appear. They waited five days in vain, beguiling the interval with frequent skirmishes, in which they were always worsted; then began hastily to retreat, carrying their wounded in the centre, while the Iroquois, sallying from their stronghold, showered arrows on their flanks and rear. The wounded, Champlain among the rest, after being packed in baskets made on the spot, were carried each on the back of a strong warrior, "bundled in a heap," says Champlain, "doubled and strapped together after such a fashion that one could move no more than an infant in swaddling-clothes. The pain is extreme, as I can truly say from experience, having been carried several days in this way, since I could not stand, chiefly on account of the arrow-wound I had got in the knee. I never was in such torment in my life, for the pain of the wound was nothing to that of being bound and pinioned on the back of one of our savages. I lost patience, and as soon as I could bear my weight I got out of this prison, or rather out of hell."

At length the dismal march was ended. They reached the spot where their canoes were hidden, found them untouched, embarked, and recrossed to the northern shore of Lake Ontario. The Hurons had promised Champlain an escort to Quebec; but as the chiefs had little power, in peace or war, beyond that of persuasion, each warrior found good reasons for refusing to lend his canoe. Champlain, too, had lost prestige. The "man with the iron breast" had proved not inseparably wedded to victory; and though the fault was their own, yet not the less was the lustre of their hero tarnished. There was no alternative. He must winter with the Hurons. The great war party broke into fragments, each band betaking itself to its hunting-ground. A chief named Durantal, or Darontal, offered Champlain the shelter of his lodge, and he was glad to accept it.

Meanwhile, Etienne Brule had found cause to rue the hour when he undertook his hazardous mission to the Carantonan allies. Three years passed before Champlain saw him. It was in the summer of 1618, that, reaching the Saut St. Louis, he there found the interpreter, his hands and his swarthy face marked with traces of the ordeal he had passed. Brule then told him his story.

He had gone, as already mentioned, with twelve Indians, to hasten the march of the allies, who were to join the Hurons before the hostile town. Crossing Lake Ontario, the party pushed onward with all speed, avoiding trails, threading the thickest forests and darkest swamps, for it was the land of the fierce and watchful Iroquois. They were well advanced on their way when they saw a small party of them crossing a meadow, set upon them, surprised them, killed four, and took two prisoners, whom they led to Carantonan,—a palisaded town with a population of eight hundred warriors, or about four thousand souls. The dwellings and defences were like those of the Hurons, and the town seems to have stood on or near the upper waters of the Susquehanna. They were welcomed with feasts, dances, and an uproar of rejoicing. The five hundred warriors prepared to depart; but, engrossed by the general festivity, they prepared so slowly, that, though the hostile town was but three days distant, they found on reaching it that the besiegers were gone. Brule now returned with them to Carantonan, and, with enterprise worthy of his commander, spent the winter in a tour of exploration. Descending a river, evidently the Susquehanna, he followed it to its junction with the sea, through territories of populous tribes, at war the one with the other. When, in the spring, he returned to Carantonan, five or six of the Indians offered to guide him towards his countrymen. Less fortunate than before, he encountered on the way a band of Iroquois, who, rushing upon the party, scattered them through the woods. Brule ran like the rest. The cries of pursuers and pursued died away in the distance. The forest was silent around him. He was lost in the shady labyrinth. For three or four days he wandered, helpless and famished, till at length he found an Indian foot-path, and, choosing between starvation and the Iroquois, desperately followed it to throw himself on their mercy. He soon saw three Indians in the distance, laden with fish newly caught, and called to them in the Huron tongue, which was radically similar to that of the Iroquois. They stood amazed, then turned to fly; but Brule, gaunt with famine, flung down his weapons in token of friendship. They now drew near, listened to the story of his distress, lighted their pipes, and smoked with him; then guided him to their village, and gave him food.

A crowd gathered about him. "Whence do you come? Are you not one of the Frenchmen, the men of iron, who make war on us?"

Brule answered that he was of a nation better than the French, and fast friends of the Iroquois.

His incredulous captors tied him to a tree, tore out his beard by handfuls, and burned him with fire-brands, while their chief vainly interposed in his behalf. He was a good Catholic, and wore an Agnus Dei at his breast. One of his torturers asked what it was, and thrust out his hand to take it.

"If you touch it," exclaimed Brule, "you and all your race will die."

The Indian persisted. The day was hot, and one of those thunder-gusts which often succeed the fierce heats of an American midsummer was rising against the sky. Brule pointed to the inky clouds as tokens of the anger of his God. The storm broke, and, as the celestial artillery boomed over their darkening forests, the Iroquois were stricken with a superstitious terror. They all fled from the spot, leaving their victim still bound fast, until the chief who had endeavored to protect him returned, cut the cords, led him to his lodge, and dressed his wounds. Thenceforth there was neither dance nor feast to which Brule was not invited; and when he wished to return to his countrymen, a party of Iroquois guided him four days on his way. He reached the friendly Hurons in safety, and joined them on their yearly descent to meet the French traders at Montreal.

Brule's adventures find in some points their counterpart in those of his commander on the winter hunting-grounds of his Huron allies. As we turn the ancient, worm-eaten page which preserves the simple record of his fortunes, a wild and dreary scene rises before the mind,—a chill November air, a murky sky, a cold lake, bare and shivering forests, the earth strewn with crisp brown leaves, and, by the water-side, the bark sheds and smoking camp-fires of a band of Indian hunters. Champlain was of the party. There was ample occupation for his gun, for the morning was vocal with the clamor of wild-fowl, and his evening meal was enlivened by the rueful music of the wolves. It was a lake north or northwest of the site of Kingston. On the borders of a neighboring river, twenty-five of the Indians had been busied ten days in preparing for their annual deer-hunt. They planted posts interlaced with boughs in two straight converging lines, each extending mere than half a mile through forests and swamps. At the angle where they met was made a strong enclosure like a pound. At dawn of day the hunters spread themselves through the woods, and advanced with shouts, clattering of sticks, and howlings like those of wolves, driving the deer before them into the enclosure, where others lay in wait to despatch them with arrows and spears.

Champlain was in the woods with the rest, when he saw a bird whose novel appearance excited his attention; and, gun in hand, he went in pursuit. The bird, flitting from tree to tree, lured him deeper and deeper into the forest; then took wing and vanished. The disappointed sportsman tried to retrace his steps. But the day was clouded, and he had left his pocket-compass at the camp. The forest closed around him, trees mingled with trees in endless confusion. Bewildered and lost, he wandered all day, and at night slept fasting at the foot of a tree. Awaking, he wandered on till afternoon, when he reached a pond slumbering in the shadow of the woods. There were water-fowl along its brink, some of which he shot, and for the first time found food to allay his hunger. He kindled a fire, cooked his game, and, exhausted, blanketless, drenched by a cold rain, made his prayer to Heaven, and again lay down to sleep. Another day of blind and weary wandering succeeded, and another night of exhaustion. He had found paths in the wilderness, but they were not made by human feet. Once more roused from his shivering repose, he journeyed on till he heard the tinkling of a little brook, and bethought him of following its guidance, in the hope that it might lead him to the river where the hunters were now encamped. With toilsome steps he followed the infant stream, now lost beneath the decaying masses of fallen trunks or the impervious intricacies of matted "windfalls," now stealing through swampy thickets or gurgling in the shade of rocks, till it entered at length, not into the river, but into a small lake. Circling around the brink, he found the point where the brook ran out and resumed its course. Listening in the dead stillness of the woods, a dull, hoarse sound rose upon his ear. He went forward, listened again, and could plainly hear the plunge of waters. There was light in the forest before him, and, thrusting himself through the entanglement of bushes, he stood on the edge of a meadow. Wild animals were here of various kinds; some skulking in the bordering thickets, some browsing on the dry and matted grass. On his right rolled the river, wide and turbulent, and along its bank he saw the portage path by which the Indians passed the neighboring rapids. He gazed about him. The rocky hills seemed familiar to his eye. A clew was found at last; and, kindling his evening fire, with grateful heart he broke a long fast on the game he had killed. With the break of day he descended at his ease along the bank, and soon descried the smoke of the Indian fires curling in the heavy morning air against the gray borders of the forest. The joy was great on both sides. The Indians had searched for him without ceasing; and from that day forth his host, Durantal, would never let him go into the forest alone.

They were thirty-eight days encamped on this nameless river, and killed in that time a hundred and twenty deer. Hard frosts were needful to give them passage over the land of lakes and marshes that lay between them and the Huron towns. Therefore they lay waiting till the fourth of December; when the frost came, bridged the lakes and streams, and made the oozy marsh as firm as granite. Snow followed, powdering the broad wastes with dreary white. Then they broke up their camp, packed their game on sledges or on their shoulders, tied on their snowshoes, and began their march. Champlain could scarcely endure his load, though some of the Indians carried a weight fivefold greater. At night, they heard the cleaving ice uttering its strange groans of torment, and on the morrow there came a thaw. For four days they waded through slush and water up to their knees; then came the shivering northwest wind, and all was hard again. In nineteen days they reached the town of Cahiague, and, lounging around their smoky lodge-fires, the hunters forgot the hardships of the past.

For Champlain there was no rest. A double motive urged him,—discovery, and the strengthening of his colony by widening its circle of trade. First, he repaired to Carhagouha; and here he found the friar, in his hermitage, still praying, preaching, making catechisms, and struggling with the manifold difficulties of the Huron tongue. After spending several weeks together, they began their journeyings, and in three days reached the chief village of the Nation of Tobacco, a powerful tribe akin to the Hurons, and soon to be incorporated with them. The travellers visited seven of their towns, and then passed westward to those of the people whom Champlain calls the Cheveax Releves, and whom he commends for neatness and ingenuity no less than he condemns them for the nullity of their summer attire. As the strangers passed from town to town, their arrival was everywhere the signal of festivity. Champlain exchanged pledges of amity with his hosts, and urged them to come down with the Hurons to the yearly trade at Montreal.

Spring was now advancing, and, anxious for his colony, he turned homeward, following that long circuit of Lake Huron and the Ottawa which Iroquois hostility made the only practicable route. Scarcely had he reached the Nipissings, and gained from them a pledge to guide him to that delusive northern sea which never ceased to possess his thoughts, when evil news called him back in haste to the Huron towns. A band of those Algonquins who dwelt on the great island in the Ottawa had spent the winter encamped near Cahiague, whose inhabitants made them a present of an Iroquois prisoner, with the friendly intention that they should enjoy the pleasure of torturing him. The Algonquins, on the contrary, fed, clothed, and adopted him. On this, the donors, in a rage, sent a warrior to kill the Iroquois. He stabbed him, accordingly, in the midst of the Algonquin chiefs, who in requital killed the murderer. Here was a casus belli involving most serious issues for the French, since the Algonquins, by their position on the Ottawa, could cut off the Hurons and all their allies from coming down to trade. Already a fight had taken place at Cahiague the principal Algonquin chief had been wounded, and his band forced to purchase safety by a heavy tribute of wampum 33 and a gift of two female prisoners.

All eyes turned to Champlain as umpire of the quarrel. The great council-house was filled with Huron and Algonquin chiefs, smoking with that immobility of feature beneath which their race often hide a more than tiger-like ferocity. The umpire addressed the assembly, enlarged on the folly of falling to blows between themselves when the common enemy stood ready to devour them both, extolled the advantages of the French trade and alliance, and, with zeal not wholly disinterested, urged them to shake hands like brothers. The friendly counsel was accepted, the pipe of peace was smoked, the storm dispelled, and the commerce of New France rescued from a serious peril.

Once more Champlain turned homeward, and with him went his Huron host, Durantal. Le Caron had preceded him; and, on the eleventh of July, the fellow-travellers met again in the infant capital of Canada. The Indians had reported that Champlain was dead, and he was welcomed as one risen from the grave. The friars, who were all here, chanted lands in their chapel, with a solemn mass and thanksgiving. To the two travelers, fresh from the hardships of the wilderness, the hospitable board of Quebec, the kindly society of countrymen and friends, the adjacent gardens,—always to Champlain an object of especial interest,—seemed like the comforts and repose of home.

The chief Durantal found entertainment worthy of his high estate. The fort, the ship, the armor, the plumes, the cannon, the marvellous architecture of the houses and barracks, the splendors of the chapel, and above all the good cheer outran the boldest excursion of his fancy; and he paddled back at last to his lodge in the woods, bewildered with astonishment and admiration.

CHAPTER XV.
1616-1627.
HOSTILE SECTS.—RIVAL INTERESTS.

At Quebec the signs of growth were faint and few. By the water-side, under the cliff, the so-called "habitation," built in haste eight years before, was already tottering, and Champlain was forced to rebuild it. On the verge of the rock above, where now are seen the buttresses of the demolished castle of St. Louis, he began, in 1620, a fort, behind which were fields and a few buildings. A mile or more distant, by the bank of the St. Charles, where the General Hospital now stands, the Recollets, in the same year, built for themselves a small stone house, with ditches and outworks for defence; and here they began a farm, the stock consisting of several hogs, a pair of asses, a pair of geese, seven pairs of fowls, and four pairs of ducks. The only other agriculturist in the colony was Louis Hebert, who had come to Canada in 1617 with a wife and three children, and who made a house for himself on the rock, at a little distance from Champlain's fort.

Besides Quebec, there were the three trading-stations of Montreal, Three Rivers, and Tadoussac, occupied during a part of the year. Of these, Tadoussac was still the most important. Landing here from France in 1617, the Recollet Paul Huet said mass for the first time in a chapel built of branches, while two sailors standing beside him waved green boughs to drive off the mosquitoes. Thither afterward came Brother Gervais Mohier, newly arrived in Canada; and meeting a crowd of Indians in festal attire, he was frightened at first, suspecting that they might be demons. Being invited by them to a feast, and told that he must not decline, he took his place among a party of two hundred, squatted about four large kettles full of fish, bear's meat, pease, and plums, mixed with figs, raisins, and biscuit procured at great cost from the traders, the whole boiled together and well stirred with a canoe-paddle. As the guest did no honor to the portion set before him, his entertainers tried to tempt his appetite with a large lump of bear's fat, a supreme luxury in their eyes. This only increased his embarrassment, and he took a hasty leave, uttering the ejaculation, "ho, ho, ho!" which, as he had been correctly informed, was the proper mode of acknowledgment to the master of the feast.

A change had now begun in the life of Champlain. His forest rovings were over. To battle with savages and the elements was more congenial with his nature than to nurse a puny colony into growth and strength; yet to each task he gave himself with the same strong devotion.

His difficulties were great. Quebec was half trading-factory, half mission. Its permanent inmates did not exceed fifty or sixty persons,—fur-traders, friars, and two or three wretched families, who had no inducement, and little wish, to labor. The fort is facetiously represented as having two old women for garrison, and a brace of hens for sentinels. All was discord and disorder. Champlain was the nominal commander; but the actual authority was with the merchants, who held, excepting the friars, nearly everybody in their pay. Each was jealous of the other, but all were united in a common jealousy of Champlain. The few families whom they brought over were forbidden to trade with the Indians, and compelled to sell the fruits of their labor to the agents of the company at a low, fixed price, receiving goods in return at an inordinate valuation. Some of the merchants were of Ronen, some of St. Malo; some were Catholics, some were Huguenots. Hence unceasing bickerings. All exercise of the Reformed religion, on land or water, was prohibited within the limits of New France; but the Huguenots set the prohibition at naught, roaring their heretical psalmody with such vigor from their ships in the river that the unhallowed strains polluted the ears of the Indians on shore. The merchants of Rochelle, who had refused to join the company, carried on a bold illicit traffic along the borders of the St. Lawrence, endangering the colony by selling fire-arms to the Indians, eluding pursuit, or, if hard pressed, showing fight; and this was a source of perpetual irritation to the incensed monopolists.

The colony could not increase. The company of merchants, though pledged to promote its growth, did what they could to prevent it. They were fur-traders, and the interests of the fur-trade are always opposed to those of settlement and population. They feared, too, and with reason, that their monopoly might be suddenly revoked, like that of De Monts, and they thought only of making profit from it while it lasted. They had no permanent stake in the country; nor had the men in their employ, who formed nearly all the scanty population of Canada. Few, if any, of these had brought wives to the colony, and none of them thought of cultivating the soil. They formed a floating population, kept from starving by yearly supplies from France.

Champlain, in his singularly trying position, displayed a mingled zeal and fortitude. He went every year to France, laboring for the interests of the colony. To throw open the trade to all competitors was a measure beyond the wisdom of the times; and he hoped only to bind and regulate the monopoly so as to make it subserve the generous purpose to which he had given himself. The imprisonment of Conde was a source of fresh embarrassment; but the young Duo de Montmorency assumed his place, purchasing from him the profitable lieuteuancy of New France for eleven thousand crowns, and continuing Champlain in command. Champlain had succeeded in binding the company of merchants with new and more stringent engagements; and, in the vain belief that these might not be wholly broken, he began to conceive fresh hopes for the colony. In this faith he embarked with his wife for Quebec in the spring of 1620; and, as the boat drew near the landing, the cannon welcomed her to the rock of her banishment. The buildings were falling to ruin; rain entered on all sides; the courtyard, says Champlain, was as squalid and dilapidated as a grange pillaged by soldiers. Madame de Champlain was still very young. If the Ursuline tradition is to be trusted, the Indians, amazed at her beauty and touched by her gentleness, would have worshipped her as a divinity. Her husband had married her at the age of twelve when, to his horror, he presently discovered that she was infected with the heresies of her father, a disguised Huguenot. He addressed himself at once to her conversion, and his pious efforts were something more than successful. During the four years which she passed in Canada, her zeal, it is true, was chiefly exercised in admonishing Indian squaws and catechising their children; but, on her return to France, nothing would content her but to become a nun. Champlain refused; but, as she was childless, he at length consented to a virtual though not formal separation. After his death she gained her wish, became an Ursuline nun, founded a convent of that order at Meaux, and died with a reputation almost saintly.

At Quebec, matters grew from bad to worse. The few emigrants, with no inducement to labor, fell into a lazy apathy, lounging about the trading-houses, gaming, drinking when drink could be had, or roving into the woods on vagabond hunting excursions. The Indians could not be trusted. In the year 1617 they had murdered two men near the end of the Island of Orleans. Frightened at what they had done, and incited perhaps by other causes, the Montagnais and their kindred bands mustered at Three Rivers to the number of eight hundred, resolved to destroy the French. The secret was betrayed; and the childish multitude, naked and famishing, became suppliants to their intended victims for the means of life. The French, themselves at the point of starvation, could give little or nothing. An enemy far more formidable awaited them; and now were seen the fruits of Champlain's intermeddling in Indian wars. In the summer of 1622, the Iroquois descended upon the settlement. A strong party of their warriors hovered about Quebec, but, still fearful of the arquebuse, forbore to attack it, and assailed the Recollet convent on the St. Charles. The prudent friars had fortified themselves. While some prayed in the chapel, the rest, with their Indian converts, manned the walls. The Iroquois respected their palisades and demi-lunes, and withdrew, after burning two Huron prisoners.

Yielding at length to reiterated complaints, the Viceroy Montmorency suppressed the company of St. Malo and Rouen, and conferred the trade of New France, burdened with similar conditions destined to be similarly broken, on two Huguenots, William and emery de Caen. The change was a signal for fresh disorders. The enraged monopolists refused to yield. The rival traders filled Quebec with their quarrels; and Champlain, seeing his authority set at naught, was forced to occupy his newly built fort with a band of armed followers. The evil rose to such a pitch that he joined with the Recollets and the better-disposed among the colonists in sending one of the friars to lay their grievances before the King. The dispute was compromised by a temporary union of the two companies, together with a variety of arrets and regulations, suited, it was thought, to restore tranquillity.

A new change was at hand. Montmorency, tired of his viceroyalty, which gave him ceaseless annoyance, sold it to his nephew, Henri de Levis, Duc de Ventadour. It was no worldly motive which prompted this young nobleman to assume the burden of fostering the infancy of New France. He had retired from the court, and entered into holy orders. For trade and colonization he cared nothing; the conversion of infidels was his sole care. The Jesuits had the keeping of his conscience, and in his eyes they were the most fitting instruments for his purpose. The Recollets, it is true, had labored with an unflagging devotion. The six friars of their Order—for this was the number which the Calvinist Caen had bound himself to support—had established five distinct missions, extending from Acadia to the borders of Lake Huron; but the field was too vast for their powers. Ostensibly by a spontaneous movement of their own, but in reality, it is probable, under influences brought to bear on them from without, the Recollets applied for the assistance of the Jesuits, who, strong in resources as in energy, would not be compelled to rest on the reluctant support of Huguenots. Three of their brotherhood—Charles Lalemant, Enemond Masse, and Jean de Brebeuf—accordingly embarked; and, fourteen years after Biard and Masse had landed in Acadia, Canada beheld for the first time those whose names stand so prominent in her annals,—the mysterious followers of Loyola. Their reception was most inauspicious. Champlain was absent. Caen would not lodge them in the fort; the traders would not admit them to their houses. Nothing seemed left for them but to return as they came; when a boat, bearing several Recollets, approached the ship to proffer them the hospitalities of the convent on the St. Charles. They accepted the proffer, and became guests of the charitable friars, who nevertheless entertained a lurking jealousy of these formidable co-workers.

The Jesuits soon unearthed and publicly burnt a libel against their Order belonging to some of the traders. Their strength was soon increased. The Fathers Noirot and De la Noue landed, with twenty laborers, and the Jesuits were no longer houseless. Brebeuf set forth for the arduous mission of the Hurons; but on arriving at Trois Rivieres he learned that one of his Franciscan predecessors, Nicolas Viel, had recently been drowned by Indians of that tribe, in the rapid behind Montreal, known to this day as the Saut au Recollet. Less ambitious for martyrdom than he afterwards approved himself, he postponed his voyage to a more auspicious season. In the following spring he renewed the attempt, in company with De la Noue and one of the friars. The Indians, however, refused to receive him into their canoes, alleging that his tall and portly frame would overset them; and it was only by dint of many presents that their pretended scruples could be conquered. Brebeuf embarked with his companions, and, after months of toil, reached the barbarous scene of his labors, his sufferings, and his death.

Meanwhile the Viceroy had been deeply scandalized by the contumacious heresy of Emery de Caen, who not only assembled his Huguenot sailors at prayers, but forced Catholics to join them. He was ordered thenceforth to prohibit his crews from all praying and psalm-singing on the river St. Lawrence. The crews revolted, and a compromise was made. It was agreed that for the present they might pray, but not sing. "A bad bargain," says the pious Champlain, "but we made the best of it we could." Caen, enraged at the Viceroy's reproofs, lost no opportunity to vent his spleen against the Jesuits, whom he cordially hated.

Eighteen years had passed since the founding of Quebec, and still the colony could scarcely be said to exist but in the founder's brain. Those who should have been its support were engrossed by trade or propagandism. Champlain might look back on fruitless toils, hopes deferred, a life spent seemingly in vain. The population of Quebec had risen to a hundred and five persons, men, women, and children. Of these, one or two families only had learned to support themselves from the products of the soil. All withered under the monopoly of the Caens. Champlain had long desired to rebuild the fort, which was weak and ruinous; but the merchants would not grant the men and means which, by their charter, they were bound to furnish. At length, however, his urgency in part prevailed, and the work began to advance. Meanwhile the Caens and their associates had greatly prospered, paying, it is said, an annual dividend of forty per cent. In a single year they brought from Canada twenty-two thousand beaver skins, though the usual number did not exceed twelve or fifteen thousand.

While infant Canada was thus struggling into a half-stifled being, the foundation of a commonwealth destined to a marvellous vigor of development had been laid on the Rock of Plymouth. In their character, as in their destiny, the rivals were widely different; yet, at the outset, New England was unfaithful to the principle of freedom. New England Protestantism appealed to Liberty, then closed the door against her; for all Protestantism is an appeal from priestly authority to the right of private judgment, and the New England Puritan, after claiming this right for himself, denied it to all who differed with him. On a stock of freedom he grafted a scion of despotism; yet the vital juices of the root penetrated at last to the uttermost branches, and nourished them to an irrepressible strength and expansion. With New France it was otherwise. She was consistent to the last. Root, stem, and branch, she was the nursling of authority. Deadly absolutism blighted her early and her later growth. Friars and Jesuits, a Ventadour and a Richelieu, shaped her destinies. All that conflicted against advancing liberty— the centralized power of the crown and the tiara, the ultramontane in religion, the despotic in policy—found their fullest expression and most fatal exercise. Her records shine with glorious deeds, the self-devotion of heroes and of martyrs; and the result of all is disorder, imbecility, ruin.

The great champion of absolutism, Richelieu, was now supreme in France. His thin frame, pale cheek, and cold, calm eye, concealed an inexorable will and a mind of vast capacity, armed with all the resources of boldness and of craft. Under his potent agency, the royal power, in the weak hands of Louis the Thirteenth, waxed and strengthened daily, triumphing over the factions of the court, the turbulence of the Huguenots, the ambitious independence of the nobles, and all the elements of anarchy which, since the death of Henry the Fourth, had risen into fresh life. With no friends and a thousand enemies, disliked and feared by the pitiful King whom he served, making his tool by turns of every party and of every principle, he advanced by countless crooked paths towards his object,—the greatness of France under a concentrated and undivided authority.

In the midst of more urgent cares, he addressed himself to fostering the commercial and naval power. Montmorency then held the ancient charge of Admiral of France. Richelieu bought it, suppressed it, and, in its stead, constituted himself Grand Master and Superintendent of Navigation and Commerce. In this new capacity, the mismanaged affairs of New France were not long concealed from him; and he applied a prompt and powerful remedy. The privileges of the Caens were annulled. A company was formed, to consist of a hundred associates, and to be called the

Company of New France. Richelieu himself was the head, and the Marechal Deffiat and other men of rank, besides many merchants and burghers of condition, were members. The whole of New France, from Florida to the Arctic Circle, and from Newfoundland to the sources of the—St. Lawrence and its tributary waters, was conferred on them forever, with the attributes of sovereign power. A perpetual monopoly of the fur-trade was granted them, with a monopoly of all other commerce within the limits of their government for fifteen years. The trade of the colony was declared free, for the same period, from all duties and imposts. Nobles, officers, and ecclesiastics, members of the Company, might engage in commercial pursuits without derogating from the privileges of their order; and, in evidence of his good-will, the King gave them two ships of war, armed and equipped.

On their part, the Company were bound to convey to New France during the next year, 1628, two or three hundred men of all trades, and before the year 1643 to increase the number to four thousand persons, of both sexes; to lodge and support them for three years; and, this time expired, to give them cleared lands for their maintenance. Every settler must be a Frenchman and a Catholic; and for every new settlement at least three ecclesiastics must be provided. Thus was New France to be forever free from the taint of heresy. The stain of her infancy was to be wiped away. Against the foreigner and the Huguenot the door was closed and barred. England threw open her colonies to all who wished to enter,—to the suffering and oppressed, the bold, active, and enterprising. France shut out those who wished to come, and admitted only those who did not,—the favored class who clung to the old faith and had no motive or disposition to leave their homes. English colonization obeyed a natural law, and sailed with wind and tide; French colonization spent its whole struggling existence in futile efforts to make head against them. The English colonist developed inherited freedom on a virgin soil; the French colonist was pursued across the Atlantic by a paternal despotism better in intention and more withering in effect than that which he left behind. If, instead of excluding Huguenots, France had given them an asylum in the west, and left them there to work out their own destinies, Canada would never have been a British province, and the United States would have shared their vast domain with a vigorous population of self-governing Frenchmen.

A trading company was now feudal proprietor of all domains in North America within the claim of France. Fealty and homage on its part, and on the part of the Crown the appointment of supreme judicial officers, and the confirmation of the titles of dukes, marquises, counts, and barons, were the only reservations. The King heaped favors on the new corporation. Twelve of the bourgeois members were ennobled; while artisans and even manufacturers were tempted, by extraordinary privileges, to emigrate to the New World. The associates, of whom Champlain was one, entered upon their functions with a capital of three hundred thousand livres.

CHAPTER XVI.
1628, 1629.
THE ENGLISH AT QUEBEC.

The first care of the new Company was to succor Quebec, whose inmates were on the verge of starvation. Four armed vessels, with a fleet of transports commanded by Roquemont, one of the associates, sailed from Dieppe with colonists and supplies in April, 1628; but nearly at the same time another squadron, destined also for Quebec, was sailing from an English port. War had at length broken out in France. The Huguenot revolt had come to a head. Rochelle was in arms against the King; and Richelieu, with his royal ward, was beleaguering it with the whole strength of the kingdom. Charles the First of England, urged by the heated passions of Buckingham, had declared himself for the rebels, and sent a fleet to their aid. At home, Charles detested the followers of Calvin as dangerous to his own authority; abroad, he befriended them as dangerous to the authority of a rival. In France, Richelieu crushed Protestantism as a curb to the house of Bourbon; in Germany, he nursed and strengthened it as a curb to the house of Austria.

The attempts of Sir William Alexander to colonize Acadia had of late turned attention in England towards the New World; and on the breaking out of the war an expedition was set on foot, under the auspices of that singular personage, to seize on the French possessions in North America. It was a private enterprise, undertaken by London merchants, prominent among whom was Gervase Kirke, an Englishman of Derbyshire, who had long lived at Dieppe, and had there married a Frenchwoman. Gervase Kirke and his associates fitted out three small armed ships, commanded respectively by his sons David, Lewis, and Thomas. Letters of marque were obtained from the King, and the adventurers were authorized to drive out the French from Acadia and Canada. Many Huguenot refugees were among the crews. Having been expelled from New France as settlers, the persecuted sect were returning as enemies. One Captain Michel, who had been in the service of the Caens, "a furious Calvinist," is said to have instigated the attempt, acting, it is affirmed, under the influence of one of his former employers.

Meanwhile the famished tenants of Quebec were eagerly waiting the expected succor. Daily they gazed beyond Point Levi and along the channels of Orleans, in the vain hope of seeing the approaching sails. At length, on the ninth of July, two men, worn with struggling through forests and over torrents, crossed the St. Charles and mounted the rock. They were from Cape Tourmente, where Champlain had some time before established an outpost, and they brought news that, according to the report of Indians, six large vessels lay in the harbor of Tadoussac. The friar Le Caron was at Quebec, and, with a brother Recollet, he went in a canoe to gain further intelligence. As the missionary scouts were paddling along the borders of the Island of Orleans, they met two canoes advancing in hot haste, manned by Indians, who with shouts and gestures warned them to turn back.

The friars, however, waited till the canoes came up, when they saw a man lying disabled at the bottom of one of them, his moustaches burned by the flash of the musket which had wounded him. He proved to be Foucher, who commanded at Cape Tourmente. On that morning,—such was the story of the fugitives,—twenty men had landed at that post from a small fishing-vessel. Being to all appearance French, they were hospitably received; but no sooner had they entered the houses than they began to pillage and burn all before them, killing the cattle, wounding the commandant, and making several prisoners.

The character of the fleet at Tadoussac was now sufficiently clear. Quebec was incapable of defence. Only fifty pounds of gunpowder were left in the magazine; and the fort, owing to the neglect and ill-will of the Caens, was so wretchedly constructed, that, a few days before, two towers of the main building had fallen. Champlain, however, assigned to each man his post, and waited the result. On the next afternoon, a boat was seen issuing from behind the Point of Orleans and hovering hesitatingly about the mouth of the St. Charles. On being challenged, the men on board proved to be Basque fishermen, lately captured by the English, and now sent by Kirke unwilling messengers to Champlain. Climbing the steep pathway to the fort, they delivered their letter,—a summons, couched in terms of great courtesy, to surrender Quebec. There was no hope but in courage. A bold front must supply the lack of batteries and ramparts; and Champlain dismissed the Basques with a reply, in which, with equal courtesy, he expressed his determination to hold his position to the last.

All now stood on the watch, hourly expecting the enemy; when, instead of the hostile squadron, a small boat crept into sight, and one Desdames, with ten Frenchmen, landed at the storehouses. He brought stirring news. The French commander, Roquemont, had despatched him to tell Champlain that the ships of the Hundred Associates were ascending the St. Lawrence, with reinforcements and supplies of all kinds. But on his way Desdames had seen an ominous sight,—the English squadron standing under full sail out of Tadoussac, and steering downwards as if to intercept the advancing succor. He had only escaped them by dragging his boat up the beach and hiding it; and scarcely were they out of sight when the booming of cannon told him that the fight was begun.

Racked with suspense, the starving tenants of Quebec waited the result; but they waited in vain. No white sail moved athwart the green solitudes of Orleans. Neither friend nor foe appeared; and it was not till long afterward that Indians brought them the tidings that Roquemont's crowded transports had been overpowered, and all the supplies destined to relieve their miseries sunk in the St. Lawrence or seized by the victorious English. Kirke, however, deceived by the bold attitude of Champlain, had been too discreet to attack Quebec, and after his victory employed himself in cruising for French fishing-vessels along the borders of the Gulf.

Meanwhile, the suffering at Quebec increased daily. Somewhat less than a hundred men, women, and children were cooped up in the fort, subsisting on a meagre pittance of pease and Indian corn. The garden of the Heberts, the only thrifty settlers, was ransacked for every root or seed that could afford nutriment. Months wore on, and in the spring the distress had risen to such a pitch that Champlain had wellnigh resolved to leave to the women, children, and sick the little food that remained, and with the able-bodied men invade the Iroquois, seize one of their villages, fortify himself in it, and sustain his followers on the buried stores of maize with which the strongholds of these provident savages were always furnished.

Seven ounces of pounded pease were now the daily food of each; and, at the end of May, even this failed. Men, women, and children betook themselves to the woods, gathering acorns and grubbing up roots. Those of the plant called Solomon's seal were most in request. Some joined the Hurons or the Algonquins; some wandered towards the Abenakis of Maine; some descended in a boat to Gaspe, trusting to meet a French fishing-vessel. There was scarcely one who would not have hailed the English as deliverers. But the English had sailed home with their booty, and the season was so late that there was little prospect of their return. Forgotten alike by friends and foes, Quebec was on the verge of extinction.

On the morning of the nineteenth of July, an Indian, renowned as a fisher of eels, who had built his hut on the St. Charles, hard by the new dwelling of the Jesuits, came, with his usual imperturbability of visage, to Champlain. He had just discovered three ships sailing up the south channel of Orleans. Champlain was alone. All his followers were absent, fishing or searching for roots. At about ten o'clock his servant appeared with four small bags of roots, and the tidings that he had seen the three ships a league off, behind Point Levi. As man after man hastened in, Champlain ordered the starved and ragged band, sixteen in all, to their posts, whence with hungry eyes, they watched the English vessels anchoring in the basin below, and a boat with a white flag moving towards the shore. A young officer landed with a summons to surrender. The terms of capitulation were at length settled. The French were to be conveyed to their own country, and each soldier was allowed to take with him his clothes, and, in addition, a coat of beaver-skin. On this some murmuring rose, several of those who had gone to the Hurons having lately returned with peltry of no small value. Their complaints were vain; and on the twentieth of July, amid the roar of cannon from the ships, Lewis Kirke, the Admiral's brother, landed at the head of his soldiers, and planted the cross of St. George where the followers of Wolfe again planted it a hundred and thirty years later. After inspecting the worthless fort, he repaired to the houses of the Recollets and Jesuits on the St. Charles. He treated the former with great courtesy, but displayed against the latter a violent aversion, expressing his regret that he could not have begun his operations by battering their house about their ears. The inhabitants had no cause to complain of him. He urged the widow and family of the settler Hebert, the patriarch, as he has been styled, of New France, to remain and enjoy the fruits of their industry under English allegiance; and, as beggary in France was the alternative, his offer was accepted.

Champlain, bereft of his command, grew restless, and begged to be sent to Tadoussac, where the Admiral, David Kirke, lay with his main squadron, having sent his brothers Lewis and Thomas to seize Quebec. Accordingly, Champlain, with the Jesuits, embarking with Thomas Kirke, descended the river. Off Mal Bay a strange sail was seen. As she approached, she proved to be a French ship, in fact, she was on her way to Quebec with supplies, which, if earlier sent, would have saved the place. She had passed the Admiral's squadron in a fog; but here her good fortune ceased. Thomas Kirke bore down on her, and the cannonade began. The fight was hot and doubtful; but at length the French struck, and Kirke sailed into Tadoussac with his prize. Here lay his brother, the Admiral, with five armed ships.

The Admiral's two voyages to Canada were private ventures; and though he had captured nineteen fishing-vessels, besides Roquemont's eighteen transports and other prizes, the result had not answered his hopes. His mood, therefore, was far from benign, especially as he feared, that, owing to the declaration of peace, he would be forced to disgorge a part of his booty; yet, excepting the Jesuits, he treated his captives with courtesy, and often amused himself with shooting larks on shore in company with Champlain. The Huguenots, however, of whom there were many in his ships, showed an exceeding bitterness against the Catholics. Chief among them was Michel, who had instigated and conducted the enterprise, the merchant admiral being but an indifferent seaman. Michel, whose skill was great, held a high command and the title of Rear-Admiral. He was a man of a sensitive temperament, easily piqued on the point of honor. His morbid and irritable nerves were wrought to the pitch of frenzy by the reproaches of treachery and perfidy with which the French prisoners assailed him, while, on the other hand, he was in a state of continual rage at the fancied neglect and contumely of his English associates. He raved against Kirke, who, as he declared, treated him with an insupportable arrogance. "I have left my country," he exclaimed, "for the service of foreigners; and they give me nothing but ingratitude and scorn." His fevered mind, acting on his diseased body, often excited him to transports of fury, in which he cursed indiscriminately the people of St. Malo, against whom he had a grudge, and the Jesuits, whom he detested. On one occasion, Kirke was conversing with some of the latter.

"Gentlemen," he said, "your business in Canada was to enjoy what belonged to M. de Caen, whom you dispossessed."

"Pardon me, sir," answered Brebeuf, "we came purely for the glory of God, and exposed ourselves to every kind of danger to convert the Indians."

Here Michel broke in: "Ay, ay, convert the Indians! You mean, convert the beaver!"

"That is false!" retorted Brebeuf.

Michel raised his fist, exclaiming, "But for the respect I owe the General, I would strike you for giving me the lie."

Brebeuf, a man of powerful frame and vehement passions, nevertheless regained his practised self-command, and replied: "You must excuse me. I did not mean to give you the lie. I should be very sorry to do so. The words I used are those we use in the schools when a doubtful question is advanced, and they mean no offence. Therefore I ask you to pardon me."

Despite the apology, Michel's frenzied brain harped the presumed insult, and he raved about it without ceasing.

"Bon Dieu!" said Champlain, "you swear well for a Reformer!"

"I know it," returned Michel; "I should be content if I had but struck that Jesuit who gave me the lie before my General."

At length, one of his transports of rage ended in a lethargy from which he never awoke. His funeral was conducted with a pomp suited to his rank; and, amid discharges of cannon whose dreary roar was echoed from the yawning gulf of the Saguenay, his body was borne to its rest under the rocks of Tadoussac. Good Catholics and good Frenchmen saw in his fate the immediate finger of Providence. "I do not doubt that his soul is in perdition," remarks Champlain, who, however, had endeavored to befriend the unfortunate man during the access of his frenzy.

Having finished their carousings, which were profuse, and their trade with the Indians, which was not lucrative, the English steered down the St. Lawrence. Kirke feared greatly a meeting with Razilly, a naval officer of distinction, who was to have sailed from France with a strong force to succor Quebec; but, peace having been proclaimed, the expedition had been limited to two ships under Captain Daniel. Thus Kirke, wilfully ignoring the treaty of peace, was left to pursue his depredations unmolested. Daniel, however, though too weak to cope with him, achieved a signal exploit. On the island of Cape Breton, near the site of Louisburg, he found an English fort, built two months before, under the auspices, doubtless, of Sir William Alexander. Daniel, regarding it as a bold encroachment on French territory, stormed it at the head of his pike-men, entered sword in hand, and took it with all its defenders.

Meanwhile, Kirke with his prisoners was crossing the Atlantic. His squadron at length reached Plymouth, whence Champlain set out for London. Here he had an interview with the French ambassador, who, at his instance, gained from the King a promise, that, in pursuance of the terms of the treaty concluded in the previous April, New France should be restored to the French Crown.

It long remained a mystery why Charles consented to a stipulation which pledged him to resign so important a conquest. The mystery is explained by the recent discovery of a letter from the King to Sir Isaac Wake, his ambassador at Paris. The promised dowry of Queen Henrietta Maria, amounting to eight hundred thousand crowns, had been but half paid by the French government, and Charles, then at issue with his Parliament, and in desperate need of money, instructs his ambassador, that, when he receives the balance due, and not before, he is to give up to the French both Quebec and Port Royal, which had also been captured by Kirke. The letter was accompanied by "solemn instruments under our hand and seal" to make good the transfer on fulfillment of the condition. It was for a sum equal to about two hundred and forty thousand dollars that Charles entailed on Great Britain and her colonies a century of bloody wars. The Kirkes and their associates, who had made the conquest at their own cost, under the royal authority, were never reimbursed, though David Kirke received the honor of knighthood, which cost the King nothing.

CHAPTER XVII.
1632-1635.
DEATH OF CHAMPLAIN.

On Monday, the fifth of July, 1632, Emery de Caen anchored before Quebec. He was commissioned by the French Crown to reclaim the place from the English; to hold for one year a monopoly of the fur-trade, as an indemnity for his losses in the war; and, when this time had expired, to give place to the Hundred Associates of New France.

By the convention of Suza, New France was to be restored to the French Crown; yet it had been matter of debate whether a fulfillment of this engagement was worth the demanding. That wilderness of woods and savages had been ruinous to nearly all connected with it. The Caens, successful at first, had suffered heavily in the end. The Associates were on the verge of bankruptcy. These deserts were useless unless peopled; and to people them would depopulate France. Thus argued the inexperienced reasoners of the time, judging from the wretched precedents of Spanish and Portuguese colonization. The world had not as yet the example of an island kingdom, which, vitalized by a stable and regulated liberty, has peopled a continent and spread colonies over all the earth, gaining constantly new vigor with the matchless growth of its offspring.

On the other hand, honor, it was urged, demanded that France should be reinstated in the land which she had discovered and explored. Should she, the centre of civilization, remain cooped up within her own narrow limits, while rivals and enemies were sharing the vast regions of the West? The commerce and fisheries of New France would in time become a school for French sailors. Mines even now might be discovered; arid the fur-trade, well conducted, could not but be a source of wealth. Disbanded soldiers and women from the streets might be shipped to Canada. Thus New France would be peopled and old France purified. A power more potent than reason reinforced such arguments. Richelieu seems to have regarded it as an act of personal encroachment that the subjects of a foreign crown should seize on the domain of a company of which he was the head; and it could not be supposed, that, with power to eject them, the arrogant minister would suffer them to remain in undisturbed possession.

A spirit far purer and more generous was active in the same behalf. The character of Champlain belonged rather to the Middle Age than to the seventeenth century. Long toil and endurance had calmed the adventurous enthusiasm of his youth into a steadfast earnestness of purpose; and he gave himself with a loyal zeal and devotedness to the profoundly mistaken principles which he had espoused. In his mind, patriotism and religion were inseparably linked. France was the champion of Christianity, and her honor, her greatness, were involved in her fidelity to this high function. Should she abandon to perdition the darkened nations among whom she had cast the first faint rays of hope? Among the members of the Company were those who shared his zeal; and though its capital was exhausted, and many of the merchants were withdrawing in despair, these enthusiasts formed a subordinate association, raised a new fund, and embarked on the venture afresh.

England, then, resigned her prize, and Caen was despatched to reclaim Quebec from the reluctant hands of Thomas Kirke. The latter, obedient to an order from the King of England, struck his flag, embarked his followers, and abandoned the scene of his conquest. Caen landed with the Jesuits, Paul le Jeune and Anne de la Noue. They climbed the steep stairway which led up the rock, and, as they reached the top, the dilapidated fort lay on their left, while farther on was the stone cottage of the Heberts, surrounded with its vegetable gardens,—the only thrifty spot amid a scene of neglect. But few Indians could be seen. True to their native instincts, they had, at first, left the defeated French and welcomed the conquerors. Their English partialities were, however, but short-lived. Their intrusion into houses and store-rooms, the stench of their tobacco, and their importunate begging, though before borne patiently, were rewarded by the newcomers with oaths and sometimes with blows. The Indians soon shunned Quebec, seldom approaching it except when drawn by necessity or a craving for brandy. This was now the case; and several Algonquin families, maddened with drink, were howling, screeching, and fighting within their bark lodges. The women were frenzied like the men, it was dangerous to approach the place unarmed.

In the following spring, 1633, on the twenty-third of May, Champlain, commissioned anew by Richelieu, resumed command at Quebec in behalf of the Company. Father le Jeune, Superior of the mission, was wakened from his morning sleep by the boom of the saluting cannon. Before he could sally forth, the convent door was darkened by the stately form of his brother Jesuit, Brebeuf, newly arrived; and the Indians who stood by uttered ejaculations of astonishment at the raptures of their greeting. The father hastened to the fort, and arrived in time to see a file of musketeers and pikemen mounting the pathway of the cliff below, and the heretic Caen resigning the keys of the citadel into the Catholic hands of Champlain. Le Jeune's delight exudes in praises of one not always a theme of Jesuit eulogy, but on whom, in the hope of a continuance of his favors, no praise could now be ill bestowed. "I sometimes think that this great man [Richelieu], who by his admirable wisdom and matchless conduct of affairs is so renowned on earth, is preparing for himself a dazzling crown of glory in heaven by the care he evinces for the conversion of so many lost infidel souls in this savage land. I pray affectionately for him every day," etc.

For Champlain, too, he has praises which, if more measured, are at least as sincere. Indeed, the Father Superior had the best reason to be pleased with the temporal head of the colony. In his youth, Champlain had fought on the side of that; more liberal and national form of Romanism of which the Jesuits were the most emphatic antagonists. Now, as Le Jeune tells us, with evident contentment, he chose him, the Jesuit, as director of his conscience. In truth, there were none but Jesuits to confess and absolve him; for the Recollets, prevented, to their deep chagrin, from returning to the missions they had founded, were seen no more in Canada, and the followers of Loyola were sole masters of the field. The manly heart of the commandant, earnest, zealous, and direct, was seldom chary of its confidence, or apt to stand too warily on its guard in presence of a profound art mingled with a no less profound sincerity.

A stranger visiting the fort of Quebec would have been astonished at its air of conventual decorum. Black Jesuits and scarfed officers mingled at Champlain's table. There was little conversation, but, in its place, histories and the lives of saints were read aloud, as in a monastic refectory. Prayers, masses, and confessions followed one another with an edifying regularity, and the bell of the adjacent chapel, built by Champlain, rang morning, noon, and night. Godless soldiers caught the infection, and whipped themselves in penance for their sins. Debauched artisans outdid each other in the fury of their contrition. Quebec was become a mission. Indians gathered thither as of old, not from the baneful lure of brandy, for the traffic in it was no longer tolerated, but from the less pernicious attractions of gifts, kind words, and politic blandishments. To the vital principle of propagandism both the commercial and the military character were subordinated; or, to speak more justly, trade, policy, and military power leaned on the missions as their main support, the grand instrument of their extension. The missions were to explore the interior; the missions were to win over the savage hordes at once to Heaven and to France. Peaceful, benign, beneficent, were the weapons of this conquest. France aimed to subdue, not by the sword, but by the cross; not to overwhelm and crush the nations she invaded, but to convert, civilize, and embrace them among her children.

And who were the instruments and the promoters of this proselytism, at once so devout and so politic? Who can answer? Who can trace out the crossing and mingling currents of wisdom and folly, ignorance and knowledge, truth and falsehood, weakness and force, the noble and the base, can analyze a systematized contradiction, and follow through its secret wheels, springs, and levers a phenomenon of moral mechanism? Who can define the Jesuits? The story of their missions is marvellous as a tale of chivalry, or legends of the lives of saints. For many years, it was the history of New France and of the wild communities of her desert empire.

Two years passed. The mission of the Hurons was established, and here the indomitable Breheuf, with a band worthy of him, toiled amid miseries and perils as fearful as ever shook the constancy of man; while Champlain at Quebec, in a life uneventful, yet harassing and laborious, was busied in the round of cares which his post involved.

Christmas day, 1635, was a dark day in the annals of New France. In a chamber of the fort, breathless and cold, lay the hardy frame which war, the wilderness, and the sea had buffeted so long in vain. After two months and a half of illness, Champlain, stricken with paralysis, at the age of sixty-eight, was dead. His last cares were for his colony and the succor of its suffering families. Jesuits, officers, soldiers, traders, and the few settlers of Quebec followed his remains to the church; Le Jeune pronounced his eulogy, and the feeble community built a tomb to his honor.

The colony could ill spare him. For twenty-seven years he had labored hard and ceaselessly for its welfare, sacrificing fortune, repose, and domestic peace to a cause embraced with enthusiasm and pursued with intrepid persistency. His character belonged partly to the past, partly to the present. The preux chevalier, the crusader, the romance-loving explorer, the curious, knowledge-seeking traveler, the practical navigator, all claimed their share in him. His views, though far beyond those of the mean spirits around him, belonged to his age and his creed. He was less statesman than soldier. He leaned to the most direct and boldest policy, and one of his last acts was to petition Richelieu for men and munitions for repressing that standing menace to the colony, the Iroquois. His dauntless courage was matched by an unwearied patience, proved by life-long vexations, and not wholly subdued even by the saintly follies of his wife. He is charged with credulity, from which few of his age were free, and which in all ages has been the foible of earnest and generous natures, too ardent to criticise, and too honorable to doubt the honor of others. Perhaps the heretic might have liked him more if the Jesuit had liked him less. The adventurous explorer of Lake Huron, the bold invader of the Iroquois, befits but indifferently the monastic sobrieties of the fort of Quebec, and his sombre environment of priests. Yet Champlain was no formalist, nor was his an empty zeal. A soldier from his youth, in an age of unbridled license, his life had answered to his maxims; and when a generation had passed after his visit to the Hurons, their elders remembered with astonishment the continence of the great French war-chief.

His books mark the man,—all for his theme and his purpose, nothing for himself. Crude in style, full of the superficial errors of carelessness and haste, rarely diffuse, often brief to a fault, they bear on every page the palpable impress of truth.

With the life of the faithful soldier closes the opening period of New France. Heroes of another stamp succeed; and it remains to tell the story of their devoted lives, their faults, follies, and virtues.

CPSIA information can be obtained
at www.ICGtesting.com
Printed in the USA
BVHW080349060820
585579BV00003B/444